MW00666972

Spire Study System

capture. cross-train. conquer.

PAX Exam

Study Guide

Spire Study System for the NLN-PAX Test Prep and Pre Nursing Practice Questions

STUDY SYSTEM + TEST PREP GUIDE + PRACTICE WORKBOOK

Proudly Printed in the United States of America
ISBN: 9781950159499

About Us

Spire was founded by individuals who wanted to drastically improve the quality of educational materials. Our goal was to create a paradigm shift in the test prep industry, just like modern technology and innovative companies have done for smartphones and computers.

To do that, we assembled a team of seasoned educators, creative professionals, and young entrepreneurs. The end result was a specially formulated study system that outperforms traditional study guides in every way.

See, just about every study guide company supplies you with a daunting volume of information, with no real instructions on how to dig through it. After you purchase their product, you're on your own.
Spire is with you every step of the way. With a 30-day system based on scientific study principles designed to increase retention, you'll know what, when and how to study. This translates into less study time, a better understanding of the material and a more prepared you on test day.

No more cramming. No more wasted studying time. No more guessing at answers and hoping for good luck.

You don't need luck. You've got Spire.

CONTENTS

INTRODUCTION

Since there have been schools, there have been tests, and there have been superstitions and myths about the best way to study for them. Maybe you've heard – or currently believe – some of these ancient yarns: "Study somewhere quiet where you won't be easily distracted." "Focus on one subject at a time." "The longer you study, the better your score will be."

These sound like good advice – in fact, they are so ingrained in us that they sound intuitively correct. The problem is that they are dead wrong.

In the last half-century, researchers and psychologists have upended a lot of conventional wisdom about the way humans learn and how we can get the most out of studying. Their discoveries have suggested several ways that students can study smarter, not harder.

However, these research findings have been slow to make their way into the school systems, if at all, and they are virtually nowhere to be found in most study guides on the market. That means that there are too many people out there working too hard for too little gain.

It's time to change that – and that's why we invented the Spire Study System. First, we assembled an experienced team of editors, educators, writers, test designers, and graphic artists. Then, we built a system around findings from decades of scientific research. Lastly, we refined and designed it for intuitive use and maximum simplicity. The result is what you hold in your hands: not a study guide, but a study system that makes preparation for any test simpler, easier and more effective.

The Spire Study System operates on the following principles:

Study multiple subjects in the same session.

You have to answer questions about multiple topics in the same test session – so why study one subject at a time? By interleaving multiple subjects in the same session, you will strengthen your powers of discrimination – which are crucial to passing a multiple-choice test! That's why this book is organized into a system of study modules, each containing multiple short chapters spanning a variety of subjects.

Change your environment often.

The more often you change your studying conditions, the better off you'll be on test day. That means studying in different locations, at different times of day, and even while listening to different kinds of music. The Spire Study System makes this easy, by providing a schedule and framework for changing your environment often enough to achieve maximum gains from your studies.

Don't study for too long.

More studying does not necessarily equal a better score. There is a point of diminishing returns that, once crossed, may actually make studying counterproductive. Come the big day of the test, you're going to want to be an expert at retrieving and re-engaging the material that you've memorized. The Spire Study System trains those skills by breaking up study sessions and spacing them out over a longer overall period of time.

Give yourself breaks.

Most of us were repeatedly told, all throughout our childhood, to "pay attention" to lectures that were much longer than our attention spans. Well, trying to pay attention is usually as effective as trying to relax or trying to fall asleep. It isn't. That's why the Spire Study System incorporates regular breaks, timed to the average person's studying speed, to help recharge the innate capacity for focus and jumpstart subconscious synthesis processes.

Start studying a month before the test.

In the time-management nightmare known as modern life, how are you supposed to carve out entire nights to devote to studying? The answer: you can't, until it's too late, when that most primal and effective of motivators – fear – sends you into a cramming frenzy the week before the test. The Spire Study System breaks up studying into short, maximally effective sessions. Rather than trying to find hours upon extra hours to study huge reams of material, you revisit small chunks of the subject matter many times, enabling more reinforcement in less overall study time.

Self-testing is very strong.

Once you've thoroughly studied the material, self-testing is your strongest tool for reinforcement. That's why this book has three practice tests. Taking the practice tests, making flash cards to test yourself, and getting someone else to quiz you are all stronger methods to build retention than an equal amount of studying.

There's so much more – but we invented the Spire Study System, so you wouldn't have to become an expert in advanced learning theories. All you have to do is stick to the following 30-day schedule, and follow the directions in the book. Easy peasy.

CALENDAR

Day 1 Pre-Test	**Day 2** Study Module 1	**Day 5** Review Module 1	**Day 6** Study Module 2	**Day 8** Review Module 2
Day 9 Study Module 3	**Day 11** Review Module 3	**Day 12** Study Module 4	**Day 13** Review Module 4	**Day 15** Practice Test 1
Day 16 Targeted Self-Study	**Day 19** Review Module 1 Self-Test	**Day 20** Review Module 2 Self-Test	**Day 22** Review Module 3 Self-Test	**Day 23** Review Module 4 Self-Test
Day 26 Targeted Self-Study	**Day 27** Targeted Self-Study	**Day 28** Review Modules 1-4 Practice Test 2	**Day 29** No Studying Allowed - Celebrate	**Day 30** Take the Test!

TARGETED SELF-STUDY
study your notes and focus on your weakest areas

SELF-TEST
flashcards or a friend

CELEBRATE
reward yourself with a day off, filled with your favorite activities and foods!

FAQ

Q: When I try to make plans, life always throws me a curveball. What should I do if I can't stick perfectly to the schedule?

A: Dwight Eisenhower once said, "Plans are useless, but planning is indispensable." If you miss a session or have to cut one short because, you know, life, the first order of business is: forgive yourself. What you have (or haven't) done is irrelevant. What matters is what you are doing. Get back to your book and stick to the schedule as best as you can.

Q: I fear change and want to keep my bad habits. Can I still use this book?

A: Of course, you can. This book contains all the information you need to pass your test, regardless of whether you follow the Spire Study System or want to do it on your own.

Q: Should I do anything specific when I take my breaks?

A: Yes: don't study. Don't think about the material. Don't talk about the material. Do some light activity like taking a walk or dancing in the living room (well, that's what we do – don't judge us. The least productive activities are those designed to distract, so avoid playing video games or anything involving your smartphone, if possible. However, if answering texts or checking the comments on your latest Instagram post are going to free your attention for more studying, then do what you got to do.

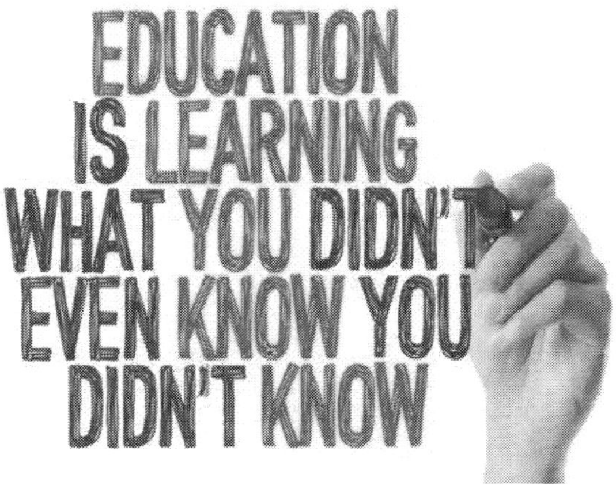

Q: AAAAAAAGGGGGGHHHHHH! I don't have 30 days! I just got this book and the test is tomorrow!

A: Hey. Take a deep breath, Lucky. We hate to break this to you, but you're in for a long, anxious night of that time-tested torture technique: Cramming. The good news is that even if you don't gain the distinct studying advantages of long-term spacing and luxurious breaks, you'll still benefit from the interleaved content and the self-testing included in the practice tests at the back of the book. Now quit reading this FAQ and turn to Practice Test 1, ASAP!

Q: What are some other bad study habits I can break?

A: We got you. Here's a handy list: Don't rewrite your notes, don't work from any test outline, and don't restudy subject material from the same module twice in one session.

Q: Should I take notes?

A: Yes. Keep them brief and focused on the main points of the subject matter and be sure to review them during Targeted Self-Study on days 16, 26 and 27.

That's it! You've got a command of the basics and you understand how the Spire Study System works: just follow the calendar and the directions in the book. Now, your first task is to head to the next section, where the Pre-test is. That's right: Before you read any of the modules, you take the Pre-test. That may sound counterintuitive, but the science is clear: Testing on the material before you start studying yields drastically better results.

So, don't even peek at the content – just get ready to take the first test. - **Good Luck!**

ABOUT THE NLN PAX EXAM

Congratulations! You've decided to enter the world of nursing. You're in for a long journey ahead, but you've chosen an excellent profession. Your study partners at Spire wish you the best of luck in your new career.

The first order of business is to successfully pass the National League for Nursing Pre-Admission Examination, commonly referred to as the NLN-PAX exam. The PAX is an admissions exam used by many nursing schools to assess potential students and their likely future success. Nursing students who take the PAX must be prepared to complete reading, math, science, and word comprehension sections on the exam.

SCORING

If you want to pass the PAX, you need to know how well you have to perform. Some nursing programs require that you score a certain percentage in each exam category, while others evaluate your overall score and compare it with your qualifications and credentials.

Minimum scores are dependent on the nursing programs you apply to, so be sure to contact the appropriate admissions offices for specific scoring requirements.

EXAM BREAKDOWN

Now that you know the score you need to get, let's talk about the actual NLN-PAX. The PAX exam evaluates your aptitude in the following categories and subtests:

SECTION	QUESTIONS/TIME
VERBAL	60/40 minutes
MATHEMATICS	40/40 minutes
SCIENCE	40/60 minutes
TOTAL	**140/140 minutes**

PRE-TEST

As you read in the FAQ, with the Spire Study System, you take the Pre-test before you look at any other material in this book.

Here's a little secret: The Pre-test is actually Practice Test 1. That's right, it's the same exact test. But there's a reason for that! Because the Spire Study System will allow you to better retain and recall the information in this book, you can compare your Pre-test and Practice Test 1 scores to see how much you've learned since you started.

After you complete the first practice test, you'll want to take a look at the answer key. That way you can establish a baseline for your current knowledge.

Then, after you work through the Spire Study System – according to the 30-day schedule – you'll take Practice Test 1...again.

Later – according to the 30-day schedule – you'll take Practice Test 2. Because you will have never seen these questions before, the second practice test will be a bit more challenging than the first.
But don't stress out! As long as you followed the Spire Study System, you'll do great. In fact, you'll be surprised at just how well you do.

But let's not get ahead of ourselves. Once you're ready to experience the magic of the Spire Study System, turn to the back of the book to begin the first test.

MODULE 1

DAY, LOCATION, MUSIC

1

MONDAY, OCTOBER 12

COFFEE SHOP ON MAIN STREET

MY FAVORITE BAND

2

3

VOCABULARY

EXPANDING YOUR VOCABULARY

The best, most natural way to expand your vocabulary is to read everything you can get your hands on. That means blogs, articles, social media, physical books, posted signs, and even the labels on your shampoo bottle. Start looking for opportunities to read a little bit more every day, from now until the day of the test.

Of course, you do have that test coming up quick, so you don't have much time to go au nature. We got your back. Here is your first and most crucial vocabulary hack: identifying root words.

WHAT IS THE WHAT?

Many words are little stories in and of themselves, which is to say that they have a beginning, middle and end. These parts are, respectively, the prefix, the root word and the suffix.

Not all words have all three parts. Sometimes it's just the prefix and root, sometimes just the root and suffix, and sometimes there are multiple roots. But – and this is important – a word is never just prefixes and suffixes. There is always at least one root word, because that's the main idea of the word. You can't have a complete, grammatically correct sentence without a subject, and you can't have a complete word without a root word.

For example, here's a word that's close to your heart lately: reviewing. It means viewing something again. Here are its parts:

Prefix = re

Root = view

Suffix = ing

Re is a prefix that means "again." View means "look." Ing is a suffix that denotes tense; it tells you the root word is happening in the present. So, if you're reviewing, you're currently viewing something again. The root word, or main idea of the word, is "view".

Let's get concrete: If you went up to one of your friends and just said, "Again," they would give you a funny look and say, "What again?"

It's the same idea if you went up to them and said, "Doing." They would say, "Doing what?"

If you went up to them and just said, "Look," they would get the point and try to see what you're seeing. They may not know what to look for, but they get the gist of what you're trying to communicate to them. That gist is the root of the word.

Almost every vocabulary word on the test will be some combination of prefixes, roots, and suffixes. If you run into one that you don't know, the first question to ask yourself is, "What is the what?"

Here is another example: unemployment
Prefix = un
Root = employ
Suffix = ment

You can't just say "un" or "ment" and expect to be understood, but when you add the main idea, employ, the word makes sense. It means the state of not having a job.

WHERE IT GETS MESSY

Of course, we speak the English language, which is a marvelous, madcap collage of many other languages, but mostly Latin, German, and Greek. That means many root words are not English words. On top of that, there are no hard-and-fast rules for how prefixes and suffixes will change root words, so each root may look a little different depending on which prefixes and suffixes are used.

However, you can usually get the gist by breaking off the parts that you know are prefixes and suffixes and asking yourself what the remaining part reminds you of.

In order to break things down, you need to have a grasp of the most common prefixes, suffixes and root words you'll encounter on the test (these are outlined below).

COMMON ROOT WORD

If you can't identify a word because it seems like it's in another language, that's most likely because it is. This isn't always true, but a good general rule is that our longer, more academic words tend to have their roots in Latin and Greek, while our shorter words tend to have their roots in German. For example, amorous and loving are synonyms, but one has its roots in the Latin amor and the other in the German lieb.

LATIN/GREEK - Because vocabulary words on the test tend toward the longer, more academic variety, you'll get the most out of studying some common Latin and Greek roots:

ROOT	VARIATIONS	WHAT IT MEANS	EXAMPLES
ASTER	Astro	Star	Astronomy, disaster
AQUA		Water	Aquatic, aquarium
AUD		Hear	Auditorium, audience
BENE		Good	Benevolent, benign
BIO		Life	Biology, autobiography
CENT		Hundred	Century, cent (money)
CHRONO		Time	Chronological, synchronize
CIRCUM	Circa	Around	Circumspect, circumnavigate
CONTRA	Counter	Against or conflict	Contraband, encounter
DICT		Speak or say	Dictate, dictation
DUC	Duct, duce	Lead or leader	Produce, conduct
FAC		Make or do	Manufacture, facsimile (fax)
FRACT	Frag	Break	Fraction, defragment
GEN		Birth or create	Genetics, generate
GRAPH		Write	Telegraph, calligraphy
JECT		Throw	Inject, projection
JUR	Jus	Law	Juror, justice
LOG	Logue	Concept or thought	Logo, dialogue
MAL		Bad	Maladaptive, malevolent
MAN		Hand	Manuscript, manual
MATER		Mother	Maternal, material
MIS	Mit	Send	Mission, submit
PATER	Pat	Father	Paternal, patriot
PATH		Feel	Sympathy, empathetic
PHILE	Philo	Love	Philosophy, anglophile
PHON		Sound	Telephone, phonetic
PHOTO		Light	Photograph, photosynthesis
PORT		Carry	Transport, portable
PSYCH	Psycho	Soul or spirit	Psychiatrist, psyche
QUI	Quit	Quiet or rest	Acquittal, tranquility
RUPT		Break	Rupture, interrupt
SCOPE		See, inspect	Telescope, microscopic
SCRIB	Script	Write	Describe, transcription
SENS	Sent	Feel	Sensory, consent
SPECT		Look	Spectate, circumspect
STRUCT		Build	Construct, obstruction
TECHNO	Tech	Art or science	Technical, technology
TELE		Far	Teleport, television
THERM		Heat	Thermometer, thermal
VAC		Empty	Vacation, evacuate

VIS	Vid	See	Visual, video
VOC		Speak or call	Vocal, vocation

PREFIXES - Here are your opposite prefixes, which you'll encounter a lot on the test:

PREFIX	VARIATIONS	WHAT IT MEANS	EXAMPLES
ANTI-	Ant-	Against or opposite	Anti-inflammatory, antagonist
DE-		Opposite	Decontaminate, deconstruct
DIS-		Not or opposite	Disagree, dis (slang for insult)
IN-	Im-, Il-, Ir-	Not	Incapable, impossible, illegitimate, irreplaceable
NON-		Not	Noncompliant, nonsense
UN-		Not	Unfair, unjust

Here is a quick list of some other common prefixes:

PREFIX	VARIATIONS	WHAT IT MEANS	EXAMPLES
EN-	Em-	Cause	Enlighten, empower
FORE-		Before	Foresee, foretell
IN-		Inside of	Inland, income
INTER-		Between	Interrupt, interaction
MID-		the middle of	Midair, midlife
MIS-		Wrong	Mistake, misdiagnose
PRE-		Before	Pregame, prefix
RE-		Again	Review, recompress
SEMI-		Half or partial	Semitruck, semiannual
SUB-		Under	Subconscious, subpar
SUPER-		Above	Superimpose, superstar
TRANS-		Across	Translate, transform

SUFFIXES - Here are some common suffixes you'll encounter on the test:

SUFFIX	VARIATIONS	WHAT IT MEANS	EXAMPLES
-ABLE	-Ible	Can be accomplished	Capable, possible
-AL	-Ial	Has traits of	Additional, beneficial
-EN		Made of	Molten, wooden
-ER		More than	Luckier, richer
-ER	-Or	Agent that does	Mover, actor
-EST		Most	Largest, happiest
-IC		Has traits of	Acidic, dynamic
-ING		Continues to do	Reviewing, happening
-ION	-Tion, -Ation, -Ition	Process of	Occasion, motion, rotation, condition
-ITY		The state of	Ability, simplicity
-LY		Has traits of	Friendly, kindly
-MENT		Process/state of	Enlightenment, establishment
-NESS		State of	Happiness, easiness
-OUS	-Eous, -Ious	Has traits of	Porous, gaseous, conscious
-Y		Has traits of	Artsy, fartsy

VOCABULARY PRACTICE TEST

For items 1-5, try to identify the root and write an English translation or synonym for it. We did the first one for you as an example.

#	WORD	ROOT	TRANSLATION/SYNONYM
EX	Description	Script	Something written
1	Irresponsible		
2	Entombment		
3	Professorial		
4	Unconscionable		
5	Gainfully		

For items 6-10, identify the prefix and write an English translation or synonym for it.

#	WORD	PREFIX	TRANSLATION/SYNONYM
EX	Prepare	Pre	Before
6	Proceed		
7	Misapprehend		
8	Antibiotic		
9	Hyperactive		
10	Cacophony		

For items 11-15, identify the suffix and write an English translation or synonym for it.

#	WORD	SUFFIX	TRANSLATION/SYNONYM
EX	Lovable	Able	Can be accomplished
11	Tedious		
12	Absolution		
13	Cathartic		
14	Merriment		
15	Inspector		

Now, it's time to test your current vocabulary:

16. Achromatic most nearly means:
    a. full of color
    b. fragrant
    c. without color
    d. vivid

17. Cursory most nearly means:
    a. meticulous; careful
    b. undetailed; rapid
    c. thorough
    d. expletive

18. Hearsay most nearly means:
   a. Blasphemy
   b. secondhand information that can't be proven
   c. evidence that can be confirmed
   d. testimony

19. Magnanimous most nearly means:
   a. Suspicious
   b. Uncontested
   c. forgiving; not petty
   d. cheap

20. Terrestrial most nearly means:
   a. of the earth
   b. cosmic
   c. otherworldly/unearthly
   d. supernatural

Answer Key

1	**response**	6	**. pro**	11	**-ious**	16	**(c) without color**
2	tomb	7	Mis	12	-tion	17	(b) undetailed; rapid
3	profess	8	. Anti	13	-tic	18	(b) secondhand information that can't be proven
4	conscience	9	hyper	14	-ment	19	(c) forgiving; not petty
5	gain	10	caco-	15	-tor	20	(a) of the earth

CRITICAL READING

FINDING THE MAIN IDEA

Many of the reading comprehension questions you will encounter on the exam are structured around finding the main idea of a paragraph. The last section on root words was all about finding the main idea of a word – notice a theme developing here?

In this section, you will need to find the main idea of a paragraph. Luckily, that's nice and simple once you know what to look for.

First, we're going to re-define a few terms you might think you already know, so don't rush through this part:

PARAGRAPH

A paragraph is a tool for organizing information. It's simply a container for sentences in the same way that a sentence is a container for words. Okay, maybe you knew that already, but you'd be surprised how many professional writers get their minds blown when they realize that almost all books are structured in the same way:

Books are made of...
Chapters, which are made of...
Sections, which are made of...
Paragraphs, which are made of...
Sentences, which are made of...
Words

It's a simple hierarchy, and smack in the center is the humble paragraph. For the purposes of the test, you need to be able to comb through given paragraphs to find two kinds of sentences: topic and detail.

TOPIC SENTENCE

A well-written paragraph, which is to say all of the paragraphs that you'll find on the test, contains just one topic. You'll find this in the topic sentence, which is the backbone of the paragraph. The topic sentence tells you what the paragraph is about. All of the other sentences exist solely to support this topic sentence, which, more often than not, is the first or last sentence in the paragraph. However, that's not always the case, so use this foolproof method: Ask yourself, "Who or what is this paragraph about?" Then find the sentence that answers your question.

DETAIL SENTENCE

Detail sentences exist to support the topic sentence. They do so with all kinds of additional information, such as descriptions, arguments, and nuances. An author includes detail sentences to explain why they're writing about the topic in the first place. That is, the detail sentences contain the author's point, which you'll need to find the main idea. To easily spot the author's point, just ask yourself, "Why is the author writing about this topic?" Then pay close attention to the detail sentences to pry out their motivations.

Got it? Good. Now, let's do some really easy math:
The topic + the author's point = the main idea.

Now, let's put that in English:
What + Why = Main Idea

IN THE REAL WORLD

All right, you've got the abstract concepts nailed down. Now, let's get concrete. Imagine a scenario where a friend is explaining the movie Toy Story to you. Also, imagine that she has already picked her jaw up off the floor, because seriously, how have you not seen Toy Story? You should fix that.
She tells you what the movie is about: There are these toys that get lost, and they have a bunch of adventures trying to get back to their owner. Then she tells you why you should see it: It's cute and funny, and it's a classic.

Two sentences: The topic (what the movie is about) and the author's point (why she's telling you about it.) And now you have the main idea: Your friend thinks you should see the movie Toy Story because it's a cute, funny classic about toys having adventures.

ILLUSTRATING THE MAIN IDEA

Here is a paragraph similar to one you might encounter on the test, followed by the types of questions that you will need to answer:

EXAMPLE 1 – FROM THE ART OF CONVERSATION BY CATHERINE BLYTH:

"Silence is meaningful. You may imagine that silence says nothing. In fact, in any spoken communication, it plays a repertoire of roles. Just as, mathematically speaking, Earth should be called Sea, since most of the planet is covered in it, so conversation might be renamed silence, as it comprises 40 to 50 percent of an average utterance, excluding pauses for others to talk and the enveloping silence of those paying attention (or not, as the case may be)."

This one is relatively easy, but let's break it down:

- Who/What is the paragraph about? Silence.
- Why is the author writing about this topic? It is often overlooked, but it's an important part of conversation.
- What is the main idea? Silence is an important part of conversation. Or, put it another way: "Silence is meaningful" - it's the first sentence!

Okay, you've seen the technique in action, so now it's your turn. Read the following paragraphs and determine the topic sentence, the author's main point, and the main idea.

EXAMPLE 2 – FROM LOVE, POVERTY AND WAR BY CHRISTOPHER HITCHENS

"Concerning love, I had best be brief and say that when I read Bertrand Russell on this matter as an adolescent, and understood him to write with perfect gravity that a moment of such emotion was worth the whole of the rest of life, I devoutly hoped that this would be true in my own case. And so, it has proved, and so to that extent I can regard the death that I otherwise rather resent as laughable and impotent."

1. The main topic of this paragraph is:
   a. gravity
   b. adolescence
   c. death
   d. love

2. The author's main point about this topic is that:
   a. it is something to be resented
   b. it is something to laugh at
   c. it makes life worth living
   d. it is brief

3. The final sentence is:
   a. the topic sentence
   b. the author's main point
   c. detail sentence
   d. the beginning of a new topic

4. The main idea of the paragraph is that:
   a. a moment of love is worth all of life's woes
   b. adolescence is something to laugh at
   c. Bertrand Russell is very wise
   d. death is something to be resented

EXAMPLE 3 – FROM RIVER OF DOUBT BY CANDICE MILLARD

"Theodore Roosevelt, one of the most popular presidents in his nation's history, had vowed never to run again after winning his second term in the White House in 1904. But now, just eight years later, he was not only running for a third term, he was, to the horror and outrage of his old Republican backers, running as a third-party candidate against Democrats and Republicans alike."

5. The topic of this paragraph is:
    a. Teddy Roosevelt
    b. early 20th century politics
    c. independent presidential candidates
    d. the election of 1912

6. Why does the author mention "old Republican backers?"
    a. Roosevelt's backers were all elderly
    b. Roosevelt used to be a Republican
    c. Roosevelt used to be a Democrat
    d. they backed Roosevelt eight years ago

7. Where is the topic sentence?
    a. the last sentence
    b. the first sentence
    c. it is likely stated before the chosen selection
    d. it is likely stated after the chosen selection

8. The main idea of the paragraph is:
    a. Roosevelt was a popular president
    b. Roosevelt ran for a third term as a third-party candidate
    c. early 20th century politics had three parties
    d. the election of 1912 had three candidates

EXAMPLE 4 – FROM LOVE IN THE TIME OF CHOLERA BY GABRIEL GARCÍA MÁRQUEZ

"To him she seemed so beautiful, so seductive, so different from ordinary people, that he could not understand why no one was as disturbed as he by the clicking of her heels on the paving stones, why no one else's heart was wild with the breeze stirred by the sighs of her veils, why everyone did not go mad with the movements of her braid, the flight of her hands, the gold of her laughter. He had not missed a single one of her gestures, not one of the indications of her character, but he did not dare approach her for fear of destroying the spell."

9. The main topic of this paragraph is:
    a. a beautiful woman
    b. fear
    c. love
    d. seduction

10. The author uses many details to:
    a. show that the man is obsessive
    b. show the vividness and intensity of love
    c. make people admire his writing ability
    d. show that the woman is unique

11. The topic sentence:
    a. is the final sentence
    b. is the initial sentence
    c. also contains many details
    d. is not present in this paragraph

12. The main idea of the paragraph is that:
    a. the man is afraid of the woman he loves
    b. the woman doesn't even know the man is alive
    c. love is vivid and intense
    d. there is no main idea because this is fiction

EXAMPLE 5 – FROM ON LOOKING BY ALEXANDRA
HOROWITZ

"Part of human development is learning to notice less than we are able to. The world is awash in details of color, form, and sound – but to function, we have to ignore some of it. The world still holds these details. Children sense the world at a different granularity, attending to parts of the visual world we gloss over; to sounds we have dismissed as irrelevant. What is indiscernible to us is plain to them."

13. The main topic of this paragraph is:
    a. what humans notice or don't
    b. human development
    c. the world's details
    d. children

14. The author's main point about the topic is that:
    a. children see more details than adults
    b. adults see more details than children
    c. aging inevitably results in wisdom
    d. the world is very complicated

15. The first sentence is:
    a. the topic sentence
    b. the author's point
    c. a detail sentence
    d. the beginning of a new topic

16. The main idea of the paragraph is:
    a. children and adults live in different worlds
    b. as you age, your experience of the world gets richer
    c. what is indiscernible to children is plain to adults
    d. as you age, you notice less than children do

Answer Key

1	d	9	a
2	c	10	a
3	b	11	b
4	a	12	c
5	a	13	a
6	a	14	a
7	b	15	b
8	b	16	a

ARITHMETIC BASICS

Before you begin studying for the arithmetic section of the exam, let's talk basics. Many math exams will test your memory of basic math definitions, vocabulary, and formulas that have become so distant that the questions on this type of exam may feel unfair. You likely don't refer to quotients and integers in your day-to-day life, so testing your recall of high school math class vocabulary and concepts doesn't exactly feel like a valid way to gauge your mathematical reasoning abilities. Well, as the French say, "C'est la vie!" or "That's life!" Perhaps the most appropriate English expression would be, "You gotta do what you gotta do."

In this section, it's best for you to begin with a refresher list so that you can master basic math terminology quickly.

INTEGER: Any whole number, i.e. any number that doesn't include a non-zero fraction or decimal. Negative whole numbers, positive whole numbers, and 0 are all integers. 3.1415 is not an integer. ½ is not an integer. -47, -12, 0, 15, and 1,415,000 are all integers.

POSITIVE AND NEGATIVE NUMBERS: A positive number is any number greater than zero. A negative number is any number less than zero. Zero is neither positive nor negative. Adding a negative number is the same as subtracting the positive value of that number. Subtracting a negative number is the same as adding a positive number.

EVEN AND ODD NUMBERS: An even number is any number that can be evenly divided by 2, with no remainder left over. -4, 2, 6, 24, and 114 are all even numbers. An odd number has a remainder of 1 when it is divided by 2. -19, 1, 3, 5, 17, and 451 are all odd numbers. Another way to think about even/odd is that even numbers are all integers that are multiples of two, and odd numbers are any integers that are not multiples of two.

FACTORS AND MULTIPLES: The factors of a number (or a polynomial) are all of the numbers that can be multiplied together to get the first number. For example, the following pairs of numbers can be multiplied to get 16: 1 * 16, 2 * 8 and 4 * 4. Therefore, the factors of 16 are 1, 2, 4, 8, and 16. Note: a polynomial is an expression that can have constants, variables, and exponents, and that can be combined using addition, subtraction, multiplication, and division.

PRIME NUMBER: An integer that only has two factors: 1 and itself. There are two things to remember: (1) out of all of the infinite integers in existence, there is only one prime number that is even, and that is the number 2 – that's it, and (2) you can handle almost any prime number question on the test by memorizing all of the primes between 0 and 100. This is not required, but you will save time and mental anguish if you do this. Here they are:

$$2, 3, 5, 7, 11, 13, 17, 19, 23, 29, 31, 37, 41, 43, 47,$$
$$53, 59, 61, 67, 71, 73, 79, 83, 87, 89, 97$$

PRIME FACTORIZATION: The prime numbers you must multiply to get a number. Take the number 24. First, you should find the factors of 24: 1, 2, 3, 4, 6, 8, and 12. Then, you need to pull out all the numbers that are not prime: 1, 4, 6, 8, and 12. What's left? 2 and 3 are the prime factors of 24! Now, that's a simple example, but the concept remains the same, no matter how large the number. When in doubt, start working from the number 2 (the smallest prime), which will be a factor of any number that ends with an even number. Be on the lookout for sneaky questions. For example, if the exam asks you for the prime factors of the number 31, recall that 31 is a prime number (but 1 is not!) so the only prime factor it can possibly have is itself – 31. The same goes for all prime numbers.

SUM: Add the number you get when you add one number to another number.

DIFFERENCE: Subtract the number you get when you subtract one number from another number.

PRODUCT: Multiply the number you get when you multiply one number by another number.

QUOTIENT: Divide the number you get when you divide one number by another number.

EXPRESSIONS

An expression is made up of terms that are numbers, variables, and operators, which are added together. If that sounds complicated, expressions are simply made up of the basic symbols used to create everything from first-grade addition problems to formulas and equations used in calculus. The individual terms of the expression are added to each other as individual parts of the expression. Remember that expressions may stand for single numbers and use basic operators like * and ÷. However, a single expression does not suggest a comparison (or equivalency). But an equation does and can be represented by a simple expression equal to a number. For example, 3 + 2 = 1 + 4 is an equation, because it uses the equal sign. So, think of 3 + 2 and 1 + 4 as building blocks – they are the expressions that, when joined together by an equal sign, make up an equation. Another way to think of an expression is that it is essentially a math metaphor used to represent another number.

ORDER OF OPERATIONS

An operation is what a symbol does. The operation of a + sign, for instance, is to add. That's easy enough, but what happens if you run into a problem like this?

$$44 - (32 * 2 + 6) = ?$$

You have to solve this equation by simplifying it, but if you do it in the wrong order, you will get the wrong answer. This is an incredibly important concept. This is where the Order of Operations comes in – here's what you have to remember.

1. **Parentheses**
2. **Exponents**
3. **Multiplication and division (from left to right)**
4. **Addition and subtraction (from left to right)**

You must do these operations in order, starting with parentheses first and addition/subtraction last, to get the correct answer.

$$44 - (3^2 * 2 + 6) = ?$$

Start by focusing on the expression in parentheses first. Inside the parentheses, you will find an exponent, so do that first so that you can do the operation within the parentheses:

$$3^2 = 3 * 3 = 9$$

then the expression becomes (9 * 2 + 6)

To complete the operation within the paragraph, you need to remember to do the multiplication operation first:

$$9 * 2 = 18$$

$$(18 + 6) = 24$$

You don't need the parentheses anymore because there are no operations left to complete inside of them. Now the problem looks like this:

$$44 - 24 = ?$$

$$20 = ?$$

You can use the phrase, **P**lease **E**xcuse **M**y **D**ear **A**unt **S**ally as a useful mnemonic. It has the same first letters as parentheses, exponents, multiplication, division, addition, subtraction.

However, the most common mistake involving the order of operations is the following: doing division after multiplication OR subtraction after addition, which results in the wrong answer. You have to do multiplication and division as you encounter it from left to right, and the same goes for addition and subtraction. Remember to do what is inside parentheses first, and that might require you to do exponents, multiplication/division, and addition/ subtraction first.

Here's another example of this concept:

$$(4^2 + 5^3 - 120) * 3 = ?$$

$$4^2 = 4 * 4 = 16$$

$$5^3 = 5 * 5 * 5 = 125$$

$$(16 + 125 - 120) * 3 = ?$$

$$21 * 3 = ?$$

$$63 = ?$$

If you didn't understand this example, you should go back and review the Order of Operations again. Occasionally, you may encounter an equation that uses brackets. You should think of brackets as super parentheses, i.e. they're at the top of the list, and so you do that first, before anything else.

EQUATIONS

Equations relate expressions to one another with an equal sign. In algebra, they can get pretty complicated, but in arithmetic, equations often center around finding the equivalent of a single expression. For instance,

$$3 + 2 = 5$$

It may seem pretty simple to say 3 + 2 expresses 5 because they have a clear and simple relationship – they are equal. Other kinds of equations, i.e. relationships, include symbols like > (greater than) and (less than), which can join two expressions together. These are often called inequalities since they are not equal. The greater than or less than relation is a sign of inequality.

Remember that equations can be rearranged by doing the same operations to each side of the equivalency. Here's an example of subtracting 6 from both sides of the equation:

$$34 - 23 = 6 + ?$$
$$34 - 23 - 6 = 6 + ? - 6$$

The number 6 subtracted on both sides of the equation cancel each other out. The equality of the relation remains unaffected.

$$11 - 6 = ?$$
$$5 = ?$$

GREATEST COMMON FACTOR

Sometimes the term Greatest Common Factor is called the Greatest Common Divisor, but either way, the concept is the same – it's the largest factor that two (or more) numbers share.

To use this concept, you should first work out all the factors for each number and then find the largest factor they have in common. For example, find the Greatest Common Factor of 18 and 30:

The factors of 18 are: 1, 2, 3, 6, 9, and 18
The factors of 30 are: 1, 2, 3, 5, 6, 10, 15, and 30

The highest number in both sets, i.e. the highest number that is common to both sets, is 6, so that's your Greatest Common Factor.

LEAST COMMON MULTIPLE

Sometimes the term Least Common Multiple is called the Lowest Common Multiple or the Smallest Common Multiple or the Lowest Common Denominator when used in a fraction, but in any case, the concept is the same – without knowing this term, you can't compare, add, or subtract fractions, and that's important.

The least common multiple is the smallest number that can be divided by two (or more) given numbers. To get this number, first write out the multiples for each number and then find the smallest multiple that they share.
For example, find the Least Common Multiple of 3 and 7:

The multiples of 3 are: 3, 6, 9, 12, 15, 18, 21, 24, 27...
The multiples of 7 are: 7, 14, 21, 28, 35, 42, 49, 56...

The lowest number in both sets is 21, so that's your Least Common Multiple. Notice that there are other multiples, but we are interested in the lowest or least of the common multiples.

EXPONENTS AND ROOTS EXPONENTS

An exponent is an algebraic operation that tells you to multiply a number by itself.
For example, 4^2 is the same as 4 * 4, and 4^3 is the same as 4 * 4 * 4. The exponent tells you how many times to multiply the number by itself.

Exponents have a few special properties (you can think of them as shortcuts or even helpful tricks if you want):

1. If two numbers with exponents share the same base number, you can multiply them by adding the exponents:

$$2^5 * 2^3 = 2^8$$

2. If two numbers with exponents share the same base number, you can divide them by subtracting the exponents:

$$2^5 \div 2^3 = 2^2$$

3. A number with an exponent raised to a negative power is the same as 1 over or the reciprocal of that number with an exponent raised to the positive power:

$$5^{-2} = 1/5^2$$
$$1/5^2 = 1/25 \, or \, 1 \div 25 = 0.04$$

4. A number raised to a fraction power is the same as a root, or radical:

91/2 = 3 (the square root indicated by the two in one half) Remember that the root of a number x is another number, which when multiplied by itself a given number of times, equals x. For example, the second root of 9 is 3, because 3 * 3 = 9. The second root is usually called the square root. The third root is usually called the cube root. Because 2 * 2 * 2 = 8, 2 is the cube root of 8. Two special exponent properties are explained more in the two examples below.

1. 1 raised to any power is 1; for example:

$$1^2 = 1$$
$$1^{-4} = 1$$
$$1^{912} = 1$$

2. Any number raised to the power of 0 equals 1 – sounds crazy, but it's true! Here's an example:

$$253^0 = 1$$

If you can remember these six properties, you'll be able to simplify almost any problem with exponents.

ROOTS AND RADICALS

Roots and radicals are sometimes held up as cliché symbols for difficult math problems, but in the real world, they're easy to understand and use to solve equations.

A radical is an expression that has a square root, cube root, etc. The symbol is a √. The number under that radical sign is called a radicand.

A square is an expression (not an equation!) in which a number is multiplied by itself. It is often said that the given number is raised to the power of 2. Here's an example: 4^2 is a square. 4 * 4 is the same square, expressed differently.

The square root of a number is a second number that, when multiplied by itself, will equal the first number. Therefore, it's the same as squaring a number, but in the opposite direction. For example, if you want to find the square root of 25, we have to figure out what number, when squared, equals 25. With enough experience, you will automatically know many of the common square roots. For example, it is commonly known that 5 is the square root of 25. Square and square root are operations that are often used to undo or cancel out each other in problem-solving situations. A mental image, kind of like a numerical mnemonic, that helps some people is to think of the given number and the square root (in the above case, 25 and 5) as the tree and its much smaller roots in the ground.

The previous example uses the number 25, which is an example of a perfect square. Only some numbers are perfect squares – those that are equal to the product of two integers. Below is a table of the first 10 perfect squares

FACTORS	PERFECT SQUARE
1 X 1	1
2 X 2	4
3 X 3	9
4 X 4	16
5 X 5	25
6 X 6	36
7 X 7	49
8 X 8	64
9 X 9	81
10 X 10	100

It is helpful to remember that if you find that the square root of any radicand is a whole number (not a fraction or a decimal), that means the given number is a perfect square.

To deal with radicals that are not perfect, you need to rewrite them as radical factors and simplify until you get one factor that's a perfect square. This process is sometimes called extracting or taking out the square root.

This process would be used for the following number:

$$\sqrt{18}$$

First, it's necessary to notice that 18 has within it the perfect square 9.

$$18 = 9 * 2 = 3^2 * 2$$

Therefore, $\sqrt{18}$ is not in its simplest form. Now, you need to extract the square root of 9

$$\sqrt{18} = \sqrt{9} * 2 = 3\sqrt{2}$$

Now the radicand no longer has any perfect square factors. $\sqrt{2}$ is an irrational number that is equal to approximately 1.414. Therefore, the approximate answer is the following:

$$\sqrt{18} = 3 * 1.414 = approximately\ 4.242$$

Note that the answer can only be an approximate one since $\sqrt{2}$ is an irrational number, which is any real number that cannot be expressed as a ratio of integers. Irrational numbers cannot be represented as terminating or repeating decimals.

FACTORIALS

If you have ever seen a number followed by an exclamation point, it's not yelling at you – it's called a factorial. Simply put, a factorial is the product of a number and all of the positive integers below it, stopping at 1. For example, if you see 5! its value is determined by doing the following example:

$$5! = 5 * 4 * 3 * 2 * 1 = 120$$

Factorials are typically used in relation to the fundamental principle of counting or for the combinations or permutations of sets.

BREAK TIME (15 MINS)

PERFORM AN ENJOYABLE ACTIVITY TO DISTRACT YOU FROM STUDYING.
READ SOMETHING LIGHT, GO FOR A WALK – WHATEVER YOU DO, TRY TO GET YOUR MIND OFF THE MATERIAL FOR A LITTLE WHILE.

ALGEBRA CONCEPTS

Algebra is a branch of Mathematics with symbols, referred to as variables, and numbers, as well as a system of rules for the manipulation of these. Solving higher-order word problems is a valuable application of the Algebra properties described in this chapter.

EXPRESSIONS

Algebra uses variables, numbers and operations as the basic parts. Variables are typically represented by letters and may have any number of values in a problem. Usually the variable is the unknown quantity in a problem. All letters can and often are used, but x, y, and z are letters that appear most often in algebra textbooks. In a testing situation, letters other than x, y, and z are often used to mislead test takers. Algebraic expressions are variables and numbers with operations such as addition, subtraction, multiplication and division. The following are all examples of algebraic expressions:

x	y	a	**(letters)**
7u	1/2 q (or q/2)	3.9 p	(product of a variable and number)
s + 5	u + v	2.3 + r	(sum of a variable and number)
z - 3.5	k- n	t - 1.3	(difference of a variable and number)
m/6	(z/2)	3.9 /p	(quotient of a variable and number)
c^2	$b^{0.5}$	√3	(variable or number with an exponent)

Finally, the sum, difference, product or quotient of these items are also expressions.

EQUATIONS

Equations are defined as algebraic expressions that are set equal to a number, variable or another expression. The simplest identifier of an equation is the equal sign (=). When an equation is written to express a condition or represent a situation for problem solving, the solution is normally completed by manipulating the equation correctly so that a variable or unknown quantity is on one side of the equal sign and the numerical answer(s) are on the other side of the equal sign. Let's review some problem-solving methods in the following examples.

If the simple equation is written in word form, the first step must be to write the equation that represents that written question. The simple problem of ages of individuals is a common example:

Example 1: Jane is 8 years older than Nancy. In 5 years, she will be 27 years old. What is Jane's age now?

The variable J will represent Jane's age and the expression J+5 will represent Jane's age in 5 years. In this example, we read that this expression is equal to a number, in this case 27. Our equation becomes:

$$J + 5 = 27$$

In the words of the problem, we have the correct expression set equal to a number. Our basic principle is to perform algebraic operations until the "J" is alone on one side of the equation and the numerical answer is on the other side. This type of solution involves the opposite of the addition (+5) so 5 is subtracted from both sides.

$$\begin{aligned} J + 5 &= 27 \\ -5 \quad & \quad -5 \\ J + 0 &= 22 \end{aligned}$$

Therefore, the answer says that the variable J, Jane's age, is now 22 years.

If the simple equation involved multiplication, the steps would involve an opposite operation that in this case would be division.

$$\begin{aligned} 7J &= 84 \\ 7J/7 &= 84/7 \\ J &= 12 \end{aligned}$$

These examples are typical of "one-step solutions" since a single operation is involved to solve the problem. Of course, there are multiple step solutions in more involved problems. But the rules are still the same, i.e.

1. Opposite operations are performed to solve
2. The same operations must be performed on both sides of the equation
3. The solution is complete when a variable is on one side and the answers are on the other side

Example 2: Jane is 8 years older than Nancy. In 5 years, she will be twice as old as Nancy. What is Jane's age now?

The first step to solving this type of problem is to identify the variable. In this solution, we will select the variable "J" to represent Jane's age and "N" to represent Nancy's age.
The two equations from the word description, become:

$$J - 8 = N$$
$$and$$
$$J + 5 = 2(N + 5)$$

Dividing both sides of the second equation by 2 means that it becomes

$$(J + 5)/2 = N + 5$$

Adding 5 to the original equation we have

$$J - 8 + 5 = N + 5$$

In this method, there are two expressions which contain "J" that are both equal to "N + 5" so therefore, they must be equal to each other. So:

$$J - 3 = (J + 5)/2$$

Multiply both sides by 2 (same operation on both sides) and the equation is:

$$2J - 6 = J + 5$$

Subtract J and add 6 to both sides and the answer becomes:

$$2J - 6 = J + 5$$
$$-J + 6 \quad -J + 6$$
$$J = 11$$

By this solution, the problem is completed, and the following statements are clarified:

1. Now, Jane is 11 years old, and Nancy is 3 years old.
2. In 5 years, Jane will be 16 years old, and Nancy will be 8 years old.

We are able to answer the question, "What is Jane's age now?" and all the other ages in the question because of an algebra principle that requires two equations for two unknowns. In the problem, there are two variables (J and N) and two relationships between them (now and 5 years from now). If we are able to formulate two equations with the two unknowns, then algebra principles will allow for the solution of a complex problem.

QUADRATIC EQUATIONS

Quadratic equations are algebraic equations where the largest variable exponent is equal to two. This is often referred to as a "second degree" equation. If there are multiple terms, it can also be referred to as a second degree polynomial, where polynomial indicates that there are multiple terms in the equation. Quadratic equations are valuable in higher-order problem solving situations, with particularly important application in Physics problem solving. Examples are depicted below:

$$7x^2 = 0$$
$$½\,(9.8)\,t^2 = 27$$
$$ax2 + bx + c = 0,$$
$$where\ a, b\ and\ c\ are\ real\ numbers$$

Note that all quadratic equations can be written in the form of the last example because coefficients can be zero and algebra operations can be performed so that the 0 is on the right side of the equation. This last statement is the standard form and is of great importance. Every quadratic equation in this form can be solved with the quadratic formula. It is presented here with a qualifying statement. In a timed testing environment, the use of the following formula is typically used when factoring is not feasible, since it is a time consuming option.

The quadratic formula for equations in the standard form states:

$$x = \frac{-b \pm \sqrt{b^2 - 4ac}}{2a}$$

Due to the complexity of the quadratic formula, it will normally be used when the term

$$(b2 - 4ac) / (2a) = 0$$
$$(b2 - 4ac) / (2a) = a\,perfect\ square$$

Since the use of technology is not allowed, any more intricate application of the quadratic formula will be too time consuming to be useful. Note that the operations before the square root sign are both correct. The plus and minus signs indicate that every quadratic equation has the possibility of two answers. It does not say that both answers will be valid to the multiple-choice word problem that is in quadratic form. This is easily explained with a simple statement. Since two negative numbers and two positive numbers multiplied together give a positive answer, any quadratic equation may have two possible correct answers. When answering questions about quadratic equations in multiple-choice problems, that statement should be considered.

FOIL – POLYNOMIAL MULTIPLICATION

Polynomial multiplication is routinely taught with a method described as FOIL, which stands for First, Outside, Inside and Last. In a binomial multiplication problem, the form will usually look like this, with A, B, C, D as whole number coefficients:

$$(Ax + B) * (Cx + D)$$

- The "First" means that Ax and Cx are multiplied together to equal ACx^2
- The "Outside" means that Ax and D are multiplied together to equal ADx
- The "Inside" means that B and Cx are multiplied together to equal BCx
- The "Last" means that B and D are multiplied together to equal BD

The polynomial answer becomes:

$$ACx^2 + (AD + BC)x + BD$$

In testing conditions, this method can be cumbersome, confusing, and unreliable because mistakes are too common. A simplified alternative is called the Box Method, and it is simpler for multiple reasons.

1. There is a box that provides the organization for the multiplication.
2. The box also provides organization for the addition of like terms.

3. This method is expandable for use with longer polynomial multiplication.

To use the Box Method for polynomial multiplication, follow these steps:

1. Create a box that has a row and column for each term in the multiplication problem.
2. Perform the multiplication of each pair of terms.
3. Place the answers in the cells of the box.
4. Add the like terms that are aligned diagonally.
5. Write the polynomial.

The following diagram explains the outcome with the previously noted example:

$$(Ax + B) * (Cx + D) \ becomes:$$

	Ax	**B**
Cx	ACx^2	BCx
D	ADx	BD

The diagonal boxes in the upper right and lower left are always the "like terms" so there are no questions as to which terms must be added. This is true if you have ordered the binomials correctly with the "x term" of the binomials on the left and on top, respectively. The final outcome is the same as the FOIL answer previously noted:

$$ACx2 + (AD + BC)x + BD$$

Notice also that the Box Method has the additional benefit of separating the addition and multiplication operations completely.
In a multiple-choice problem such as this, there is a significant benefit in using the box method as a time saving technique.

Example: (x + 6) (4x + 8) = (choose a correct answer below)

	x	**6**
$4x$	$4x^2$	$24x$
8	$8x$	48

A	$4x^2 + 32x + 48$
B	$4x^2 + 32x + 32$
C	$4x^2 + 32x + 14$
D	$4x^2 + 14x + 48$

The lower right box entry means that the last term in the answer must be 6 * 8, or 48. So, both answers B and C can be eliminated because the last term is not 48.

The upper right and lower left box entries are added and the middle term must be 24x + 8x = 32x. So, answer D can be eliminated because the middle term is not 14x.

The correct answer must be A, a choice that can be made logically by looking at the box entries. Eliminating choices is expedited with the Box Method because the box entries can be easily compared to coefficients in the answer choices.

SUBSTITUTE VARIABLES

Many mathematical applications involve using equations and then substituting via terminology. This means that the algebraic equation will typically have a single variable with all other parameters defined as whole, decimal, or fractional numbers. Then to solve a specific problem, the value of the specific variable will be uniquely defined (in some cases, multiple values may be supplied for comparison) and the variables used to determine a solution. For example, let's use the previously discussed, for a car travelling at miles per hour:
Distance traveled equals 70 mph multiplied by time t in hours
Without the words, in strictly algebraic terms:

$$D = 70t \ (t \ in \ hours)$$

To find the amount of distance traveled, solve the equation by substituting the value of time that is appropriate for the problem. If the problem stated that the equation would be solved with the following:

$$D = 70 * 2.5$$

After multiplying, the answer for the distance traveled is 175 miles.

In some equations, you may be asked to evaluate an equation that involves a second-degree variable. For example, a word description might read as follows:

Distance traveled is equal to one-half 9.8 m/sec^2 multiplied by the time squared
Again, without words, in strictly algebraic terms the equation would be:

$$D = 1/2 * 9.8 * t^2$$

Evaluating this equation for a time of 2 second becomes:

$$D = 1/2 * 9.8 * 2^2 = 1/2 * 9.8 * 4 = 2 * 9.8 = 19.6 \, meters$$

The answers have distance units that are determined by the units of measure that are given in problem statement. Miles per hour multiplied by hours gives distances in miles. Meters per second per second multiplied by seconds square will provide distances in meters. The units of time and distance within the problem must be consistent. Substituting variables will be simple if the variables are consistent.

INEQUALITIES – GREATER THAN AND LESS THAN

Inequalities are an algebra topic that is often misrepresented and taught in a more difficult manner than necessary. When we find solutions to algebra equations there is a single number (or two numbers in the case of a quadratic equation) that represents the set of all numbers that are equal to the algebraic expression on the other side of the equal sign.

Inequalities represent the set of all numbers that are either greater than or less than that specific solution. If the number 3 represents the solution equation, then the following number line will help visualize what the inequalities may look like:

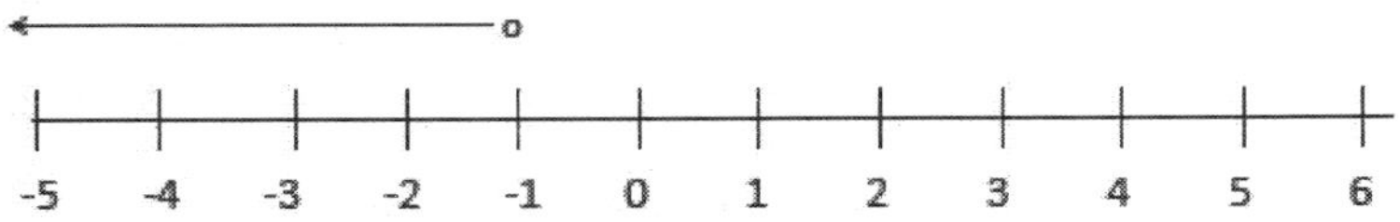

The arrow on the left side of the "o" is the less than inequality, and the arrow on the right side of the "o" is the greater than inequality. Of course, the "o" represents the exact solution of the inequality. This simplicity tells us that the simplest way to solve the inequality is to first solve the equality and then find out which arrow is required. The solution with quadratics will be discussed at the end of this section.
The inequality 7x + 2 > -5 will be solved by first solving the equality:

$$7x + 2 = -5$$

Following the steps discussed in section 2, the first step is to subtract 2 from both sides and divide both sides by 7. The solution of the equality says:

$$x = -1$$

To see which way the arrow points, we will use the value of x = 0 in the inequality to see if it is true. If it is true, then the arrow pointing to the right is correct (>), which is what we would expect. If x = 0 is not true then the arrow must point the other direction (<). The test helps by ensuring that the point at x = 0 is or is not in the solution set of the inequality, allowing the correct answer to be chosen.

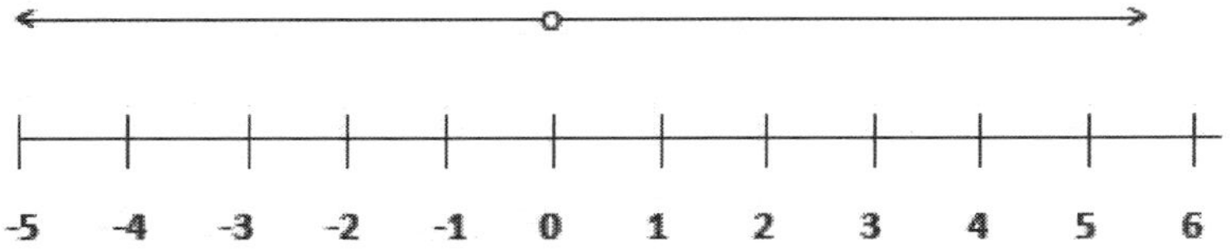

Therefore, substituting x = 0 means: $7(0) + 2 > -5$

Since 2 is greater than negative 5, the answer looks like the following diagram:

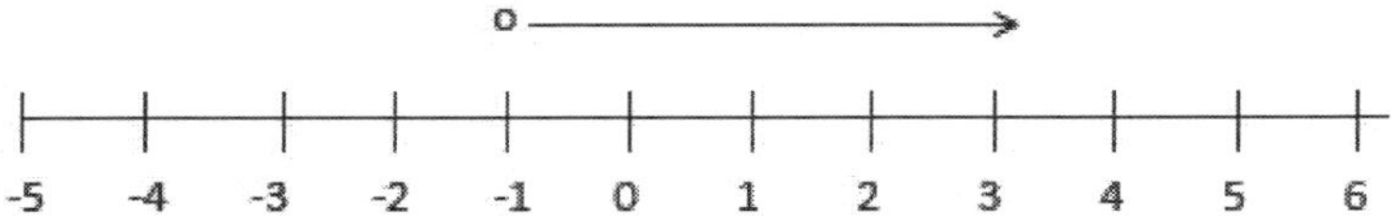

The arrow includes the point "0" on the number line because the "Zero Test" tells us that that point satisfies the inequality. If the "0" is not included then the arrow must point to the left of the point at -1, which was the answer to the equality. For this reason, both "Greater Than" and "Less Than" are addressed in this section. They are determined the same way, specifically:

First, find the solution to the equality.
Second, test to see if x = 0 is true for the inequality.
If the test is true, the solution must include the point x = 0.
If the test is not true, the inequality goes the opposite direction.

There may be the question as to why the value of x = 0 is chosen for the test. Simply, it represents the simplest solution for evaluating algebra equations with variables. Any term which has an "x" (or x^2 or higher order) simply disappears when x = 0, leaving only the constant numerical terms.

If there is a need to solve an inequality where the equality solution is $x = 0$, then the inequality test can be performed with $x = 1$. The test is almost as simple as the zero test, and it applies if the equality solution is 0. The same logical decision process used for the zero test also applies here.

MODULE 2

DAY, LOCATION, MUSIC

1

MONDAY, OCTOBER 12

COFFEE SHOP ON MAIN STREET

MY FAVORITE BAND

2

3

LIFE AND PHYSICAL SCIENCE

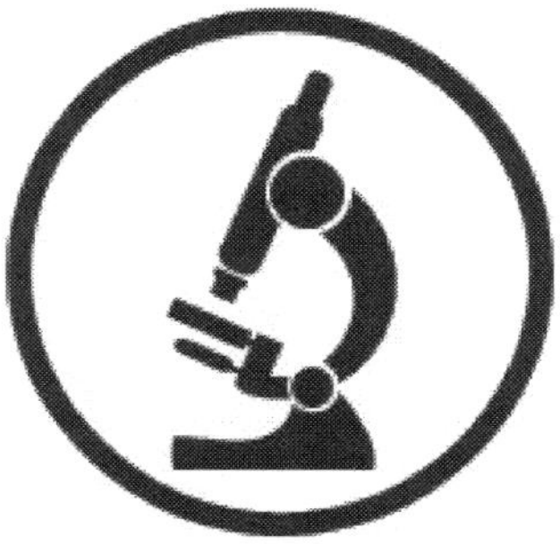

The questions contained in the science sections of the PAX are designed to evaluate one's level of knowledge of the chemical basis of life, cellular biology, human anatomy and human physiology. This includes virtually the entire range of content of a full year of introductory high school level biology and general chemistry. Additionally, the PAX will likely include questions that test for knowledge of topics that are often not well covered by the introductory high school level courses in biology and general chemistry. In particular, these topics may include material that is usually addressed in higher level courses such as organic chemistry, biochemistry, cell physiology, human physiology, human anatomy, human embryology, and human genetics.

It is obviously not practical to provide a complete science review within a single manual that includes the entire range of material that is covered in multiple years of science coursework at a high school or college level. No study manual can claim that it covers everything in the TEAS. The information provided in this manual is – in our opinion – likely to be high-yield. In other words, it is material that is very likely to be encountered as topics of actual PAX science questions. We also present the material as a logical progression of topics – as a storyline that makes sense and is (we hope) reasonably interesting. It is also our judgement that by far most of lower-yield science information that is actually encountered on PAX science questions is likely within this section of the manual.

We also – when necessary – may introduce concepts that are unlikely to be directly tested for on the TEAS, but that greatly clarify and simplify the explanation of high-yield information. This material will allow one to avoid the need to use rote memorization of a large amount of high-yield facts as preparation for the TEAS. It will also provide a deeper level of understanding of a large amount of otherwise confusing information and allow us to introduce much of the more advanced science topics in an efficient and more easily grasped manner. Although we cannot guarantee that this manual will prepare you for every possible PAX science question, we are confident it will prepare you to succeed at the highest levels of the PAX science section.

Properties of Matter

Physical properties of matter are those that can be observed or measured, such as color, elasticity, mass, volume, and temperature.

Mass measures the amount of a substance is in an object. **Weight** is the amount of gravitational pull of Earth on an object. **Volume** is the amount of space the object occupies. **Density** is the amount of mass per unit volume.

Mass

Nearly everything in the universe relevant to the PAX can be defined as matter or as energy. Matter is essentially everything that has mass. Nearly all matter on earth is composed of atoms, and atoms are composed of three basic subatomic particles: the proton, the neutron, and the electron. All three of these subatomic particles have a fundamental physical property called mass.

Any physical object on earth should be thought of as being composed entirely of atoms. All physical objects on earth therefore have mass. This mass is the sum of the mass of all the atoms that comprise the object. The mass of the atoms of the object is the sum of the masses of all the protons, neutrons, and electrons that compose the atoms of the object.

For macroscopic objects such as a rock, a glass of water, or a balloon full of helium gas, the SI unit of mass is the kilogram (kg). In the laboratory, it is more common to work with smaller units of mass than kilograms. The most common of these mass units are grams and milligrams. Grams (g) are 1/1000th of a kilogram and milligrams (mg) are $1/1000th$ that of a gram. It is unusual that the kilogram is the standard SI unit for mass since a kilogram is equal to 1000 grams.

At the atomic scale, masses are incredibly small. The mass of a proton is $1.6726\ x\ 10^{-27}$ kg, and the mass of the neutron is slightly more than the mass of a proton, but the mass of the electron is 1827 times lighter than the mass of the proton. For atomic scales, masses are given in atomic mass units (AMUs). The AMU unit is vastly smaller than a kilogram unit. The mass of a proton in AMUs is approximately 1.007 AMU. The mass of the electron is so small that it can be approximated as zero for most cases likely to be encountered in the TEAS.

Density

In addition to mass, all matter also has a volume. For any given sample of matter, that volume is the amount of space that the sample occupies. The mass of a sample of matter divided by the volume of the sample of matter is the mass per unit volume of the sample (m/V).

Density is mass divided by volume.
D = m/V

The density of liquid water at a temperature of 4° C is equal to 1 gram per cubic centimeter ($1\ g/cm^3$).

Weight
The physical quantities of weight and mass are often misunderstood. Mass is an intrinsic property of matter that is determined by the type and number of atoms that comprise a given sample of matter. Weight is a force that acts on matter in a gravitational field.

Basic Atomic Structure

The Atom
The atom is the smallest unit of matter that can retain the physical and chemical properties of a specific substance. Atoms are composed of three subatomic particles; electrons – which are fundamental (not composed of smaller subatomic particles) – and protons and neutrons which are each composed of quarks. Quarks are fundamental subatomic particles.

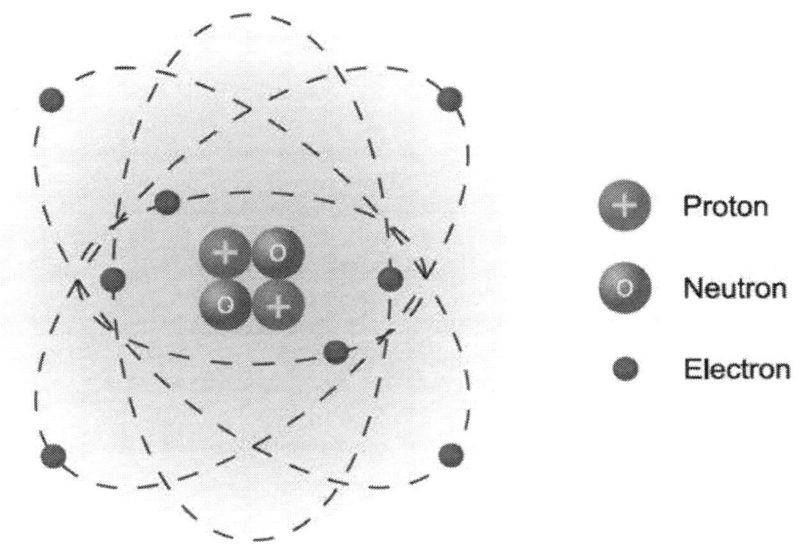

Atomic and Molecular Weights
The terms atomic and molecular weights are often used in science and should be equivalent to the terms atomic mass and molecular mass where the units of mass in grams is substituted for the number of AMU units. If, for example, an atom has an atomic mass of 10 AMU, then the corresponding atomic weight is 10 grams. This is equivalent to the number of atoms that, as a sample, would have a total mass of 10 grams. We have discussed that a single atom's atomic mass is approximately the sum of the masses of the protons and neutrons contained in the atom's nucleus. The unit of mass at the atomic level is the atomic mass unit (AMU). When the term atomic weight is used, it is referring to the average mass of an atom of an element.

The Atomic Nucleus
The central region of an atom – the nucleus – is composed of protons and the neutrons. The only exception to this statement is that one isotope of the element hydrogen – hydrogen 1 – consists of atoms that have a nucleus that contains one single proton and no neutrons. Protons and neutrons are more generally classified as nucleons. The nucleons of an atomic nucleus are held together by the strong nuclear force.

Atomic Mass

The mass of a proton is equal to exactly one atomic mass unit (1 AMU). The mass of a neutron is nearly equal to but slightly higher than that of the proton. For the TEAS, the mass of the neutron is also 1 AMU. The mass of an electron is several thousand times less than 1 AMU and for the PAX the mass of the electron is so small that it will irrelevant in comparison to proton and neutron masses. The mass of a single atom therefore is almost entirely due to the sum of the masses of the nucleons (protons and neutrons) in the atom's nucleus. For example, an atom whose nucleus contains six protons and seven neutrons has an atomic mass of 6 AMU + 7 AMU = 13 AMU.

Electrons and Atomic Charge

The nucleus is surrounded by electrons. Electrons have an electric charge of -1, protons have an electric charge of +1, and neutrons have zero charge. Particles with opposite electric charges are attracted to one another by the electromagnetic force (particles with the same electric charge repel each other). It is the electromagnetic force that attracts electrons to an atom's positively charged nucleus. When an atom contains the same number of electrons and protons, the positive charge due to the protons in the nucleus and the negative charge of the electrons surrounding the nucleus cancel out. As a result, the atom has a net electric charge of zero. When this is the case, the atom is called a neutral atom.

Elements

An element is the group of all atoms that have the same number of protons in their nucleus. For instance, the element carbon refers to all atoms that have exactly four protons in their atomic nuclei. Most carbon atoms also have four neutrons in their nuclei, so most carbon atoms have an atomic mass of approximately 8 AMU (4 protons + 4 neutrons). Some carbon atoms have more than 4 neutrons in their nuclei, so these carbon atoms have a mass larger than 8 AMU. On average, the mass of a carbon atom is somewhat larger than 8 AMU due to the existence of the carbon atoms that have nuclei with more than 4 neutrons. The actual average value depends on the naturally occurring percentages of heavier carbon atoms. This average elemental atom mass is defined as the element's atomic mass – but also is frequently described as the element's atomic weight.

In the laboratory, the term atomic weight is the equivalent to the element's atomic mass in grams. This is a very important definition to understand because it is used as a scientific basis for designing almost all chemical experiments. The reason for this is because the atomic masses of all the elements have been determined experimentally. The absolute values of these elemental masses are less important than the fact that we also know what the elemental masses are relative to the other elemental masses. For instance, the atomic mass (average mass) of a carbon atom is approximately 12 AMU (21.01), and the atomic mass of an oxygen atom is approximately 16 AMU.

Ions

Atoms can have fewer or more electrons than protons. When the number of electrons exceeds the number of protons, the atom has a net negative charge. When the number of protons exceeds the number of electrons, the atom has a net positive charge. The net charge is equal to the sum of the positive charges due to protons and negative charges due to electrons. For instance, if an atom has eight electrons and six protons, then the net charge of the atom is $(-8) + (6) = -2$.

Atoms (and molecules) with net charges are called ions. Negative ions are called anions, and positive ions are called cations.

Larger particles such as molecules and even macroscopic objects can have a net charge, but this net charge always is due to an unbalanced number of electrons and protons within the particle or object
We will discuss the electromagnetic force at the atomic and molecular level in greater detail in the chemistry review section, but it is important to note that nearly all of the macroscopic mechanical forces such as mechanical friction, air resistance, and the pressures exerted by fluids and gases are actually due to the repulsive electromagnetic force at the atomic level between the electrons of different atoms.

Isotopes

The simplest atom is the hydrogen atom. Any atom that has one and only one proton in its nucleus is an atom of the element hydrogen. Hydrogen atoms may also have one or two neutrons in their atomic nucleus. These three types of hydrogen nuclei – one with one proton only, one with one proton and one neutron and one with one proton and two neutrons – all have one proton in their nucleus, but the nuclei have different numbers of neutrons. Elemental atoms with different numbers of neutrons in their nucleus are designated as isotopes of the element. Therefore, there are three isotopes of the element hydrogen.

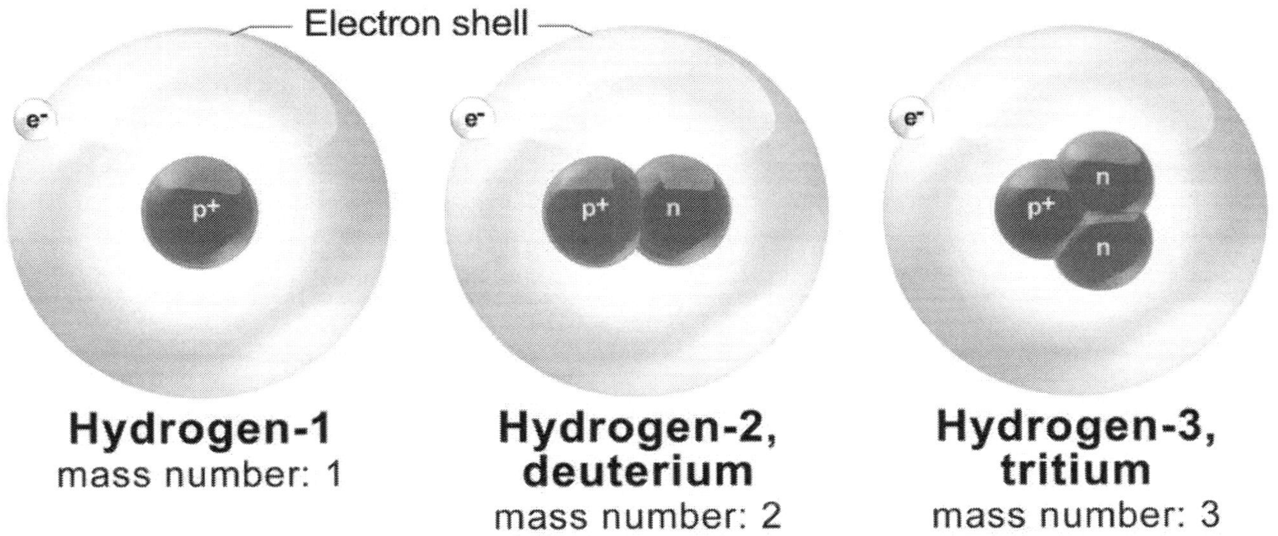

The other elements have varying numbers of isotopes. Atoms with nuclei that contain different numbers of protons are different elements. The atoms of every individual element have a unique set of physical and chemical properties. Isotopes of an element have virtually identical chemical properties but can have different physical properties due to the difference in mass among the isotopes.

Atomic Weight

The atomic weight of an element is defined as the average atomic mass of atoms of an element. Since almost every element has at least two isotopes, the average mass of the elemental atoms depends on the masses of the isotopes and the fractional percentage (relative abundance) of the isotopes that occur in nature.

Hypothetically, imagine that hydrogen's three isotopes occur naturally in percentages of 50% H-1 (one proton or 1 AMU), 20% H-2 (1 proton and 1 neutron or 2 AMU) and 30% H-3 (one proton and 2 neutrons or 3 AMU). The average atomic weight of hydrogen atoms in general would be

$$(0.5)(1\,AMU) + (0.2)(2\,AMU) + (0.3)(3\,AMU) = 0.5 + 0.4 + 0.9 = 1.8$$

If these were the actual percentages of hydrogen's three isotopes, the average mass of hydrogen atoms would be 1.8 AMU and the atomic mass of the element hydrogen would be 1.8. Nearly all hydrogen (99.99%) is the isotope H-1; therefore, the tiny fractions of heavier isotopes are too small to change the mass except at several digits to the right of the decimal point. Therefore, the atomic mass of the element hydrogen is very nearly equal to that of the hydrogen-1 isotope, which is 1.008.

For the lighter elements, usually the most common isotope by far is the isotope that has equal numbers of protons and neutrons, so most atomic weights are close to twice the element's atomic number (the number of protons in the elemental atom nucleus). This is not always true. For instance, the element chlorine has an atomic number of 17 and an atomic weight of 35.45. This indicates that the element chlorine contains a relatively large percentage of the heavier chlorine isotopes.

The Periodic Table

The periodic table arranges the elements in a modified grid-like chart. Each element occupies a unique position in the table. The position correlates with the element's atomic number (as we have mentioned, the atomic number of an element is equal to the number of protons contained in the nucleus of atoms of the element). The first element – hydrogen – occupies the upper left corner position in the table. Elements of sequentially increasing atomic number are added to the next available position in the same row of the chart immediately to the right until the row of the table is complete. The element with the next higher atomic number is assigned to the first position on the left of the row immediately below the completed upper-row of the table.

Groups and Periods

The rows of the periodic table are called periods; the columns of the table are called groups. The first two columns on the left side of the table, beginning with the first column on the left, are the group I elements and – for the adjacent column on the right – the group II elements. The last column on the right side of the table is designated as the group XIII elements. The columns that are located to the immediate left of the group VIII column, beginning with the adjacent column, are the group VII, VI, V, IV, and III elements,
The first period (top row) of the table has only a group 1 position – hydrogen – and a group VIII position – helium. They are separated by a wide gap in the periodic row. The second period has eight positions that include all the groups I-VIII. The group I and group II positions are separated by another large gap from the group III-VIII positions. The third period has eighteen positions. Between the group II and the group III positions are ten new positions. The elements corresponding to these ten new positions are designated as transition metal elements.

The gaps in the periods ultimately reflect differences and similarities in properties of the elements that emerge as electrons arrange themselves in various configurations. We will describe the manner of how electrons are arranged around an atomic nucleus shortly.

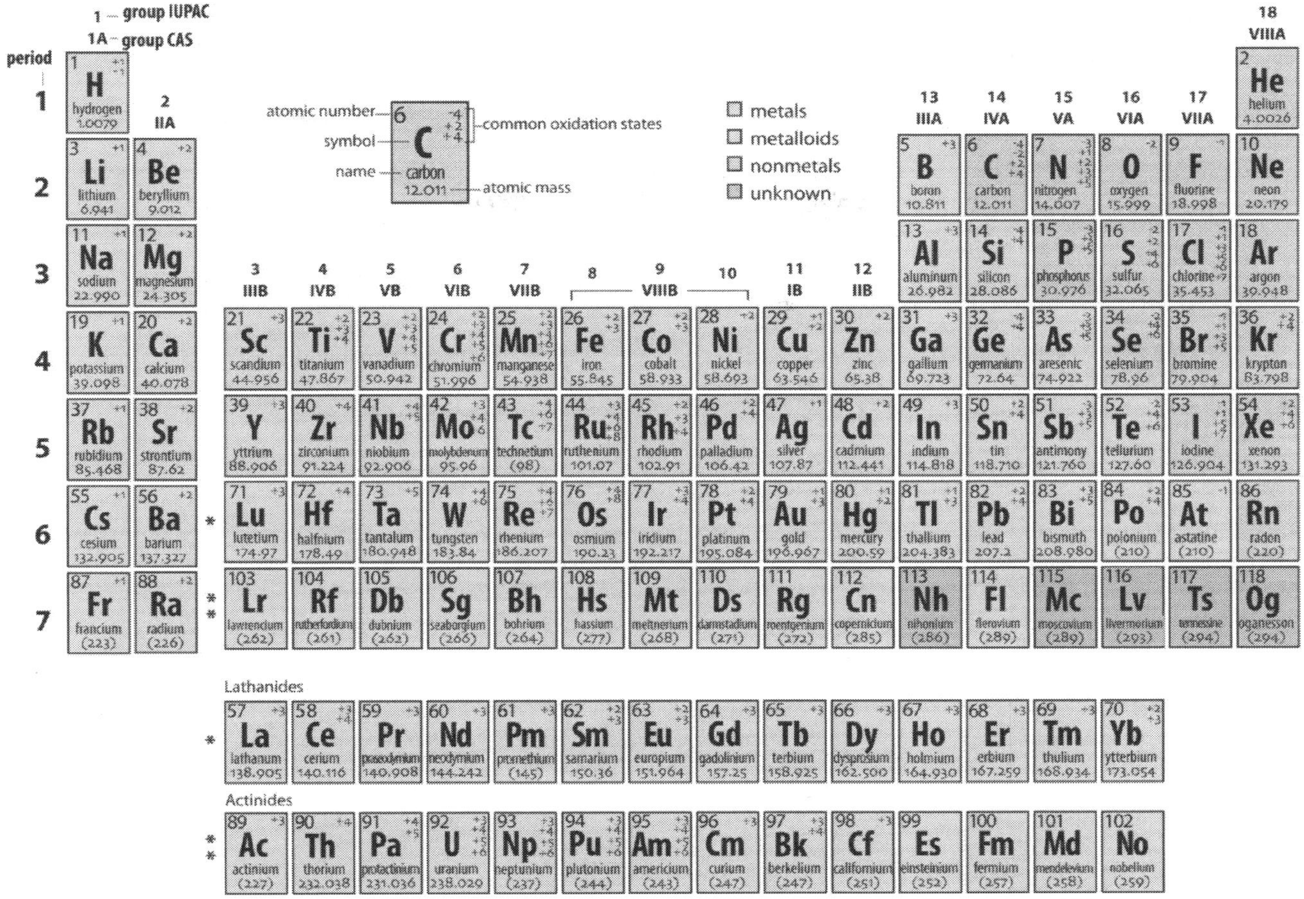
1 group IUPAC
1A group CAS
period
atomic number
symbol
name
common oxidation states
atomic mass
6 C carbon 12.011
metals
metalloids
nonmetals
unknown
Lathanides
Actinides

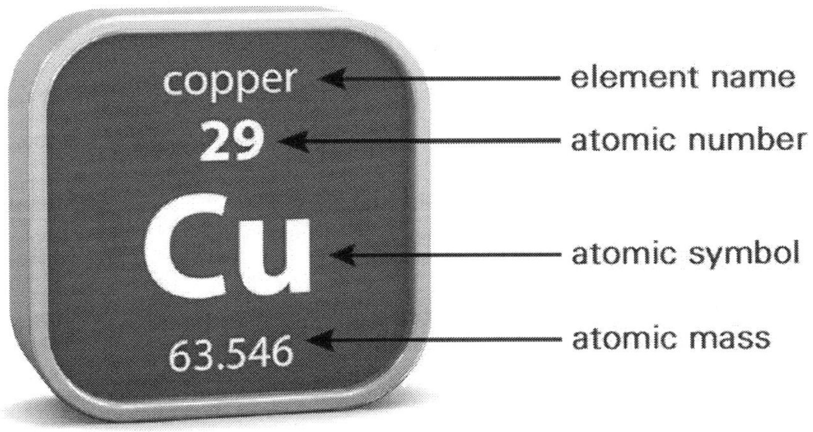
copper
29
Cu
63.546
element name
atomic number
atomic symbol
atomic mass

Atomic Energy States

All atoms strive to attain their lowest possible energy states. First, this is favored by achieving charge neutrality for the atom. The nuclei of atoms have a positive charge equal to the number of protons in the atom's nucleus. All protons have a charge of +1. The most energetically favorable state for an atom in terms of charge is the neutral state. An electron has charge of -1, the exact opposite charge of a proton. When an atom contains equal numbers of protons and electrons the proton and electron charges cancel out and the atom's net charge is zero. Neutral atoms have a net charge of zero. Neutral atoms, however, can lower their overall energy state even further if they can achieve an arrangement of electrons.

Electron Shells - the N levels

Electrons that are electromagnetically bound to an atom arrange themselves in concentric electron shells around the nucleus. In an atom, the innermost electron shell is the "n=1" electron shell. The "n=1" electron shell contains the lowest energy level positions available to electrons. For this reason, the n=1 shell is the first to be filled by electrons. The n level can be any positive integer n=1,2,3... the larger the integer value for n, the higher the energy of the n electron shell.

Electron Subshells (Orbitals)

The regions within an electron shell that electrons may occupy are called subshells or electron orbitals. The n=1 level shell has only one type of subshell/ orbital. This is a spherical orbital called an "s" orbital. Since this s orbital is located at the n=1 shell, it is designated as the "1s" orbital. Individual subshell orbitals can accommodate no more than 2 electrons. There is only one "s" orbital at any n shell level. Therefore, only two electrons can be accommodated at the n=1 level.

An atom achieves a significant lowering of its energy state when it fills its n=1 shell. Atoms of the element helium have two protons and therefore will achieve charge neutrality by acquiring 2 electrons. Additionally, these two electrons will fill the 1s orbital. This also simultaneously completes the n=1 electron shell. There is no additional electron configuration that will further lower the energy state of helium atoms. Helium is therefore chemically inert – it will almost never participate in any chemical reactions with other elements.

Period 2 Elements and p Orbitals

For elements with atomic numbers higher than 2 (by definition, atoms that have nuclei containing more than 2 protons), additional electrons must be acquired for the atoms to achieve charge neutrality. Beginning with helium, the n=1 electron shell is filled. For all elements with atomic numbers greater than 2, additional electrons must occupy higher energy positions within orbitals beginning at the n=2 electron shell.

At the n=2 level, there are two types of orbitals – the s orbital and a new type of orbital, the "p" orbital. At the n=2 shell level, and at all subsequently higher shell levels (n= 3, 4 ...) there are one "s" orbital and three "p" orbitals. Within any n level electron shell, this new type of orbital – the p orbital – is at a higher energy level in comparison to the s orbital.

Since the maximum electron capacity of any single orbital is always 2 electrons, the n=2 shell can accommodate a total of eight electrons: 2 in the single s orbital and 2 electrons in each of the three p orbitals. These orbitals at the n=2 level is designated as the 2s orbital and the 2px, 2py and 2pz orbitals. Elements in the second period (row) of the periodic table have electrons that occupy positions within the orbitals of the n=2 electron shell. There are eight elements in the second period of the table, beginning with lithium on the left in the group I column directly beneath hydrogen. The elements to the right of lithium sequentially add one additional electron to the n=2 level orbitals. At the final position on the right (and the 8th position of the period) is the element neon (atomic number 10). Notice that neon has completed the n=2 electron shell and that neon is in the group VIII column directly below helium.

Electron Configuration Notation

The electron configuration (positions) of an atom can be specified by listing the electron shells and orbitals that contain electrons. The electron positions are specified beginning with the lowest energy orbital on the left and then to progressively higher energy orbitals. For hydrogen, this would be indicated by the following notation: $1s^1$

For helium (atomic number 2) this would be: $1s^2$
For neon (atomic number 10) this would be: $1s^2 2s^2 2p^6$

Since at any given n electron shell level, the s orbitals are lower energy than the p orbitals, the s orbitals fill before electrons begin to occupy positions in p orbitals.

NOTE: The electron energy level notation indicates the lowest possible electron energy state for an atom. This is called the ground state for electrons in an atom. Electrons can acquire energy by absorbing photons and consequently jump to higher energy level orbitals. This is termed an excited energy state. If an electron absorbs energy it can escape from the parent atom entirely. The energy required for this is equal to the parent atom's elemental ionization energy.

Valence Electrons

At this point we can begin to explain and even predict the chemical properties of the elements as well as many physical properties of the elements. For the ten period 2 elements, the n=2 electron shell is the outermost electron shell. Recall that all ten of the period 2 elements have an innermost n=1 electron shell that is filled by 2 electrons. These electrons are very tightly bound to their atomic nuclei and under normal circumstances never participate in chemical reactions. It is the electrons in the outermost or highest energy shells of an atom that participate in chemical reactions. These outermost shell electrons are usually called valence electrons.

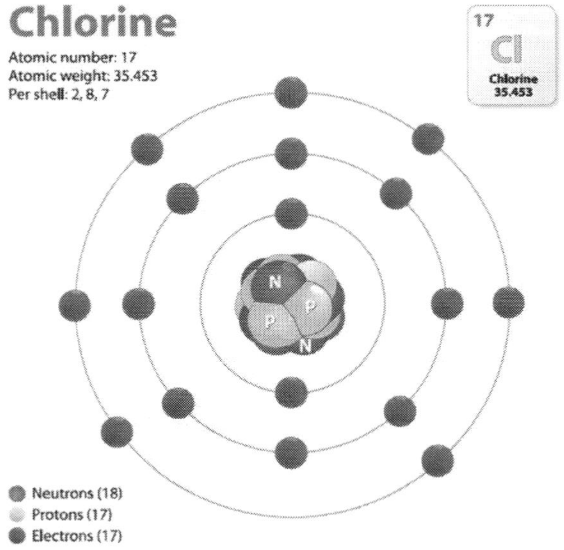

The Octet Rule

The energy of an atom is lowered by a large amount when the n=1 electron shell is completed by the acquisition of 2 electrons that occupy the 1s orbital. Beginning at the n=2 energy level, an additional large reduction of energy occurs when the 2s orbital and the three 2p orbitals of the shell are filled by electrons. This is an underlying explanation for the octet rule.

The octet rule states that there is a fundamental reason that atoms engage in chemical reactions. The reason is atoms strongly desire to acquire exactly eight valence electrons in their valence s and p orbitals. The reason for this desire is that this eight-electron configuration in the valence s and p orbitals results in a large reduction in an atom's electron energy level. Atoms that do not have a filled valence octet can "fill" the octet by taking electrons from other atoms (and consequently becoming an anion). Alternatively, atoms may achieve a valence octet by sharing additional electrons with other atoms through the formation of covalent chemical bonds with those other atoms.

Periodic Properties of the Elements

The term periodic in the periodic table reflects the fact that the chemical and many physical properties of the elemental atoms tend to periodically repeat. This is because elemental atoms with the same number of s and p orbital valence electrons attempt to satisfy the octet rule in the same manner. Atoms of the elements that are in the same column of groups I through VIII have the same number of s and p valence electrons.

Except helium, all the elements in group VIII (the noble gases) have satisfied the octet rule as neutral atoms. They have no energetic advantage to gain by participating in chemical reactions with other elemental atoms. Consequently, the noble gases are chemically inert.

The Trends in the Periodic Table - From Left to Right Electronegativity

The ability of an elemental atom to draw electrons from other atoms to share in a covalent bond or, in extreme cases, to take an electron away from an atom is determined by the electronegativity of the atom. The electronegativity of elemental atoms is primarily determined by how near the atom is to complete a valence octet. The group VII element atoms (the halogens) are one electron short of completing their valence octets and are therefore the most electronegative of the group I through VII elemental atoms. The group I elemental atoms (the alkali metals) are 7 electrons short of completing their valence octets. They are the farthest away from completing their valence octet and have little to gain by attempting to acquire additional electrons. The group I elemental atoms therefore have the lowest electronegativity of the groups, I through VII elemental atoms.

The trend in the electronegativities of elements in the periodic table is that electronegativities increase from left to right across a period. This trend is broken at the last element on the right of a period. This is the group VIII element. The noble gases (group VIII) have no desire for additional electrons and therefore have almost zero electronegativity.

ELECTRONEGATIVITY

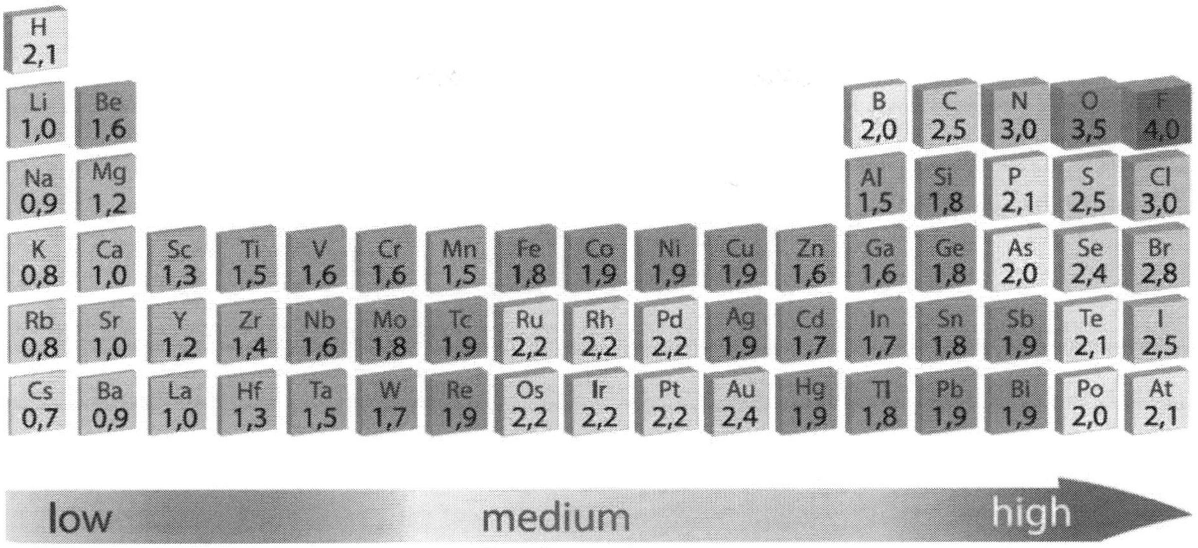

Ionization Energies

The ionization energy for an atom is the amount of energy required to overcome the electrons attraction to its nucleus. The extraction of the first electron from an atom requires the lowest amount of energy. This is called the first ionization energy. This process results in a $+1$ charged atomic ion. Extracting a second electron requires a larger amount of energy. This process results in a $2+$ atomic ion. Each subsequent ionization requires progressively higher amounts of energy.

An elemental atom's ionization energies are usually correlated to the elemental atom's electronegativity. Elements with the lowest first ionization energies are the Group I elements and those with the highest first ionization energies are the group VIII elements. The exception to this correlation is the noble gases. The noble gases have the lowest electronegativities of the all the periodic groups but have the highest ionization energies of all the periodic groups.

The trend in the ionization energies of elements in the periodic table is that ionization energies increase from left to right across a period.

Atomic Radius

The electrons of an atom orbit the atom's nucleus. The outermost orbiting electrons define the surface boundary of the atom and define the size of the atom. Usually this size is given in terms of atomic radius or atomic diameter. The trend from left to right in the periodic table for the atomic radii of the elemental atoms is that the atomic radius decreases from left to right. The reason for this is that in the periodic table the progression from left to right correlates with an increasing number of protons contained in the nucleus and therefore an increasing positive nuclear charge of the elemental atoms. This increasing positive nuclear charge exerts a stronger electromagnetic force on the electrons orbiting the nucleus. As a result, the electrons are physically drawn closer to the nucleus, including the electrons located in the outermost electron shell. Since the outermost electron shell determines the outer boundary surface of an atom, increasing nuclear charge will decrease the atom's atomic radius.

The Trends in the Periodic Table - from Top to Bottom

Electronegativities and ionization energies decrease from top to bottom in the periodic table and atomic radii increase from top to bottom in the periodic table. There is a common phenomenon that explains all three trends. This is the phenomenon of electron shell shielding of the atomic nucleus.

Physical Properties of Transition Metals Malleability and Ductility

The ability of transition metal nuclei to move relatively easily in relation to other transition metal nuclei within the solid state of a transition metal sample explains the physical properties of transition metals of ductility and malleability. The metals can be shaped (malleability) and stretched (ductility) and yet the atoms within a transition metal object are still strongly attracted to one another. Although the metal objects can be forged or stretched into different shapes, including very thin wires, it is extremely difficult to separate a metal object into two or more separate objects. These properties of ductility, malleability and tensile strength make the transition metals ideal elements for use as structural materials. They are strong yet can be machined into a wide variety of useful shapes – tools, weapons and parts of complex machinery.

Electrical and Thermal Conductivity

The mobile electrons in the conduction bands of transition metal also make the transition metals excellent conductors of electricity. Transition metals have very high specific heats of fusion and vaporization. It requires very large amounts of heat to melt or vaporize transition metal objects, but the specific heats of transition metals are very low, so they are excellent conductors of heat (and extremely poor insulators).

Nonmetals

The PAX expect that one understands several chemical and physical properties of the group of elements that are classified as nonmetals. These properties should be appreciated in contrast to the same properties of the elements of the transition metal category and the Group I category – the alkali metals. Further discussion of the underlying physical principles that distinguish these categories becomes too technical and counterproductive for preparation for the TEAS. It is best to simply memorize that the most significant nonmetal elements are carbon (C), nitrogen (N), oxygen (O) phosphorus (P), sulfur (S) and all of the group VII elements - the halides.

These properties of nonmetals are generally the opposite of the transition metals. The nonmetals – in their elemental form and as molecular compounds with other elemental atoms – tend to form small molecules that are strongly covalently bonded but with weak intermolecular attractions. These compounds in the solid state tend to be brittle or powdery. The nonmetals are extremely poor electrical and thermal conductors and therefore excellent electrical and thermal insulators.

Metalloids

There are one or two elements that are located at the positions in each period, beginning with boron at group III in period two and then advancing to group IV, V and VI in a descending stair step fashion moving from top to bottom of the periodic table that have properties that are partially metallic and partially those of the nonmetal elements. The second period group IV through VI elements - carbon, nitrogen and oxygen are all nonmetals. Several other of the group IV through VI elements including phosphorus and sulfur are nonmetals and all the group VII (halogens) and group VIII (noble gases) are nonmetals. The metalloids most notably have intermediate electrical conductivity and are often classified as semiconductors. Semiconductors are critical materials used in the electronics industry. The most familiar metalloids are the elements silicon and germanium.

The Fifth and Higher Periods of the Periodic Table

At the $5th$ and higher periods of the periodic table, additional electrons begin to be added to new types of orbitals. At the fourth period, the "f" orbital becomes available and at the fifth period a "g" class orbital becomes available. Elements that are adding electrons to these new orbitals are the lanthanide and actinide elements. Once these f and g orbitals are filled, then d orbitals begin to fill. The chemistry of the lanthanide and actinide orbitals are beyond the scope of the TEAS. The group I (alkali metals) the group II (alkali earths), group VII (halogens) and the group VIII (noble gases) at all higher periods of the periodic table retain their specific group properties – and this is expected knowledge for the TEAS.

Chemical Bonds Between Atoms

Except the group VIII elements, all elemental atoms to varying degrees will engage in chemical reactions with other atoms. The groups I through VII elemental atoms attempt to satisfy the octet rule either by taking one or more electrons away from other atoms (ionization) or by sharing electrons with other atoms through the formation of interatomic bonds.

Ionic Bonds

When an atom succeeds in taking one or more electrons from another atom, the atom that takes the electron(s) becomes a negatively charged ion (an anion). The atom that loses the electron(s) becomes a positively charged atom (a cation). Usually the electron donor and the electron acceptor atoms become strongly bonded due to the electromagnetic force between the negative and positive charges of the two atoms. This type of interatomic or molecular bond is called an ionic bond.

Atoms with very high electronegativities can take electrons away from atoms with very low electronegativities. Ionic bonds therefore occur between atoms of very high electronegativity and those with very low electronegativity. The tendency to form ionic bonds is highest for elements located on the left and right of the periodic table – groups I and II as cations and groups VI and VII as anions – and progressively lower towards the middle of the table. The formation of the cation in an ionic bond requires less energy and is therefore more likely progressing from top to bottom, but the formation of an anion is less energetically favorable and therefore less likely progressing from top to bottom in the periodic table.

Hydrogen Bonds

Hydrogen bonds are the strongest type of bond. They occur between molecules that have hydrogen atoms that have a partial positive charge and separate regions that have a partial negative charge. Important examples of molecules that experience intermolecular hydrogen bonding in the solid and liquid state are water molecules and ammonia (NH_3) molecules.

Covalent Bonds

In most cases, the difference in electronegativity between bonding atoms is insufficient for one atom to take an electron away from the other bonding atom. The two atoms instead share one electron each through a covalent bond. Atoms can share additional electrons through the formation of additional covalent bonds with other atoms or by forming additional covalent bonds with the same atom resulting in double or triple covalent bonds.

The number of covalent bonds that an atom forms depends on how many electrons the atom requires to complete its valence octet. For instance, oxygen, with 6 valence electrons, is 2 electrons short of completing its valence octet. Therefore, oxygen typically forms two covalent bonds with other atoms. This results in the sharing of two additional electrons by the oxygen atom through the two covalent bonds with other atoms. In this manner, the oxygen atom has completed its valence octet.

Polar Bonds

In covalent bonds, electrons are not equally shared when there is a significant difference in electronegativity between the bonding atoms. For example, in the molecule hydrogen fluoride (HF), fluorine is much more electronegative than hydrogen and the hydrogen fluoride molecule has a partially negative pole near the fluorine atom and a partially positive pole near to the hydrogen atom. The covalent bond between hydrogen and fluorine is said to have a partial ionic character.

Ionic bonds also have some covalent character, more so as the difference in electronegativities between the bonding atoms decreases. Some covalent bonds are pure covalent bonds and when the molecule consists of atoms of the same element such as O_2 or N_2. Importantly, the carbon-hydrogen bonds in hydrocarbon atoms have almost no ionic character, and hydrocarbon molecules are nonpolar molecules. This is significant because nonpolar molecules will not dissolve in polar liquids such as water. Water molecules are very polar and liquid water is a powerful polar solvent. Hydrocarbons and molecules composed in large part of hydrocarbons (fats and other lipid molecules) are insoluble in water but will dissolve in nonpolar liquids such as benzene or other hydrocarbon liquids.

Changes in States of Matter

The Four Phases of Matter

At the human or macroscopic scale, matter in the form of large collections of atoms and molecules can exist in four phases or states. These phases are the solid phase, the liquid phase, the gas phase, and the plasma phase. When we are discussing the phases of matter, we are usually describing a macroscopic sample of a substance. That substance is usually a pure sample of a molecule.

A molecule is a particle that consists of more than one atom, and those atoms are strongly bound together by electromagnetic forces either in the form of ionic bonds between oppositely charged atoms, or in the form of electrons in covalent bonds that form between the nuclei of two atoms. These binding forces are called intramolecular forces and except for the fourth state of matter – the plasma phase – the intramolecular covalent binding forces are not disrupted or broken during phase changes of the substance. Ionic bonds are a different story – they are the forces that bind positive and negative ions together in an ionic crystalline solid. They are very strong, and they must be disrupted for the ionic compound to transition from a solid state to a liquid or gaseous state. Also, ionic solids are not composed of small molecules – instead they are composed of a three-dimensional lattice of alternating anions and cations. For the TEAS, discussions of the phases and phase changes of matter are almost certain to be referring to substances that are covalent molecular compounds and not ionic crystalline solid or liquid compounds.

Temperature and pressure impact the phase of a substance. Increasing the temperature will move the matter particles apart, increasing pressure packs the matter particles closer together.

Intermolecular Forces

The forces that are responsible for the unique properties of the solid and liquid phases are the attractive electrical forces that occur between molecules – intermolecular forces. These forces are weaker than the intramolecular forces of covalent bonds but can be surprisingly strong in the case of hydrogen bonds.

Temperature

In most cases heat – on the atomic and molecular scale – is energy that ultimately is converted to kinetic energy. Although an object that is motionless has no net kinetic energy, every object has a temperature. The temperature of an object is proportional to the average kinetic energy of the atoms that are contained in the object (to be precise the temperature of a substance is directly proportional to the square root of the statistical mean of the kinetic energy of the particles – atoms or molecules – that comprise the substance). This is true not only for substances in the solid state, but for substances in the liquid and gas states as well. The higher the temperature of a substance the greater the average kinetic energy of the individual particles contained in the substance. The addition of heat to a substance usually increases the temperature of the object.

The Temperature Scales - Celsius, Kelvin and Fahrenheit

The Fahrenheit (°F) temperature scale defines the freezing point of water as 32 °F and the boiling point of water as 212 °F. The Celsius (°C) temperature scale defines the freezing point of water as 0 °C and the boiling point of water as 100 °C.

The Kelvin (K) temperature scale is equivalent to the Celsius scale with the exception that the Kelvin scale defines absolute zero as 0 °K, and the triple point of water as exactly 273.16 degrees (we will discuss what a triple point is in the phases of matter discussion). Absolute zero on the Celsius scale is $-273.15\ °C$. Absolute zero is the theoretically lowest possible temperature of matter. It corresponds to a state where the atoms of matter have no kinetic energy at all – in other words, they are completely motionless. The laws of quantum mechanics show that this temperature can never occur in nature – it is physically impossible to cool anything down to a temperature of absolute zero.

The conversion formula for Celsius to Fahrenheit $\quad T\,(°C) = (T\,(°F) - 32) \times 5/9$

The Celsius to Kelvin conversion $\quad T\,(°C) = T\,(°K) - 273.15$

Solids

In a solid, intermolecular forces are sufficiently strong to prevent individual particles from changing position relative to other particles in the solid. The kinetic energy of particles in a solid is manifested as vibrational motion. The particles in a solid have no translational velocity, but they are vibrating at a certain frequency. As the particles in the solid acquire more energy, they vibrate faster, and the temperature of the solid increases. Matter in the solid state maintains a constant 3-dimensional configuration (shape), solid matter has definite volume and definite shape.

Liquids

As heat is continuously added to a solid, the temperature of the solid eventually rises to the solid's melting point. At the melting point, the individual particles' vibrational kinetic energy will allow the particles to begin to move or flow freely among the other particles in the solid. This process represents a phase change from the solid phase to the liquid phase. In the liquid phase, the particles in the liquid still have little if any net translational motion. The continued addition of heat to a liquid increases the particles' kinetic energy by increasing the vibrational motion of the particles. At temperatures below the liquid's boiling point, the particles do not have energy to completely overcome the intermolecular force present within the liquid. The particles in a liquid remain in contact with one another.

The ability of particles in a liquid to move freely within the liquid results in one of the defining physical properties of a liquid – the ability to conform to the interior shape of the vessel that contains the liquid. The liquid has definite volume but no definite shape. Liquids will seek the lowest spaces available within a container and form a continuous horizontally level surface while occupying (filling) all the accessible interior volume of the container that is below this liquid level surface.

As heat is continuously removed from a liquid, the liquid's temperature will eventually drop to the liquid's freezing point. At the freezing point, the reverse of the solid-to-liquid phase transition, the liquid-to-solid phase transition begins to occur. Notice that the freezing and boiling point temperatures of a substance are identical.

Gases

With the continuing addition of heat energy, the particles of a liquid move around faster and faster, both vibrationally and translationally. When the particles acquire enough kinetic energy, they can overcome their attraction to other particles. The particles in the liquid then begin to escape as individual particles into the surrounding environment. This corresponds to the temperature of the liquid's boiling point. At this temperature, the liquid particles begin to escape from the liquid and travel freely into the surrounding environment. This is the liquid-to-gas phase transition. The term for this process is evaporation.
The kinetic energy of gas particles is no longer due to vibrational motion; it is due to translational motion – the linear distance that an object travels per unit time. This kinetic energy is the form most of us are familiar with. The average speed (the magnitude of the velocity) of gas molecules can be calculated based on the temperature. The average speed of air molecules at 20 °C is 500 m/s. This is equivalent to approximately 1100 miles per hour. Particles in the gas phase behave as if there are no intermolecular forces among the particles.

As gas molecules lose heat energy, the gas temperature eventually decreases to the condensation point (this is identical to the substance's boiling point) and the gas particles return to the liquid phase. This is the gas to liquid phase transition, the reverse of the liquid to gas phase transition; The term for this phase transition is condensation. Gases are highly compressible and change in volume, but liquids and solids are non-compressible.

Plasmas

The plasma phase of matter occurs when matter reaches extremely high temperatures. At sufficiently high temperatures, the kinetic energy of individual molecules overcomes the strength of intramolecular bonds and molecules are torn apart into individual atoms. The atom's electrons absorb additional energy and eventually are energetic enough to overcome the attractive electromagnetic force that binds electrons to atoms.

As electrons are stripped away from atomic nuclei, a collection of naked positively-charged atomic nuclei and intermingling negatively charged free electrons form. This represents the plasma phase of matter. The plasma phase seldom occurs on earth except when artificially generated by highly specialized and sophisticated technological processes. Elsewhere in the universe, the plasma phase of matter is the most common phase since it is the phase of matter that exists within stars and interstellar dust. It is unlikely that PAX questions will involve any more detailed knowledge regarding the plasma phase of matter.

Sublimation and Deposition

Under certain conditions, substances in the solid phase may transition directly to the gas phase. This is called sublimation. Similarly, substances in the gas phase may transition directly to the solid phase. This phase transition is called deposition. The temperature at which this occurs is the sublimation and deposition point for the substance. An example of this is carbon dioxide, which transitions directly from a solid to a gas at atmospheric pressure with a sublimation and deposition point of -78.5 °C.

Evaporation and Condensation

Reaction participants can also be removed by heating the reaction solution so that the participant becomes a gas, thereby escaping from the reaction solution. In the gas phase, reaction participants can be removed from the reaction environment by cooling the reaction vessel to the condensation point of the participant so that a specific participant becomes a liquid that can be drained away from the reaction vessel.
Each method can also result in preventing reactions from reaching equilibrium and drive reactions to completion in the desired direction. These methods can be combined using various laboratory techniques. In general, these separation methods are termed distillations.

Specific Heat Capacity

The amount of heat energy that is required to increase the temperature of a given amount of a substance by a given number of degrees Celsius depends on the physical nature of the substance. Several factors determine the magnitude of this heat value, but the actual value must be determined experimentally for each substance.

This measured quantity is designated as the specific heat of a substance; it is given in units of energy per unit mass per degree Celsius, usually either Joules/g-degree Celsius or calories/g-degree Celsius.
An example, the specific heat capacity of liquid water is 4.18 J/g·°C. This means that it requires 4.18 joules of heat energy to raise the temperature of 1 gram of water by 1 degree Celsius. The specific heat capacity of water is one of the highest values for any substance; for instance, the heat capacity of solid iron is 0.45 J/g·°C, This means it requires approximately ten times more heat energy to raise the temperature of one gram of liquid water by one degree Celsius than is required to raise the temperature of one gram of solid iron by one degree Celsius.

An example of a specific calculation is to calculate the amount of energy required to raise the temperature of 20 grams of liquid water by 15 °C. The calculation is shown below.

$$(4.18\, J/g \cdot °C)(10\, g)(15\, °C) = 1254\, J$$

Characteristic Properties of Substances

Cellular Homeostasis

Cell Membranes

For biological cells, homeostasis requires a physical barrier in the form of a cell membrane to separate the cell's internal environment from the surrounding external environment. The external cell membrane is a selective, semi-permeable membrane. The cell membrane is permeable to water, oxygen and carbon dioxide molecules. These molecules are free to cross the membrane, but most other atomic ions and molecules are not.

Osmolality

We have discussed the general topic of osmolality in detail. In the context of human cellular biology, all intracellular processes occur in solutions where the solvent is water. The particles dissolved in intracellular water include oxygen, carbon dioxide, electrolytes, small molecules such as glucose, and a vast number of other chemicals and proteins. The total concentrations of all these dissolved particles is defined as the osmolality of the intracellular fluid or simply the osmolality of the cell

Hypertonic and Hypotonic Solutions

Outside of the cell there is usually a liquid environment as well - and this environment also has an osmolality. The tendency of water is to diffuse between regions so that the osmolality of regions equalizes. For cellular homeostasis, the internal and external osmolality levels are slightly different. The internal cellular osmolality is artificially maintained at a slightly higher concentration level. This tends to draw water into cells via osmosis and the result is that the cells have a higher internal fluid pressure. The desired homeostatic state for cells is that they are surrounded by a hypotonic solution. - meaning the surrounding external solution of the cell has lower osmolality than the cell's internal osmolality.

If the external environment has higher osmolality this is called a hypertonic external solution environment. In this case water moves out of the cell via osmosis and the cell shrivels - if the situation continues the cell will die. Conversely, if the outside osmolality is too low -a hypotonic external solution environment - so much water will enter the cell that the cell membrane will burst. This phenomenon can be observed microscopically by adding red blood cells to a Petri dish filled with pure water - which has no (zero) osmolality.

Semipermeable Membranes

Semipermeable membranes are typically thin sheets of material that separate (at least) two fluid compartments. The barrier is generally permeable to the solvent liquid within the compartments. Permeable means "able to pass through". The semipermeable membrane is impermeable to some or all the solutes in the solutions within the compartments. Impermeable means "unable to pass through".

Semipermeable membranes are critical in biology because the membrane of a cell – which separates the interior contents of the cell from the external environment of the cell – is a semipermeable membrane. The cell's semipermeable membrane is permeable to water (which is the solvent in biological solutions). The membrane is impermeable to most other substances that are dissolved in biological solutions.

Diffusion

Diffusion is the passive (non-energy requiring) process that occurs when solvents and solutes are moving from one local region to another local region due to differences in the concentrations of solutes between the two regions. When a concentration gradient exists between two regions, the solute particles in the region of higher concentration will move or flow to the region of lower concentration. The greater the difference in concentration between the two regions, the greater the driving force for the movement of solutes from higher to lower concentrations.

The other consideration in determining how strong the driving force of diffusion is the distance that the separates the highest and lowest concentration regions. The shorter the distance between the high and low concentration regions, the stronger the driving force of diffusion. Diffusion will continue until the concentrations of the two regions are equal.

If a semipermeable barrier exists between the high and low concentration regions, where the barrier is permeable to the solvent but not to the solutes, the solutes will be unable to diffuse between high and low concentration regions. In this case, the solvent liquid will diffuse through the semipermeable barrier in attempt to dilute the higher concentration region and thereby equalize the concentration of the solution between the two regions.

Simple Diffusion

We have discussed the details of diffusion in general. To review: All dissolved particles in a solution will, if possible, move by diffusion spontaneously from regions of higher particle concentrations to regions of lower particle concentration. This is referred to a movement with or down a concentration gradient. This diffusion process does not require energy. In fact, diffusion processes can be a source of chemical energy that drives chemical reactions. Within the human body oxygen will typically diffuse into and carbon dioxide will typically diffuse out of the cells via simple diffusion.

Facilitated Diffusion

Other solubilized particles – those that are impermeable to the cell membrane – can move across the cell membrane down their concentration gradients, but this diffusion requires the participation of transmembrane cell structures that provide a pathway through the membrane. This type of diffusion is called facilitated diffusion. It is a process that does not require energy use by the cell.

Osmotic Pressure

Osmotic pressure is a colligative property that is present in solutions when there is a semipermeable barrier between two solutions with different solute concentrations. To explain the phenomena of osmotic pressure, we first need to describe what a semipermeable membrane is and second to describe the process that drives fluid and solutes across a semipermeable membrane. This process is called diffusion.

Chemical Reactions

The concept of chemical equilibrium is a state where chemical reactions will proceed from initial conditions to reach an equilibrium state. This equilibrium state refers to the concentration of chemical participants that exist when a chemical reaction appears to have stopped – with no further changes in the concentrations of chemical participants occurring over time.

General Form of a Chemical Reaction

The convention for writing chemical reactions is to place the reactants on the left followed by a rightward pointing arrow followed by the products of the reaction.

$$aA + bB \rightarrow cC + dD$$

The small letters, a, b, c, d are the relative amounts in number of particles for each participant A, B, C, D in the reaction (called the stoichiometric coefficients of the reaction).

The General Types of Chemical Reactions

Simple chemical reactions can be categorized as one of four types of reactions. These are the synthesis reaction, decomposition reaction, single replacement reaction and double-replacement reaction. The general formula for each of these types of reactions are shown below

Synthesis:	$A + B \rightarrow AB$
Decomposition:	$AB \rightarrow \ + A + B$
Single Replacement:	$AB + C \rightarrow \ + A + BC$
Double Replacement:	$AB + CD \rightarrow \ + AD + BC$

The general formulas for these four types of reactions should be self-explanatory in terms of what occurs during the reactions. There are more complex reactions where combinations of these four basic reactions occur simultaneously. This categorization of reactions actually provides very little useful information, other classifications of reaction types are much more important to recognize, in particular whether the reaction is an acid-base reaction, a reduction-oxidation reaction, a hydrolysis or dehydration reaction, a polymerization reaction, or phosphorylation or dephosphorylation reaction.

Stoichiometric Coefficients

In most cases, this chemical reaction involves molecules on the right side "A" and "B" whose atoms react to rearrange themselves into new types of molecules "C" and "D". The molecules A and B on the left side of the equation are called reactants, and the molecules C and D on the right side of the equation are the products of the reaction. The reactant molecules rearrange into the product molecules by breaking existing chemical bonds and forming new chemical bonds. The lowercase letters, a, b, c, and d are called stoichiometric coefficients. They are integer numbers that indicate the proportional numbers of the molecules A, B, C, and D that participate in the reaction. For instance, this could be

$$2A + 3B \rightarrow C + 4D$$

This indicates a reaction where two molecules of A and three molecules of B react to produce one molecule of C and four molecules of D. Notice that when the stoichiometric coefficient is 1 that the number 1 is not used, in this case for the product molecule C. When reactant or product molecules are not preceded by a coefficient, it is understood that the coefficient is 1.

As we have discussed, the coefficients may be thought of as numbers of individual molecules, but more often they are considered to be very large collections of molecules as given by moles – for the example above this would be interpreted as two moles of A and three moles of B react to produce one mole of C and four moles of D. The key concept is that the stoichiometric coefficient describes the relative amounts of reactants and products participating in the chemical reaction.

Balancing Reactions

Balancing chemical reactions is a process that begins with the elements and elements of molecules that constitute the reactants and products of a chemical reaction but with no ratios of the elements that compose molecules nor stoichiometric ratios of elements or molecules that participate in the reaction.

To balance a chemical reaction the total numbers of each type of atom on the left must equal the total numbers of each type of atom on the right. When the ratios of elements are unknown for the molecules that participate in chemical reactions, the information provided in the periodic table and in the octet or equivalent rule for individual elements can be used to predict what the ratios of elements should be.

Once this information is known, the stoichiometric coefficients can be reasoned out using common sense or simple algebra. To illustrate this balancing process, several examples are provided below.

Reaction 1: Synthesis of liquid water from molecular hydrogen gas and molecular oxygen gas. Perhaps the most basic chemical reaction is the reaction of hydrogen molecules (H_2) and oxygen molecules (O_2) to form a hydrogen-oxygen molecule:

$$H_2(g) + O_2(g) \rightarrow HO\ (l)$$

The reaction shown above is an unbalanced chemical reaction where hydrogen and oxygen combine to form a molecule consisting of hydrogen and oxygen. The (g) for H_2 and O_2 indicate that, in this reaction, both O_2 and H_2 react as gasses. The (l) for HO indicates the product "HO" is a liquid.

There are two atoms of hydrogen and two atoms of oxygen on the right and one atom each of hydrogen and oxygen contained on the molecule HO on the left. One could write a balanced reaction 1 as:

$$H_2(g) + O_2(g) \rightarrow 2HO\ (l)$$

This is a balanced reaction - there are the same number of hydrogen and oxygen atoms on the left and right sides of the reaction, but it is incompatible with what we know atoms are attempting to do in chemical reactions - namely to satisfy the octet rule. Recall that oxygen requires two additional electrons to satisfy the octet rule. Hydrogen is unique in that it does not have an octet rule but does have the equivalent.
When hydrogen has 2 electrons it achieves a substantial lowering of energy by filling the $n = 1$ electron shell. Oxygen therefore wishes to share 2 electrons by creating two covalent bonds and hydrogen wishes to share one electron by creating one covalent bond. Therefore, we can predict that one oxygen atom will form 2 covalent bonds, one with each of 2 hydrogen atoms. The Lewis dot structure for this is as follows:

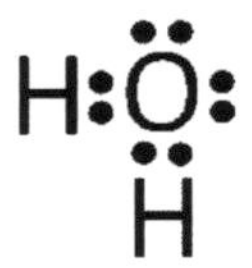

The two dots between the hydrogen and oxygen atoms represent covalent bonds between hydrogen and oxygen atoms. Each atom is sharing one of its valence electrons in each covalent bond.

This structure demonstrates that both hydrogen and the oxygen atoms have all attained a desired electron configuration; each hydrogen has 2 electrons that are shared in a covalent bond with oxygen and oxygen has eight octet valence electrons, an additional two which are acquired through sharing of electrons in single covalent bonds with the two hydrogen atoms. This indicates the correct chemical reaction for reaction 1 is:

$$2H_2(g) + O_2(g) \rightarrow 2H_2O\ (l)$$

Reduction-Oxidation (Redox) Reactions

A major alternative classification of reactions is the reduction-oxidation or "redox" class of chemical reactions. Any of the four categories of general chemical reactions – synthesis, dissociation (or decomposition), single replacement, and double replacement can be redox reactions. The critical element in determining whether a reaction is a redox reaction is to determine whether during the reaction, any atom participating in the reaction has changed its oxidation number.

Combustion Reactions

Combustion reactions for the PAX are the oxidation-reduction reaction where oxygen molecules and molecules containing carbon hydrogen and sometimes oxygen are the reactants and carbon dioxide and water are the products. A typical combustion reaction is the reaction which occurs in an internal combustion engine with the reactant's oxygen and the mixture of hydrocarbon molecules in gasoline.

An example of this type of combustion reaction – in which ethane and oxygen are the reactants – is shown below:

$$2C_2H_6 + 7O_2 \rightarrow 4CO_2 + 6H_2O$$

This is a balanced reaction, but it is more commonly written as:

$$C_2H_6 + 3\tfrac{1}{2}\,O_2 \rightarrow 2CO_2 + 3H_2O$$

All combustion reactions are self-sustaining and highly exothermic, and therefore generate a large amount of heat energy.

Pressure Change Effects on Reactions

Another way to drive reactions in a desired direction is to take advantage of the effects that changes in the partial pressures of chemical participants can have on chemical reactions. In the example of a pure gas phase reaction $A(g) + B(g) \rightleftharpoons C(g) + 2D(g)$, the forward reaction produces 3 moles of product (1 mole of C and 2 moles of D) from 2 moles of reactant (one mole of A and one mole of B). The forward reaction therefore produces a larger amount of gas molecules from a smaller amount of gas molecules.

In a sealed reaction vessel, the forward reaction tends to increase the partial pressures of the reaction participants within the reaction vessel. If the reaction vessel is a piston, external force can be exerted by the piston head on the gas in the reaction vessel. As the partial pressures increase, the reaction moves farther away from the equilibrium partial pressures and the reverse reaction becomes more favorable since this causes lowering of the partial pressures of participants within the vessel by converting a larger number of gas molecules into a smaller number of gas molecules via the reverse reaction.

By increasing the volume of the reaction vessel, the forward reaction is favored by the same reasoning. It is important to realize that this effect is due to increasing the concentration of the participant gases. Other methods of increasing the pressure of the reaction vessel – such as pumping additional non-reactive gas into the vessel – will not have any effect on the reaction.

Temperature Effects on Reactions

For exothermic reactions, increases in temperature drive the reverse reaction, which removes heat from the system. Lowering the temperature increases the forward reaction, which adds heat to the reaction environment. The reverse is true for endothermic reactions. Increasing the temperature of the reaction environment will favor the forward reaction since this removes heat from the reaction environment and decreasing the temperature will favor the reverse reaction by the same reasoning.

Enzymes

Catalysts are substances that increase the rate of chemical reactions without themselves being transformed or consumed by the chemical reaction. Enzymes are biological catalysts. They are not simple metallic surfaces but extremely complex three-dimensional protein structures. They lower activation energies of biological reactions by attracting reactants to a specific site on the enzyme known as the active site. As reactants bind to the active site, the configuration of the site changes in a manner that orients the reactants in the optimum manner for the chemical reaction to occur. This process is called the induced fit mechanism for enzymatic activity. The activity of an enzyme is defined as the rate at which the reaction catalyzed by the enzyme occurs. The higher the enzyme activity, the greater the rate of enzyme catalyzed reaction.

Acids, Bases, and pH Balance

In living organisms, there are very important acid-base reactions that must occur. Living organisms must maintain a carefully regulated narrow range of pH values for the fluids located inside of their bodies. This range for humans is between pH of 7.35 and 7.45. The metabolic processes of living organisms produce organic acids as waste products, and these acids must be neutralized or excreted from the body, otherwise the organism's internal fluids will become increasingly acidic and will rapidly reach fatally low pH levels. One of the most important series of reactions used by biological organisms to neutralize and/or excrete excess acid involve reactions involving the weak acid carbonic acid.

Acids

Acids are molecules that, in solution, partially or nearly completely dissociate into hydrogen ions and a conjugate base. One definition of an acid is that an acid is a proton (hydrogen ion) donor molecule.

Bases

Bases, by one definition, are molecules that accept hydrogen ions. Acids and bases react together to produce water and salt.

pH

For solutions that contain hydrogen ions (H^+), the negative log of the hydrogen ion concentration is defined as the pH of the solution. As we discussed, in pure liquid water, the hydrogen ion concentration is $1x10^{-7}$. Therefore, the pH of pure liquid water is 7, a neutral pH, Solutions with higher concentrations of H^+ have pH values lower than 7. These solutions are acidic solutions. Solutions with lower concentrations of H^+ have pH values higher than 7. These solutions are basic solutions. The pH of body fluids in humans is tightly regulated to an ideal pH of 7.4.

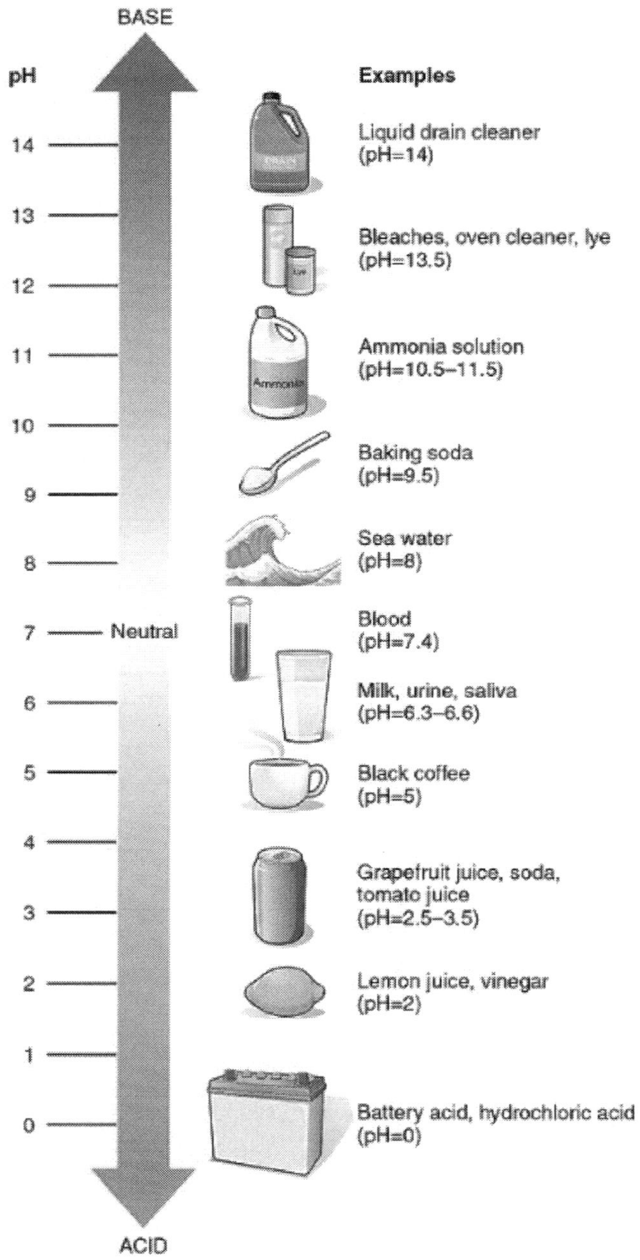

Majority of questions on the PAX are based on material from the PAX category identified as Human Body Science. The Biochemistry & Cell Biology and General Human Anatomy sections cover the material equivalent to the PAX human body science topics. In this section, Biochemistry & Cell Biology, we proceed logically from the general chemistry and begin to introduce the chemical reactions and molecular structures that can be classified as topics in biochemistry and cell biology. These topics are focused on the biochemical and cellular processes that include humans and are essential for a rational understanding of human body science that is continued in General Human Anatomy.

Basic Macromolecules in a Biological System

Carbohydrate Chemistry in Biology

Carbohydrates play a crucial role in human biology. In addition to providing a source of chemical energy for cells, sugars and other carbohydrates have many other critical functions within living organisms, such as structural and recognition of molecules . We briefly described the general chemical definition of carbohydrates as molecules that are individual sugars or are molecules that are composed of sugars. The sugars are in general classified as saccharides - a single sugar is a monosaccharide, two sugars covalently bonded form a disaccharide molecules and multiple sugars that are covalently bonded form polysaccharide molecules.

Glucose

The molecule $C_6H_{12}O_6$ is the sugar glucose.

Sugars a class of molecules called carbohydrates. Carbohydrates are molecules that consist of carbon chains where carbons are also single bonded to hydrogens and double bonded to the oxygen (creating an aldehyde or a ketone functional group) or single bonded to oxygens of hydroxide groups (creating an alcohol functional group). Hydroxide groups consist of one oxygen atom single bonded to one hydrogen atom (O-H). The carbon-hydroxide molecular subunit is called an alcohol. The chemical structure of glucose ($C_6H_{12}O_6$) is shown below.

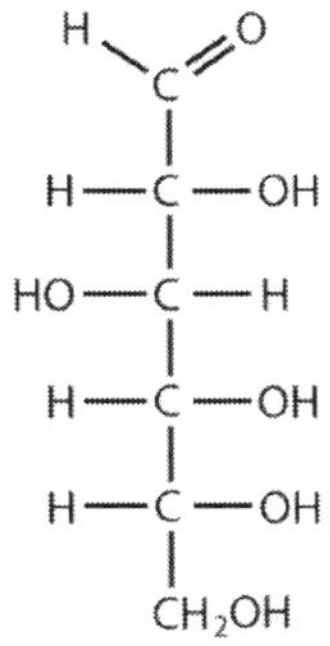

Monosaccharides (Single or Simple Sugars)

Nearly all monosaccharides are classified as "single" or "simple" sugars. They are the chemical subunits or building block of all more complex carbohydrates. The naming of monosaccharides that are sugars begins with the Latin prefix of the number of carbons in carbon chain backbone the sugar – "tri" for three, "pent" for five and "hex" for six – and end in the suffix "-ose". The sugar "ribose" is a five-carbon sugar, so it is a pentose. Glucose is a six-carbon sugar, so it is a hexose.

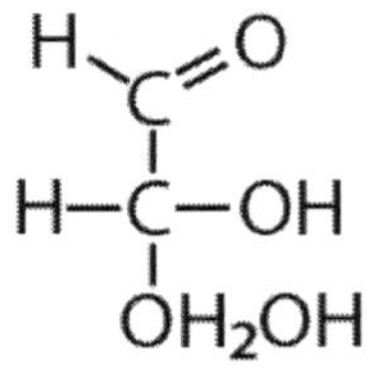

Starches and Cellulose

Dietary carbohydrates are usually consumed in the form of starches contained in grains and vegetables. Starches are another polymerized form of glucose. Cellulose is a glucose polymer that has glyosidic bonds that cannot be broken by human digestion. Cellulose forms majority of non-digestible fiber in the human diet.

Nucleotides

Another critical role of cyclic sugars is the structural roles that the sugars ribose and deoxyribose provide into the genetic information storage molecule DNA and genetic information messenger and protein assembly molecule RNA. Both DNA and RNA molecules are very-large linear-chain polymers composed of nucleotide subunits. Nucleotides have the following structure:

RNA nucleotide

$$PO_4 - (C5)\ Ribose\ (C1) - (N)\ base$$

DNA nucleotide

$$PO_4 - (C5)\ Deoxyribose\ (C1) - (N)\ base$$

Lipid Chemistry in Biology

Lipids are a broad class of molecules that have a wide range of functions in the human body including energy storage in the form of triglycerides stored in adipose (fat) cells, major components of cell membranes in the form of phospholipid molecular subunits, cholesterol and cholesterol derivatives such as the steroid hormones, cell signaling and immune mediating molecules in the form of prostaglandins, and other types of lipid based immunes system pathway molecules and as vital components of numerous cellular biochemical processes in the form of the fat-soluble vitamins A, D, E, and K. Nearly all of the types of lipids in biological processes are derivatives of either fatty acids or cholesterol.

Most dietary fat and the storage form of fat in adipocytes is in the form of triglycerides. Dietary triglycerides are hydrolyzed in the small intestine by the enzyme lipase to monoglyceride molecules and fatty acid molecules. After absorption, some fatty acids are recombined with monoglycerides to reform triglycerides. Most of these triglycerides are stored in fat cells but some remain in the circulation as free triglycerides. The remainder of fatty acids are packaged along with cholesterol molecules and proteins into circulating complexes called lipoproteins. Most notable of these are the high-density lipoprotein (HDL) and low-density lipoprotein (LDL) complexes. Fatty acids and cholesterol molecules are transferred from lipoprotein complexes in the bloodstream into cells where they serve raw materials for construction of cell membranes, as a source of energy production and many other functions.

The concentrations of triglycerides and lipoproteins in the bloodstream is a major factor in the risk for development of atherosclerosis and coronary artery disease. These two conditions are the primary causes of heart disease and cerebral stroke. Together these two conditions are by far the most common causes of death in the industrialized world. High levels of triglycerides and LDL increases the risk of these diseases and HDL lowers the risk of these diseases.

Cholesterol

Cholesterol is a four-ringed lipid-based molecule that is an important component of cell membranes and a precursor molecule for the synthesis of the steroid hormones, cortisol, aldosterone progesterone and the sex hormones testosterone and estrogen. It is also the precursor for the synthesis of vitamin D. Most of the cholesterol used in the body is synthesized rather that of dietary origin.

Amino Acids and Proteins

No class of biological molecules is more essential than the proteins. Amino acids are the small molecules that are used to assemble proteins. The general form of an amino acid is a central carbon atom single bonded to a hydrogen atom and to three functional groups - an amine (-NH_2) group, a carboxylic acid (-COOH) group and a side group designated as an "R" group.

```
    H
    |
H2N-C-COOH
    |
    R
```

The R group is not the R group designated for hydrocarbons but is the amino acid side group that can be any of 20 unique functional groups. Each individual type of amino acid has a unique functional side group. The R or side group of the simplest amino acid – glycine – is a hydrogen atom. It is not likely that the PAX expects memorization of the R groups for all 20 amino acids, but it is useful to know that the R groups include hydroxyl groups $-OH$ as in the amino acid serine, hydrocarbon groups such as CH_3 in the amino acid alanine, amine groups NH_2 as in the amino acid lysine, and carboxylic acid groups $-COOH$ as in the amino acid glutamic acid (glutamate).

In a typical American diet, most protein is acquired by eating meat, but all amino acid requirements can be supplied by a properly selected vegetarian diet. Excess dietary proteins can be converted to fat by the body. Inadequate protein intake during early childhood development can result in the starvation state known as kwashiorkor.

Protein Structure

With 20 different amino acids to choose from for every amino acid position in a single polypeptide chain corresponding to a complete biological protein the number of possible linear sequences of amino acids in the polypeptide chain is astronomical and therefore the range of different single-chain proteins is practically unlimited.

Structural Proteins

One of the primary functions of proteins in the human body is to provide a physical structure for elements within the body. These may be microscopic structures inside of cells and in the extracellular spaces between cells or they may be macroscopic structures that extend over body surfaces These structural proteins are designed to provide the mechanical properties that are required by the structural role that they provide. These properties also are designed to respond in particular ways to the forces that the proteins experience in their structural roles. Some roles require that the proteins can stretch or flex in one or more directions, but to resist forces in other directions. In general, structural proteins have an overall fibrillar (fiber-like) shape - as opposed to globular proteins, which typically have enzymatic or transport functions.

Collagen

The most important extracellular structural protein is collagen. There are many different forms of collagen, each with its own unique mechanical properties. The collagen found in bone is rigid, but in tendons that connect muscles to bone, collagen is elastic and able to stretch and relax as muscles contract and relax. Collagen in cartilage has mechanical properties intermediate between rigidity and elasticity in its role of providing a protective layer over the ends of bones at movable joints and as structural elements in the nose, ears and within the skeletal system and elsewhere throughout the body. Collagen also is a major component of ligaments - which connect bones at joints - and in the integumentary system where it provides the ability of skin to stretch but to resist mechanical penetration by foreign objects and to contain the internal contents of the body. Collagen is also a major structural element of blood vessels.

Overall collagen comprises approximately 30% of the total protein mass of the human body. Collagen is synthesized by many types of cells, but the most important producer is the fibroblast cells. These cells are found throughout the body and are constantly producing collagen particularly in inflammation and tissue regeneration and repair processes.

Keratin

Keratin is the other major extracellular structural protein in humans. It provides protective and mechanical support to the outer layers of skin and the primary component of hair and nails in humans. In other animals, it also forms horns and claws.

Heredity Material

Nitrogenous Bases

All cells contain the nucleic acids DNA and RNA. The DNA molecules within a cell contain all the genetic information required to synthesize all the proteins that the cell requires to carry out its metabolic, physiological and structural functions. This information is stored as a linear sequence of nitrogenous bases. The nitrogenous bases occur in two forms, purines and pyrimidines. Both forms are small nitrogen-containing molecules that have either one structural ring - the purines, or a double ring - the pyrimidines.
The nitrogenous bases in DNA are the purines adenine (A) and guanine (G) and the pyrimidines thymine (T) and cytosine (C). The nitrogenous bases found in RNA molecules are the same as those found in DNA molecules with the exception that in RNA, another pyrimidine, uracil, is substituted for thymine.

The DNA Double-Helix

The structure of a DNA molecule in a cell is usually the double-stranded form of DNA. This double-stranded structure is a spiraling (helical) ladder consisting of linear backbones of alternating deoxyribose sugars and phosphate groups. One deoxyribose phosphate polymer backbone forms the left side rail of the DNA ladder and another one forms the right-side rail of the DNA ladder.

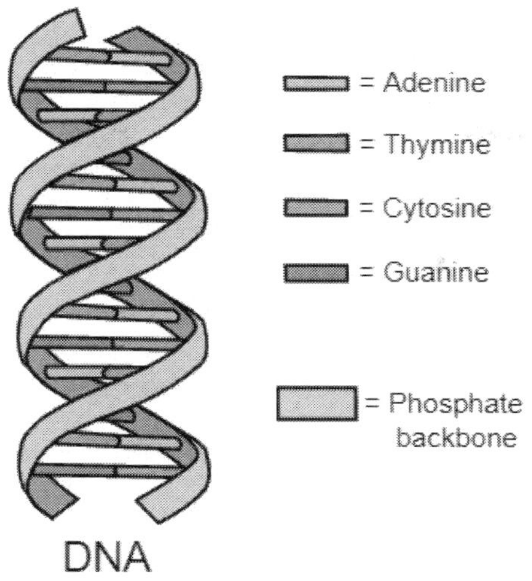

Complementary Base Pairing in Double-Stranded DNA

Each deoxyribose sugar is also bonded to a single nitrogenous base. Additionally, in double-stranded DNA, each of these bases is hydrogen bonded to its complementary base, which is similarly bonded to a deoxyribose sugar on the opposing sugar-phosphate backbone of the DNA molecule. These hydrogen-bonded nitrogenous base pairs form the rungs of the double stranded DNA ladder.

The term "complementary" in complementary base pair bonding refers to the fact that each nitrogenous base will pair bond with one and only one specific complementary base, Adenine (A) will only pair bond with thymine (T) and guanine (G) will only pair bond with cytosine (C). There are two hydrogen bonds formed between base-pairing adenine and thymine and three hydrogen bonds formed between base-pairing guanine and cytosine in double stranded DNA.

Nucleotides

A nucleotide is the term for a nucleic acid molecular subunit consisting of either a ribose or a deoxyribose sugar bonded to a phosphate group and to a nitrogenous base is referred to as a nucleotide. Any DNA molecule can be assembled entirely from deoxyribose containing nucleotides. Any RNA molecule can be assembled entirely from ribose containing nucleotides.

Chromosomes

In eukaryotic cells, DNA is usually in an extended linear form that allows the cells to access the nitrogenous base sequences for DNA replication and for transcription of DNA base sequences into messenger RNA molecules. During cell division, these DNA strands are highly condensed into structures called chromosomes. The formation of chromosomes during cell division cycle involve a series of coiling and supercoiling actions of the DNA molecule This process involves the physical wrapping of the DNA molecule around specialized spherical proteins called histone proteins or histones.

Chromatids

Each chromosome can exist in two forms. One is as a single condensed strand of DNA. The other form consists of two condensed identical strands of DNA. These two condensed DNA strands are called chromatids individually, and together they are called sister chromatids. The sister chromatid form occurs only after replication of an entire DNA strand is completed.

Homologous Chromosomes

Human somatic cells have 46 chromosomes. These 46 chromosomes occur as 23 pairs of chromosomes - 22 pairs of autosomes and 1 pair of sex chromosomes. The pairs of chromosomes are called homologous chromosomes. The sex chromosome pair in males is not an actual pair - it consists of one "X" chromosome and one "Y" chromosome. In females, the sex chromosomes are a chromosome pair - consisting of two X chromosomes.

Protein Synthesis

When a cell begins the process of constructing a protein, it first must expose the DNA base sequences of the gene that codes for the desired protein. During protein synthesis, the region of the DNA that contains the gene that will be transcribed is exposed by disrupting the hydrogen bonds between the nitrogenous base pairs. This separates the left and right halves of the DNA ladder as if it were being unzipped down the middle of the nitrogenous base pair rungs.

Transcription of DNA into mRNA - The 3' to 5' Direction

A protein complex called RNA polymerase then inserts itself into the cleft created by the disruption of the hydrogen bonds between complementary base pairs. The RNA polymerase then begins to assemble a single-strand RNA molecule that is complementary to the DNA strand that contains the base sequence code for the protein that will be constructed. The DNA strand that is transcribed is transcribed beginning at the 3' end of the DNA molecule and continues in the 5' direction.

The Sense and Antisense Strands of DNA

The DNA strand that is transcribed by RNA polymerase is called the "antisense strand" The other DNA strand - the complementary strand of the sense strand - is called the sense strand. Since the base sequence of the sense strand is the complementary sequence of the antisense strand, the sense strand does not code for functional proteins and it is not read by RNA polymerase. The mRNA base sequence is identical to the sense strand DNA sequence with the exception that the nitrogenous base uracil in the mRNA base sequence replaces the nitrogenous base thymine in the sense strand of the DNA molecule.

Genes

The base sequence in the sense strand that codes for a single-chain protein is called a gene. One gene always code for one and only one polypeptide chain - a polypeptide chain is a linear molecule composed of amino acids. All polypeptide chains are single-chain proteins. Some complex proteins are composed of more than one type of polypeptide chain.

Codons

The individual amino acids that will form the protein's chain are coded for by three-base sequences. These three-base sequences are called codons. Since there are four different bases that can occur at any point in the DNA base sequence, there are statistically 64 possible combinations of three-base sequences. Therefore, there are 64 possible codons. There are only 20 amino acids that are used to assemble proteins, so there may be more than one codon that specifies for a given amino acid. The reverse is NOT true - None of the individual codons ever codes for more than one specific amino acid.

Transcription of DNA

As RNA polymerase assembles an RNA molecule, a new nitrogenous base, uracil (U), is used in place of the base thymine, Uracil is the RNA base that is complementary to adenine. The process of constructing an RNA molecule that contains a complementary base sequence to a DNA gene sequence is defined as transcription.

Anticodons and Ribosomes

Once a complete RNA transcript of a gene has been completed, the transcript, known as a messenger RNA (mRNA) molecule leaves the nucleus and enters the cell cytoplasm. Eventually the mRNA molecule encounters a ribosome that attaches to the mRNA transcript. The ribosome then reads the RNA as three-base compliments of the DNA codons. These three- base RNA sequences are called anticodons.

Translation of mRNA

When the ribosome reads an anticodon, it inserts the amino acid that corresponds to the anticodon onto a growing polypeptide chain. When the entire mRNA molecule has been processed by the ribosome the result is a newly synthesized single chain protein. This polypeptide chain is the protein coded for by the gene that was transcribed at the beginning of this process. The reading of mRNA by ribosomes and the construction of the corresponding protein is called translation.

Transfer RNA

During the assembly of a protein chain at a ribosome, the individual amino acids are transported to the ribosome by transfer RNA (tRNA) molecules. These molecules are short segments of RNA that have a three-leaf-clover configuration. One end of the stem of the clover binds to an amino acid. There are 20 different types of tRNA molecules and each bind to one and only one type of amino acid. There is a complementary tRNA molecule type for each of the 20 amino acids.

DNA Replication

During DNA replication, the unzipping of double-stranded DNA is accompanied by the construction of a new complementary DNA for each of the original strand of the double stranded DNA. The synthesis of these two new complementary strands continues for the entire length of the DNA molecule. The result is that exact two copies of the original DNA molecule are created. Each of the new DNA molecules contains either the right or the left strand of the original DNA molecule and a complete newly synthesized complementary strand. This type of replication of DNA is called semi-conservative replication.

DNA Polymerase

During the replication of DNA, DNA polymerases are the enzyme complexes that insert themselves into gaps created by disruption of complementary base pair hydrogen bonds. These DNA replication molecules synthesize complementary DNA strands to both the original DNA sense and antisense strands simultaneously.

Genetic Variability

Recall that homologous chromosome pairs do not in general have identical genes, but often have variants of each gene, different versions of a gene called alleles. Therefore, the two daughter cells resulting from the first cell division of meiosis have one half of the total number of chromosomes – 23 instead of 46 – and these cellular sets of genes, but these are not identical sequences of DNA. The individual chromosomes from homologous chromosome pairs which are now in different cells, almost certainly have a wide variety of differing alleles for a wide variety of individual genes. Also, during the pair separation process in anaphase of meiosis 1, small segments from chromatids on different chromosomes of the homologous pairs can be exchanged. This creates hybrid chromatids. This process is called crossing over and it increases the genetic variability of the chromosomes.

Meiosis 2

The next round of cell division follows immediately without any replication of DNA. This is the Meiosis 2 phase of meiotic cell division. The events of Meiosis 2 cell division are identical to the events of mitosis cell division. In each of the two daughter ells created by the meiosis 1 cell division, the 23 individual chromosomes align at the metaphase plate of each daughter cell and individual sister chromatids of each chromosome are pulled apart and separated into the second generation of daughter cells.
This process - beginning with the original diploid progenitor cell - results in the production of four haploid cells. Each haploid cell contains one chromosome on the form of a sister chromatid, from each of the 23 pairs of chromosomes contained in the progenitor cell. In the human male, meiosis results in the production of sperm cells. In the human female, meiosis results in the production of ova,

Molecular Genetics

In individual members of a species, the total amount of genetic information contained in the genes of a diploid cell of the individual represents the individual's genome. The specific types of genes within the genome are the individual's genotype. The manner of an individual's genotype is expressed in physical form is the individual's phenotype.

Calculating Gene Frequencies

For species where there are multiple alleles for a given gene, individual members of the species may have different combinations of these alleles in their individual genomes. When there are two alleles for a given gene - for instance if we indicate these to be the alleles "A" and "a" for a specific gene, individuals may possess one of three possible combinations of the two alleles within their genotype. These are "AA", "aa" and "Aa". The combinations AA and aa are the two possible homozygous genotypes and the combination Aa is the heterozygous genotype. This type of mating is often described as an "Aa x Aa" cross. When a mating Aa male and Aa female pair of a species create a zygote (an Aa x Aa cross), the probability or predicted frequencies of the alleles in the zygote can be calculated using a Punnett square.

	A	a
A	AA	Aa
a	Aa	aa

A Punnett square representation of a cross between two heterozygous (Aa) parents (an Aa x Aa cross).
The Punnett square above shows the possible combinations of zygotes resulting from a mother and father where both are heterozygous for the gene with alleles A and a. Since each parent can contribute only one

allele to any zygote, the alleles for one parent are separated into an "A" column and an "a" column. The other parent's alleles are represented by an "A" row and a little "a" row. The four squares show the combination of alleles that results from combining a parental row with a corresponding parental column.

Notice that for two heterozygous individuals there is one AA square, one aa square and two Aa squares. This indicates that there is a 1 in 4 probability (25% chance) that the parents with produce a zygote with AA alleles, a 1 in 4 probability (25% chance) that the parents with produce a zygote with aa alleles and a 2 in 4 probability (50% chance) that the parents with produce a zygote with Aa alleles. Since zygotes can develop into children, for humans these are the probabilities of heterozygous parents having children with the AA, Aa and aa genotypes.

The expected gene frequencies resulting from mating between parents with other genotypes can be calculated in the same fashion using the Punnett square technique. The gene frequencies for the gene with two alleles A and a in the offspring of one heterozygous (Aa) parent and one homozygous (AA) parent (an AA x Aa cross) is shown in the Punnett square below.

	A	A
A	AA	AA
a	Aa	Aa

A Punnett square representation of a cross between one heterozygous parent (Aa) and one homozygous parent (AA) - an AA x Aa cross.

There is only 1 possible gamete for the homozygous parent (AA) for the gene. this is the allele A. The homozygous parent gametes are represented in the horizontal orientation as A and A at the top margin of the 2 × 2 Punnett square. The heterozygous parent (Aa) can produce two different gametes for the gene - either the allele A or the allele a. The heterozygous parent gametes are represented in the vertical left margin orientation as A and a.

We see that there are two possible zygotes from this heterozygous/homozygous cross - AA and Aa. Of the four possible crosses (represented by the allele pair in each of the four individual squares), two are AA and two are Aa. The gene frequencies for both AA and Aa are 2/4 or 50%. Notice that there is a zero percent chance of a homozygous aa offspring.

There is another possible cross for the homozygous/heterozygous state. This would be a cross between a parent homozygous for the "a" allele of the gene (aa) and a parent heterozygous for the gene (Aa). This would be an Aa x aa cross.

	A	a
a	Aa	aa
a	Aa	aa

Notice the gene frequencies are the same as for an AA x Aa cross except that it is the aa homozygous state that is 50% (instead of the AA homozygous state) and that there is a zero percent chance of an AA homozygous state (instead of an aa homozygous state) state. The heterozygous state (Aa) has the same 50% probability as it does for the AA x Aa cross.

There are three other possible crosses for a single gene with two alleles (A and a). Two are homozygous crosses of aa x aa and AA x aa. It should be obvious that each has only one possible zygote outcome. For the aa x aa cross, there is only an a allele, and so all offspring must be homozygous for the a allele (aa). By similar reasoning only one combination of alleles AA is possible for offspring of an AA x AA cross. The final possible combination for a cross of a single gene with two alleles (a and a) is the cross between a homozygous AA parent and a homozygous aa parent

	A	A
a	Aa	Aa
a	Aa	Aa

A Punnett square representation of a cross between two homozygous parents one parent is homozygous for the allele A (AA) and the other parent is homozygous for the allele a (aa). There is only one possible combination of zygotes from this cross - the heterozygous combination (Aa).

Dominant and Recessive Alleles

Often the phenotypic appearance or the physical trait that results from a gene depends on whether the alleles for the gene are dominant or recessive. The classic example is eye color - where the brown allele is "B" and blue allele is "b".

Brown (B) is the dominant allele and blue (b) is the recessive allele. Homozygous brown eyed individuals - those who are BB, and heterozygous individuals - who are Bb, always have brown eyes. Only homozygous blue (bb) individuals have blue eyes. Notice that the offspring of parents who are heterozygous for eye color (Bb), will have the same expected genotype frequencies as shown in the Punnett square example above; but the blue-eyed phenotype is only the bb genotype. Therefore, heterozygous brown-eyed parents will have a 1 in 4 or 25% chance of having a blue-eyed child.

Notice that two blue-eyed parents will never have brown-eyed children, since both parents possess only the blue eye color allele. Finally notice that in any couple where at least one parent is homozygous brown (BB), there is no possibility of offspring who will be homozygous blue (Bb) and therefore these parents have no chance of having a blue-eyed child.

Dihybrid Crosses

A classic topic in Mendelian genetics is the calculation of the types of different gene combinations that can occur in offspring of parents for two genes - each with two alleles that assort independently. This type of cross is classified as a dihybrid cross.

If we represent the two alleles for these two genes as A and a for the alleles of the first gene and B and b as the alleles for the second gene, then we can construct a Punnett square to calculate the possible gene combinations and frequencies for the offspring of any two parents with any possible combination of the alleles for the two genes (A, a, B and b).

We have partially completed the construction of a Punnett square to calculate these gene combinations and frequencies for a dihybrid cross where both parents are heterozygous for both genes. This would be a diploid state of AaBb for each parent. As the Punnett square illustrates, each parent can generate gametes with four possible combinations of the alleles for the two genes.

These possible combinations are AB, Ab, aB and ab. Each of the four combinations is listed at the top margin for one parent and at the left margin for the other parent. Notice that the possible zygote for any square is the combination of the horizontal and vertical gametes that correspond to the row and column of the square.

	AB	Ab	aB	ab
AB	AABB			
Ab		AAbb		
aB			aaBB	
ab				aabb

There are sixteen squares for a dihybrid cross, but the actual number of different combinations of alleles that are possible for the parental offspring depends on the alleles of the genes possessed by each parent. For instance, in our example of a dihybrid cross where both parents are heterozygous for both genes, several of the 16 possible combinations are equivalent. For example, an AaBb combination is identical to an aAbB combination. Both combinations have exactly one of each allele (A, a, B, and b) - it makes no difference which parent contributed an allele.

	AB	Ab	aB	ab
AB				AaBb
Ab			AaBb	
aB		AaBb		
ab	AaBb			

The Punnett square above shows that there are four squares that have the equivalent allele combination of AaBb. The frequency for this combination is therefore 4/16 (or ¼) or 25%. At this point we have partially completed the Punnett square as shown below.

	AB	Ab	aB	ab
AB	AABB			AaBb
Ab		AAbb	AaBb	
aB		AaBb	aaBB	
ab	AaBb			aabb

If we continue the process of assigning allele combinations to the remaining empty squares the result is the square shown below.

	AB	Ab	aB	ab
AB	AABB	AABb	AaBB	AaBb
Ab	AABb	AAbb	AaBb	Aabb
aB	AaBB	AaBb	aaBB	aaBb
ab	AaBb	Aabb	aaBb	aabb

We have listed capital alleles (A, B) before lowercase alleles (a and b) in the squares to make it easier to identify equivalent combinations. It is still difficult to recognize all the possible combinations by looking at the squares. The PAX will unlikely ask a question of the degree of difficulty required to determine exactly the frequencies of all the allele combination from this type of dihybrid cross, but one should be able to construct the Punnett square itself for any dihybrid cross and to identify frequencies for simpler examples of a dihybrid cross.

SCIENTIFIC REASONING

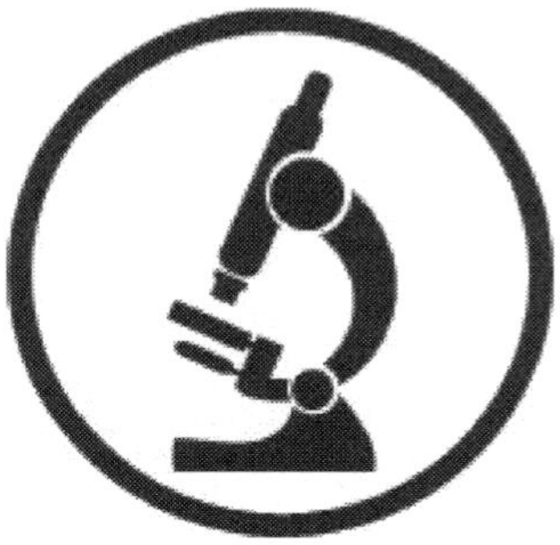

Basic Scientific Measurements Using Laboratory Tools

Accurate measurements, recording, and charting data is essential when performing scientific investigations and writing reports.

SI Units

The International Systems of Units or known as the metric system supports measurement in meters, kilograms, seconds, amperes (electric current), Kelvin, candela (luminous intensity), and moles (amount of substance). The metric system uses base unit of 10 and prefixes to increase or decrease the base unit's size.

Mass is the amount of material an object consumes by giving the object weight in a gravitational field. The mass of an object is measured in kilograms (kg).

The length measures the distance from end to end of an object. The length of an object is measured in meters (m).

The duration of time that something will or has occurred is measured in increments of 1 second (s or sec).

The volume of a three-dimensional object is measured according to length, height, and width. All measurements are recorded as length measurements, with the meter as a base.

The volume of a container measuring 10 cm x 10 cm x 10 cm = 1,000 cm^3. A liter (L) more accurately describes the volume of the container.

SI Unit Measurements				
Prefix	**Symbol**	**Base 10**	**Decimal**	**English Word**
milli-	m	10^{-3}	0.001	One-thousandth
centi-	c	10^{-2}	0.01	One-hundredth
deci-	d	10^{-1}	0.1	One-tenth
Base		10^{0}	1	one
deca-	da	10^{1}	10	ten
78hecto-	h	10^{2}	100	hundred
kilo-	k	10^{3}	1000	thousand

Scale Unit

When measuring, it is essential to use the most appropriate scaled unit. Use kilograms when measuring a larger volume, rather than centigrams. When measuring something small, such as a chocolate chip, it is more appropriate to use millimeters instead of meters. It is more logical to state one chocolate chip measures 0.004 mm than a million chocolate chips measures 4 meters.

Tool Selection

The triple beam balance and the electronic balance are tools that measure mass of an object. The electronic or digital balance is more common due to ease of use. An electronic scale is much faster and easier for weighing smaller amounts. However, balance beam scales are the most precise measuring device.

Glassware

Numerous types of glassware are available to measure the volume of liquids. A volumetric flask provides the most accurate measurement when measuring large volumes. A volumetric pipette provides efficiency when measuring small volumes. Graduated cylinders provide less accurate measurement data. The volume of solids is calculated by multiplying the length, width, and height of the object by using rulers, meter sticks, or measuring wheels.

Scientific Explanation Using Logic and Evidence

Using logic and evidence to analyze the scientific process and developing conclusions from data is vital to draw logical scientific explanations. Additionally, analyzing scientific arguments for evidence will help determine the scientific information, content, and to construct meaning.

Empirical Evidence

Empirical evidence is the evidence generated through conducting experiments. Striving to only collect the logical explanations when reviewing or reproducing data will benefit the scientist is appropriately collecting relevant data and understand how to make logical conclusions based by the data.

Conclusions

Many scientists associate a cause-and-effect relationship as a conclusion in their scientific explanation. Conclusions depend on the evidence that supports them. When utilizing and analyzing the strengths of evidence used to support an argument is imperative to understanding the conclusion. Strong conclusions are demonstrated by replicable and convincing data. The process of analyzing data must include, presence of bias (intentional or unintentional), a controlled setting by allowing only one variable change at a time, accurate data collection and impeccable record keeping, and the ability to reproduce the results.

Relationships Among Events, Objects, and Processes

Relationships and processes are everchanging, the need to differentiate between the magnitude of events, objects, and processes is essential.

Every measurement requires a specific unit and the unit determines the scale.

Determining a causal relationship may be challenging but are necessary to determine the cause and effect relationship from the given scientific information. May need to also determine the sequence of events leading to a consequence as additional information relevant to the scientific investigation.

The Design of a Scientific Investigation

Scientists review investigations to determine an evidence supported hypotheses and then design investigations to test their hypotheses. These investigations are published and targeted towards knowledgeable people in that field to receive confirmation and validation of the scientist's information.

Hypotheses are informed opinions about causal relationships as determined by observation and the collection of initial data. The scientists do not divulge too deep in their investigation and begin developing hypotheses once they form ideas about the relationships. The context of the hypotheses establishes the strength of the investigation. Hypotheses may be accepted, rejected, the creation of new hypotheses, or revision of initial hypotheses.

During the investigation, the collection of experimental data develops theories. The scientist must implement strategies to control variables. The goal is to have and manipulate only one variable, the independent variable, what is measured as the possible cause of the hypotheses. A controlled investigation manages all other variables and kept the same. The dependent variable is the observed condition that responds to the manipulation of the independent variable, creating a causal relationship between the independent and dependent variables.

The scientist analyzes data for possible conclusions at the completion of the investigation. The conclusions are supported by evidence, the investigation will be published in journals and scrutinized by other scientists and either accept or reject hypotheses through this process.

PERFORM AN ENJOYABLE ACTIVITY TO DISTRACT YOU FROM STUDYING.
READ SOMETHING LIGHT, GO FOR A WALK – WHATEVER YOU DO, TRY TO GET YOUR MIND OFF THE MATERIAL FOR A LITTLE WHILE.

VOCABULARY

WORDS IN CONTEXT

When reading through a chapter in a book or a passage on a test, you will sometimes encounter a word you've never seen before. You may not know what it means, but don't worry! You can still figure out a basic definition of the word, even if you don't have a dictionary in hand (or if you don't want to get off the sofa and get one).

In every sentence, any given word is surrounded by clauses, phrases and other words. When you find a word you don't recognize, you can learn more about it by studying the context surrounding it. These surrounding words, phrases and clauses are called context clues. Using these, you can determine the definition for almost every unfamiliar word you encounter. This is a skill that will become especially helpful when you start reading higher level texts with fancy words or training manuals with lots of jargon.

TYPES OF CONTEXT CLUES

As you read, you can use several different types of context clues to help you discover the meaning of unknown words. Some important and common types of context clues are outlined below. Try to use the specific context clue to determine the meaning of the bolded word.

ROOT WORD & AFFIX

This is a context clue that uses your existing knowledge of common root words.
EXAMPLE: SCIENTISTS WHO DIG UP DINOSAUR BONES ARE EXPERTS IN PALEONTOLOGY.
This context clue assumes you have knowledge of dinosaurs and can relate that to the study of "paleontology."

COMPARE/CONTRAST

This is a context clue that signals a similarity or difference by using words or phrases that denote a comparison or contrast. Words that imply similarity (or comparison) include like, also, just as, too, etc. Words that imply difference (or contrast) include whereas, opposed to, unlike, versus, etc.
EXAMPLE: A COMET, LIKE AN ASTEROID, IS MADE FROM LEFTOVER MATTER IN THE UNIVERSE.
This context clue compares an "asteroid" with a comet to imply a similarity to the given definition of a comet.

LOGIC

This is a context clue wherein you must infer the definition of the unknown word by using the relationships within the sentence.

EXAMPLE: BUILDERS ROUTINELY USE FASTENERS THAT WILL HELP HOLD THEIR STRUCTURES AND BUILDINGS IN PLACE.

This context clue describes the job that "fasteners" do.

DEFINITION

This is a context clue that includes a basic definition of the unknown word.

EXAMPLE: NEW BIOLOGICAL SPECIES CAN BE FORMED THROUGH A PROCESS CALLED SPECIATION.

This context clue defines "speciation" outright.

EXAMPLE OR ILLUSTRATION

This is a context clue that uses an example or illustration of the unknown word.

EXAMPLE: ANIMALS CLASSIFIED IN THE PHYLUM PORIFERA LIVE IN A MARINE HABITAT LIKE THE ATLANTIC AND PACIFIC OCEANS.

This context clue uses Atlantic and Pacific Oceans as examples of "marine" habitats.

HOMOGRAPHS

Now that you've had a refresher on context clues, let's talk about homographs. A homograph is a word that is spelled exactly like another word, but has a different meaning. For example, "bass" can mean "a low, deep sound" or "a type of fish." Here's a more complex homograph: "minute" can mean "a unit of time" or "something very small."

Although questions with homographs aren't necessarily difficult, you'll need to pay extra attention to the context clues. If you're rushing or don't read the entire sentence, you can accidentally mark an incorrect answer by mistaking the homograph for the wrong meaning. As long as you take your time and use the context clues, you'll most likely have no problem.

Here's something to consider when you take the exam. Within the question, replace the vocabulary term with your selected answer choice. Read the sentence and check whether or not it makes sense. This won't guarantee a correct answer, but it will help identify an incorrect one.

Another point to keep in mind is that sometimes there will not be an answer choice that exactly fits into the sentence. Don't panic! You probably did not misread the context clues or come up with an incorrect meaning. Many times, questions will ask you to select the best word from the given answer choices, even though that correct answer choice may not be the best possible answer overall. These types of questions want you to choose the most correct answer choice. These can be tricky to tackle, but expect to see questions like this on the exam.

CRITICAL READING

DETAIL QUESTIONS

Reading passages and identifying important details is an important part of the critical reading process. Detail questions ask the reader to recall specific information about the main idea. These details are often found in the examples given in the passage and can contain anecdotes, data or descriptions, among other details. For example, if you are reading a passage about certain types of dogs, you may be asked to remember details about breeds, sizes and coat color and patterns. As you read through the passage, make sure you take note of numbers, figures and the details given about the topic. Chances are you will need to remember some of these.

There is a wealth of information, facts, pieces of data and several details that can be presented within any passage you read. The key to uncovering the main idea and understanding the details presented is to take your time and read through everything contained in the passage. Consider each example and figure presented. Think about how they relate to the main idea, how they support the focus, and how those details add to the information and value of the passage.

Strategies for Answering Detail Questions:

- Identify key words in the question that help you find details and examples to answer the question.
- Take note of how words are used and if phrases are repeated. Look for the overall meaning of each paragraph and passage.
- Some questions will pull words or phrases from the passage and quote them in the question. In this case, find those quotes and make sure they are being used the same way in the passage and the question. Many questions will change the meaning of these to make the question wrong or confuse the reader.
- Some questions will ask you to determine if a particular statement or topic is true. In this case, look over the paragraphs and find the overall theme or idea of the passage. Compare your theme or idea to the statement in the question.

UNDERSTANDING QUESTION STEMS

In addition to careful reading of the passages (including marking up the text for topic and concluding sentences, transitional words and key terms), you must also be able to identify what is being asked of you in each of the questions. Recognition of the task in each question can be easily accomplished if you are familiar with the question stems, or the most commonly phrased wording that will be associated with each type of question on the test. Keep reading for an explanation of each question type, along with sample stems, and suggested approaches for tackling them.

Supporting Details

Supporting details are those that back up the main ideas presented in the passage. These can include examples, clarifying explanations, or elaborations of basic ideas presented earlier in the reading. Supporting details are directly stated in the passage, so you must rely on your careful reading to guide you to the correct answer. Answers may not be stated in the original language of the passage, but the basic ideas will be the same. Here are some common ways this type of question is asked:

- The passage states...
- The author says...
- According to what you read...

Main Idea

Questions asking you to identify the main idea expect that you will be able to determine the overall point of the passage (often called the thesis), NOT secondary details or supporting points. Attempting to put the main idea into your own words after reading WITHOUT looking at the text again is a very helpful strategy in answering this type of question. If you can sum up the author's main point in your own words, then you will find it very easy to find the right "match" amongst the answers provided for you. Alternately, the main idea may often be found in the opening or concluding paragraphs, two common places where an author may introduce a topic and his perspective about said topic, or he summarize the main points.
Here are some common ways this type of question is asked:

- The main idea for this paragraph...
- The central point of the passage...
- A possible title for the passage...
- The author's primary point...

Inference

Inferences are those ideas which can be gleaned from the suggestions that may be implied in other statements made by the author. They are never explicitly stated, but we understand that they are true from "reading between the lines". The answers to inferences questions, therefore, are assumptions, and cannot be found from direct statements in the text. You will have to rely on your ability to logically deduce conclusions from your careful reading. More than one answer may sound correct, but only one is. Make sure that, whichever answer you choose, you can find statements in the text which would support that idea. If you cannot do that, then that choice is likely not the right answer.
Here are some common ways this type of question is asked:

- The passage implies...
- The author suggests...
- The reader could logically conclude that...
- The reader would be correct in assuming that...

Tone/Attitude

Some questions will ask you about the author's tone or attitude. A good place to start with this type of question is to consider whether the passage is positive, negative or neutral. Does the author seem angry? Maybe sad? Or torn between two points of view? The language that an author uses can be very telling about his tone and attitude. Is the author critical? Praiseworthy? Disappointed? Even if you find some finer details of passage difficult to understand, the tone and attitude are often fairly easy to identify. Look for adjectives and statements that reveal the author's opinion, rather than facts, and this will help you know his tone or attitude.

Here are some common ways this type of question is asked:

- The tone of the passage is...
- The attitude of the author is...
- The writer's overall feeling...

Style

Style refers to a writer's "way with words". Most seasoned writers have a well-developed and easily recognizable style, but often the topic of a written work can dictate style. If the topic is serious, the language will likely be more formal. Works for academic settings may be heavy with the jargon of that discipline. Personal reflections can be rife with imagery, while instructional manuals will use simple and straightforward language. Identifying style is not difficult; simply pay attention to the words used (simple or fancy?), the sentence structure (simple or compound-complex?), as well as the overall structure of the piece (stream of consciousness or 5-paragraph essay?). You must answer these questions in order to determine the style of the passage.

Here are some common ways this type of question is asked:

- The overall writing style used in the passage...
- The author's style is...
- The organizational style of the passage is...

Pattern of Organization

Pattern of organization questions want you to consider how the writing of a piece was developed. What features did the writer utilize to make his point? Did he include personal anecdotes? Data or statistics? Quotes from authorities on the topic? These are all modes of organizing a passage that help the writer support his claims and provide a logical focus for the work.

Here are some common ways this type of question is asked:

- The author proves a point through...
- In the passage, the author uses...
- Throughout the passage, the author seems to rely on...

Purpose and Attitude

Questions asking about purpose and attitude require you to consider why the author took the time to write. The author's motivations are directly behind the purpose of the piece. What question did he wish to answer? What cause did he want to show support for? What action did he wish to persuade you to take? Identifying these reasons for writing will reveal the purpose and attitude of the passage.

Here are some common ways this type of question is asked:

- The purpose of the passage is...
- The author's intent for writing the passage is...

- The attitude the author displays is...

Fact/Opinion

There will be some questions on the test that will ask you whether a statement is a fact or an opinion. Without being able to fact-check, how will you do this? A rule of thumb would be that opinions reflect only the thoughts, feelings or ideas of the writer, whereas facts are verifiable as true or false, regardless of one's feelings. If a writer cites a statistic about the environmental effects of oil drilling on migratory mammals in the Pacific Northwest, then that is verifiable and can be considered factual. If, however, the writer claims that oil drilling in the Pacific Northwest United States is bad and should be stopped, then that is his opinion. He may at some point provide examples of why this is so, but that viewpoint is based on his thoughts and feelings about oil drilling and can only be considered opinion.

Here are some common ways this type of question is asked:

Which statement is a fact rather than an opinion?

- This statement is meant to be...
- An example of fact is when the author says...
- An example of opinion is when the author states that...

ELIMINATING WRONG ANSWERS

An author often writes with an intended purpose in mind, and they will support their main idea with examples, facts, data and stories that help the overall meaning of their written text to be clear. You may be asked a question regarding one of these details or examples, or you may be asked something about the overall theme or main idea of the passage. These types of questions require you to read the passage carefully for meaning and to look at all the supporting details used. However it's also important to learn how to identify incorrect answer choices and eliminate them right away. This will help you narrow down the answer choices that are likely to be correct

ARITHMETIC REASONING

ADDITION, SUBTRACTION, MULTIPLICATION, DIVISION OPERATIONS WITH DECIMALS

The sign conventions for positive and negative decimal arithmetic operations are the same as those for whole number operations outlined in Module 1. But, there are special details to recall when performing arithmetic operations with decimal values to ensure correct answers.

When adding and subtracting decimal values, it is important to make sure that the decimal points are aligned vertically. This is the simplest method to ensure a reliable result. For example adding 0.522 and 0.035 should be performed as follows:

$$\begin{array}{r} 0.522 \\ \underline{+0.035} \\ 0.557 \end{array}$$

Subtraction operations should be aligned similarly.

$$\begin{array}{r} 0.522 \\ \underline{-0.035} \\ 0.487 \end{array}$$

It is important to note that multiplication requires a different convention to be followed. When multiplying decimals, the operations are NOT aligned necessarily the same way as addition and subtraction. For example, multiplying 0.7 and 2.15 is performed as follows:

$$\begin{array}{r} \underline{2.15} \\ \times\ 0.7 \\ 1.505 \end{array}$$

When multiplying decimal values, the decimal point placement in the answer is determined by counting the total number of digits to the right of the decimal point in the multiplied numbers. This detail is often overlooked in testing choices where the same numbers may appear in several multiple-choice answers, but with different decimal point placements.

Division of decimal values is simplified by first visualizing fractions that are equivalent. The mathematics terminology is that a dividend / divisor = quotient. For example:

$7.35 / 1.05$ is the same as $73.5 / 10.5$, which is the same operation as $735 / 105$.

The last fraction, in the example above, means that to solve $7.35 / 1.05$ we can divide $735 / 105$ and find the correct whole number answer. This method just requires that when dividing by a decimal number, the divisor must be corrected to be a whole number. This requirement is achieved by moving the decimal points in both the dividend and divisor the same number of decimal places. If the dividend still contains a decimal point, the place is maintained in the long division operation, and the correct quotient is still achieved. The quotient remains in the form of a decimal number.

ADDITION, SUBTRACTION, MULTIPLICATION, DIVISION OPERATIONS WITH FRACTIONS

The sign conventions for positive and negative fractional arithmetic operations are the same as those for whole number operations outlined in Module 1. However, there are special details to recall when performing arithmetic operations with fractional values to ensure correct answers.

Remember that fractions are made up of a numerator and a denominator. The top number of the fraction, called the numerator, tells how many of the fractional parts are being represented. The bottom number, called the denominator, tells how many equal parts the whole is divided into. For this reason, fractions with different denominators cannot be added together because different denominators are as different as "apples and oranges." So, when adding or subtracting fractions with different denominators, a common denominator must be found. In this case, simple geometric models will be used to explain the common denominator principle. Usually, this principle is illustrated with circles divided into "pie slices." A simpler and more effective example involves the use of squares or rectangles divided into fractional parts.

Representing fraction parts, $1/3$ and $1/4$ will be demonstrated with the following square diagrams. In this case a whole square is the number "1" and the fractional parts will be the slices of the square as follows:

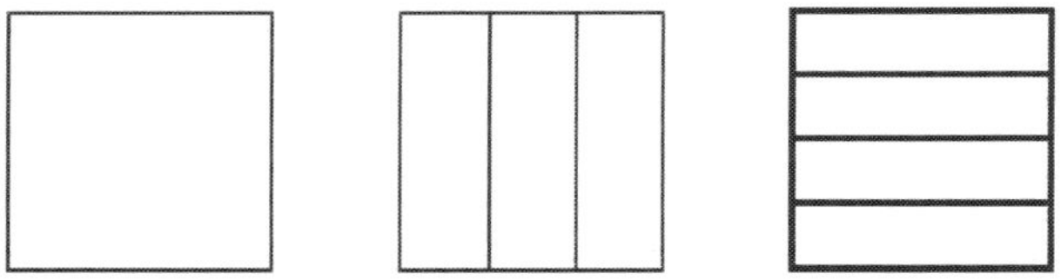

WHOLE (1) THIRDS FOURTHS

If we superimpose the four horizontal slices over the three vertical slices, there are twelve separate parts of the whole as follows:

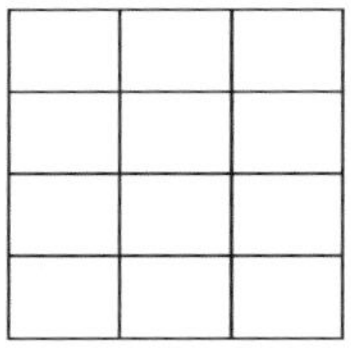

In the last diagram, any column representing a third, has four of the twelve small rectangles from the diagram, or $4/12$ as the equivalent fraction. Similarly, any row of the last diagram, representing a fourth, has three of the twelve small rectangles from the diagram, or $3/12$ as the equivalent fraction. With this modification of the two fractions, both are now in the form of a common denominator, and the addition of the two fractions can be completed:

$$1/3 + 1/4 = 3/12 + 4/12 = 7/12$$

Notice that this result is exactly analogous to the simple diagram above. Common denominator fractions need not be simplified with this type of diagram, but it is a valuable example to explain the principle. The common denominator is required whenever adding or subtracting fractions with different denominators. If the denominators are the same, then the addition or subtraction of numerators is all that is required. If more assistance is needed on how to find common denominators, the Arithmetic Reasoning chapter in Module 1 will provide information on finding the Least Common Multiple, or the lowest common denominator, required for addition and subtraction. Remember that the individual fractions will retain the same value only if the numerator and denominator are multiplied by the same value.
Multiplication of fractions is a simple operation because fractions multiply as follows:

$$7/8 * 3/4 = (7 * 3)/(8 * 4) = 21/32$$

This fraction is in its simplest form because there are no common factors. If common factors exist in the numerator and denominator of a fraction, then that fraction must be simplified.
Division of fractions should never be attempted in the form of a ratio. The method is confusing, elaborate and unreliable in a testing situation. Instead, every fraction division problem is a simple operation because the division operation can be rewritten as a multiplication operation. To begin, as stated previously:

$$dividend/divisor = quotient$$

This can be rewritten as:

$$dividend * (1/divisor) = quotient$$

This yields exactly the same outcome as division. The quantity (1/divisor) is called a reciprocal, and for a fraction, it's as simple as flipping the fraction upside down. Therefore:

$$(5/8)\ /\ (1/4) = 5/8 * 4/1 = 20/32 = 5/8 \text{ (in simplified form)}$$

FRACTION TO DECIMAL CONVERSIONS

Every fraction represents a division problem. The decimal value of any fraction is represented by the numerator, (top value), divided by the denominator (bottom value). Certain combinations, such as $1/3$, will result in repeating decimals that will always be rounded in a multiple-choice testing situation.
The fraction 1/2 has a decimal value of 0.5, which is the value of 1 divided by 2. The values of improper fractions such as $3/2, 5/2$, or $7/2$ (larger numerator than denominator) are determined by dividing as previously stated or more easily by multiplying the numerator by 0.5. So the improper fraction of $7/2\ is\ 7 * 0.5$, or 3.5. Often, the determination of the unit fraction (1 divided by the denominator) followed by the decimal multiplication is simpler in a testing situation.

The fraction $3/5$ has a decimal value of 0.6, which is the value of 3 divided by 5. Alternately, the value of the unit fraction of $1/5$ is 0.2, and that unit fraction multiplied by 3 is 0.6. If you know the unit fractions for common fraction values, the answer selection process may be simplified.

When a fraction such as $5/7$ is evaluated, the quotient of 5 divided by 7 results in a lengthy decimal value of 0.71428 .... That extended value will never appear as a multiple-choice test answer selection. Typically, that value will be rounded to either 0.71 or 0.714. Remember that testing instructions say to choose the best answer. Your best choice may be a rounded number.

DECIMAL TO FRACTION CONVERSIONS

All decimals are also fractions and can be written in that form. The fractions that result all have powers of 10 in the denominator and usually need to be simplified in order to be compared to multiple-choice answers in a testing situation. For example, simple decimal values, such as 0.25, can be written as the fraction $25/100$. This fraction must be simplified to be correct. $25/100$ can be rewritten as a product:

$$(25 * 1)/(25 * 4)$$

or

$$25/25 * 1/4$$

The fraction can be expressed correctly as $1/4$ since the fraction $25/25$ is simplified to 1. Recognizing the common factors in the numerator and denominator is the essential element in making these conversions. For testing purposes, decimal conversions will often be based on common fraction values. For example, $1/16$, if divided with long division, is 0.0625. Any integer multiple of this value results in a fraction with 16 in the denominator. The value 0.0625 is first rewritten as the fraction:

$$625/10000$$

Simplifying with factors of 5 in the numerator and denominator gives the fraction:

$$125/2000$$

Simplifying with factors of 25 in the numerator and denominator gives the fraction:

$$5/80$$

Simplifying with factors of 5 in the numerator and denominator one more time gives the simplified fraction:

$$1/16$$

While either of these methods may require an extra amount of time to complete, usually the answer choices may be logically reduced to two of the four examples. Testing the answer choices is simply a matter of multiplying the decimal value by the denominator to determine if the numerator is correct. Another solution method, logical deduction, can be used as a simple, reliable and time saving approach to finding the fractional value of 0.435. In this example, the following is a list of possible multiple-choice answers:

$3/16$
$5/16$
$7/16$
$9/16$

Logically, any fraction greater than $1/2$ is immediately eliminated since:

$$0.435 < 0.5$$

So, first eliminate answer D. Incorrect answer choices will be eliminated with this type of logical deduction.
Second, notice that in the answer choice:

$$3/16 < ¼$$

and in decimal form

$$3/16 < 0.25$$

So, choice A can logically be eliminated since our answer comparison is with 0.435.
Third, notice that in the answer choices:

$$5/16 > 1/4$$

and in decimal form

$$5/16 > 0.25$$

Since $5/16$ is just slightly more than $1/4$, choice B can be eliminated since our comparison is with 0.435.
Finally, C is chosen as the most likely answer choice.
It is the logical choice since:

$$7/16 < 1/2$$

and

$$0.435 < 0.5$$

PERCENTAGES

Percentages is a concept you are most likely familiar with from real-world applications, so these are some of the less scary math problems that appear on tests. However, test writers take that confidence into account and can use it against you, so it's important to be careful on problems with percentages. Let's look at an example:

A sweater went on sale and now costs 25.20. If the original price was 42.00, what is the percent discount?

16.8%
20.0%
25.0%
40.0%
60.0%

Take a minute to work out the problem for yourself. If you get the wrong answer, it will be helpful to you to see where you went wrong – several of the answer choices are distinct traps that often appear on test questions like this.

SOLUTION:

With percentages, you can always set up a fraction. First, you want to know what percent the sale price is of the original price. The reference point, or original price, will go on the bottom of the fraction. The numerator will be the sale price. The ratio of $25.2 / 42$ is equal to $6 / 10$.
The sale price, 25.20, is 0.6, or 60%, of the original price. A percentage is just the decimal times 100%. This is answer choice E. However, the question did NOT ask what percent the new price is of the original

price. Read carefully: it asks for the percent discount. This language is commonly used for questions with prices. Here's what it means, in math terms:

$$Percentage\ discount = 100\% - Percentage\ of\ the\ Sale\ Price$$

The percent discount is the amount less than 100% that the sale price is of the original price. We can use this equation to solve, which yields:

$$(42 - 25.2) / 42 = 0.40$$

Remember, a percent is a decimal times 100%. So, we can convert the decimal on the right side to a percentage by multiplying by 100%:

$$100\% * 0.40 = 40\%$$

The sale price is 40% less than the original price, which is answer choice D. Another mathematical reasoning approach would be to take the original fraction subtracted from 1:

$$1 - 25.2 / 42 = 0.4$$

From here, just recognize that if the sale price is 60% of the original price, then it is 40% less than the original price. You can solve for the discounted amount and then find that as a percent of the original amount to solve for the percentage of the discount:

$$42 - 25.2 = 16.80$$
$$16.80 / 42 = 0.4$$

Those are three different ways to approach one problem, using the same concept of percentage and recognizing that a percent discount requires subtraction from the original. Here's another percentage problem, this time with a different trick:

$$168\ is\ 120\%\ of\ what\ number?$$

SOLUTION:

First, convert 120% to a decimal. Remember, converting a percentage to a decimal is done by dividing by 100%:

$$120 / 100 = 1.2$$

We are told that 168 is this percent of some other number. This means that 168 goes in the numerator of our percent fraction equation. Here is the resulting equation:

$$168 / x = 1.2$$

Here, x signifies the unknown number in the problem. Writing the percent equation is indispensable to solving this type of problem. Multiply both sides by x and then divide both sides by 1.2 to isolate the variable:

$$168(x) / x = 1.2(x)$$
$$168 = 1.2x$$

$$168 / 1.2 = 1.2x / 1.2$$
$$140 = x$$

Therefore, 168 is 120% of 140. We can verify this answer by plugging the numbers back into the original equation:

$$168 / 140 = 1.2$$

This problem is tricky because the percentage is greater than 100%, or greater than 1.0, so it violates our intuition that the bigger number should go on the bottom of the fraction. Usually, percentages are less than 100. However, when percentages are larger than 100, the numerator is bigger than the denominator.
The inverse of this question could be the following:

$$168 \textit{ is what percent of } 140?$$

Many people, after reading this question, would automatically set up the following fraction equation:

$$140/168 = 0.83$$

83% would likely be an answer choice, but it's the wrong answer. The question is asking for 168 / 140. Read these questions carefully, and don't automatically place the larger number in the denominator.
Let's look at one more example, which combines these concepts, and then do a couple practice problems:
An ingredient in a recipe is decreased by 20%. By what percentage does the new amount need to be increased to obtain the original amount of the ingredient?

SOLUTION:
Here is a pro's tip for working with percentages:
When a problem is given only in percentages with no given numbers, you can substitute in any value to work with as your original amount. Since you are solving for a percent, you'll get the same answer no matter what numbers are used because percentages are ratios. The easiest number to work with in problems like this is 100, so use that as the original recipe amount. 100 what? Cups of flour? Chicken tenders? Chocolate chips? Doesn't matter. Here's how your equation should look:

$$x / 100 = 0.20$$

Solve for x, which gives the amount the ingredient has been decreased by:

$$x = 100 * 0.20$$

Remember that 20% is a decimal, so $0.20 * 100 = 20$. The ingredient has been decreased by 20 units. What is the new amount?

$$100 - 20 = 80$$

What was the question asking for? By what percent does the new amount need to be increased to obtain the original amount of the ingredient? Let's parse this mathematical language. We've found the new amount of the ingredient, 80. The original amount, we decided, was 100.
The next step in answering the question is to find the amount that we would need to add to get back to the original amount. This part is pretty easy:

$$80 + x = 100$$
$$x = 20$$

It's the same amount that we subtracted from the original amount, 20. But the question asks what percentage of 80 is required to add 20?
Set up the percentage equation. 80 times what percent (x / 100) will give that extra 20 units?

$$80 * x / 100 = 20$$

Solve as normal by dividing both sides by 80 and then multiplying both sides by 100:

$$x / 100 = 0.25$$
$$x = 25$$

The new amount must be increased by 25% to equal the original amount.

MATHEMATICS KNOWLEDGE

RATES AND SYSTEMS OF EQUATIONS

These are some of the most common questions on standardized math exams and also some of the most criticized. How many pop culture references are there to the nightmare of the "if train A is traveling west of Detroit at 70 miles an hour and train B is traveling north of Denver at 90 miles an hour, what is the weight of the moon" variety? Excluding the nonsensical nature of the joke (would we weigh the moon in terms of its own gravity, or Earth's? Do bodies in orbit actually weigh anything? Wait, wrong subject), this is simply a rate problem! Train A has a speed and a direction, Train B has a speed and a direction, and given those facts, you can answer all kinds of questions easily.

A rate is anything that relates two types of measurement: distance and time, dollars and workers, mass and volume, x per y. Exchange rates tell us how much of one currency you can get for a certain amount of another currency. Speedometers tell us how many miles we travel per unit of time. Growth rates tell us how much additional population we get over time. Rates are everywhere in the world, and they are everywhere on standardized math tests. To express a rate mathematically, think of the following:
All rates express one measurement in terms of another. For example, miles per hour gives us a measurement of distance (miles) for one unit of time (an hour). "Per" is a term that means divide. It looks like this:
If a car is traveling 70 mph, it goes 70 miles for every one hour of time that passes.
All rates work this way. If you can get €0.81 (Euros) for one American dollar, the exchange rate is:

$$\text{€}0.81\ (Euros)\ /\ 1\ Dollar\ =\ 0.81\ Euros\ per\ Dollar$$

A rate is written as a fraction. A rate equation gives you a value of one of the measurements if you know the rate and the value of the other measurement.

If a car travels 70 mph: $Distance\ =\ 70\ miles/\ hour\ *\ hours$

This recipe for the equation always works for a rate problem:
Examine the mph example: when you multiply 70 miles/hour times a number of hours, the hours units cancel out, leaving you with a number of miles. This works for any type of rate. The thing being measured on the top (numerator) of the rate measurement is equal to the rate times the unit being measured on the bottom of the rate measurement.

TO SOLVE A RATE PROBLEM, FOLLOW THESE STEPS:
Read the question carefully to determine what you will be solving for. Is it an amount of time? A distance? Something else? Make sure you understand this before anything else. It can be helpful to name the variables at this point.

Write equations to express all of the information given in the problem. This is just like we've demonstrated for percentage problems, averaging problems, etc. The ability to express information in an equation is one of the main mathematical reasoning abilities that you can demonstrate to succeed on tests like these.
Remember the equation:

$$Distance = Rate * Time$$

Solve!

First, a simple example:
A train is traveling west at 75 mph. How long will it take to travel 60 miles?

Step 1: Identify what the question is asking for: in this instance, it's how long, or the time it takes to travel 60 miles.

Step 2: Write an equation: $60 = 75 * time$

Step 3: Solve! We know that the rate is 75 miles per hour and that the miles traveled is 60. To solve for time, just plug those values into the equation:

Isolate the "x hours" by dividing both sides by 75 mph:

$$60\ miles\ /\ 75\ miles\ per\ hour = 0.8\ hours$$

$$0.8\ hours * 60\ minutes\ per\ hour = 48\ minutes$$

Rate problems can also require a system of equations. This just means that you need to write two equations to relate two unknown variables, instead of one equation to solve for one unknown variable, like the problem above. The algebra is not any more difficult for these types of problems. They just require the extra step of writing another equation.

For example: Jessica assembles one model airplane per hour. James assembles one model airplane per 45 minutes. If they work for the same amount of time and assemble twelve planes all together, how many planes did James assemble?

Step 1: Identify what the question is asking for: the number of planes that James assembled.
Step 2: Write equations:

$$x = 1\ Airplanes\ per\ hour * T\ hours$$

$$y = 1/0.75\ Airplanes\ per\ hour * T\ hours$$

$$x + y = 12$$

You convert "45 minutes" to 0.75 hours, since $45/60 = 0.75$. If you'd rather not do that, you could leave the rate in minutes, but then change Jessica's rate to 60 minutes instead of one hour. The important thing is to use the same units for time across the whole equation.

Step 3: Solve! Notice that the "T hours" term is the same in both of the rate equations. The problem stated that the two of them worked for the same amount of time. To solve for the number of planes James assembled, first we need to find T hours. The number of planes Jessica assembles and the number of planes James assembles can be added together since we know that the sum is 12. This is the new equation from adding those together:

$$12 = 1\, Airplanes\ per\ hour * T\ hours + 1/0.75\, Airplanes\ per\ hour * T\ hours$$

The algebra here is a little bit hairy, but we can handle it! To solve for time, isolate T step by step. First, multiply every term in the equation by "1 hour":
Now, the unit "hour" cancels out of both terms on the right side of the equation. Remember, when you multiply and divide a term by something, that cancels out:
Now, we have:

$$12\, plane\ hours = 1\, plane * T\ hours + 1/0.75 * T\ hours$$

We need to isolate "T hours." Gather together the "T hours" terms on the right side of the equation. Right now, they are separated into an addition expression. If we add them together, they will be collected into one term. Since $1/0.75$ is equal to $4/3$, change that term first:

$$12\, plane\ hours = 1\, plane * T\ hours + 4/3\, plane * T\text{hours}$$

Now add:

$$12\, plane\ hours = (1\, plane + 4/3\, plane) * T\ hours$$
$$12\, plane\ hours = (1\ and\ 4/3\, plane) * T\ hours$$

You add together 1 and $4/3$. This is the same as saying that $1x + 2x = 3x$. We just collected the like terms.

Now, divide both sides by 1 plane to isolate the T hours term. Since mixed fractions are difficult to work with, change this into an improper fraction:

$$12\, plane\ hours = (7/3\, plane) * T\ hours$$

The planes unit cancels out on the right side. So, we are left with:

$$12\, hours\ /\ (7/3) = T\ hours$$

One arithmetic trick: dividing by a fraction is the same as multiplying by the inverse of the fraction. If you are comfortable dividing by fractions on your calculator, you can do the rest of the problem that way, or else you can flip the fraction over and simplify the arithmetic:

$$12 * 3/7 = T\ hours$$
$$36/7 = T\ hours$$
$$5\,1/7 = T\ hours$$

The answer is $x = 5\frac{1}{7}$ hours, or approximately 5.14 hours.

That was a long problem! But it included rates, a system of equations, unit conversions (changing minutes into fractions of an hour) and algebra with complex fractions. That is about the most difficult type of rate problem you would ever see on a standardized math exam, so if you were able to follow along with the solution you're in good shape.

Remember, on exams like this, the vast majority of points come from the easier problems. The harder problems (which on most exams tend to be at the end of a section) are always worth giving a shot, but they are not necessary to get a good score. Problems like these are great for practice because they include a lot of different concepts. Don't be discouraged if you don't always get the tougher problems correct on the first try. They are preparing you to do well on a wide range of different problem types!

MODULE 3

DAY, LOCATION, MUSIC

1

MONDAY, OCTOBER 12

COFFEE SHOP ON MAIN STREET

MY FAVORITE BAND

2

3

VOCABULARY

LET'S FACE IT. VOCABULARY JUST ISN'T THAT INTERESTING. SO, LET'S CHANGE IT UP! BELOW IS A CROSSWORD PUZZLE TO HELP YOU LEARN SOME NEW WORDS AND EXPAND YOUR VOCABULARY.

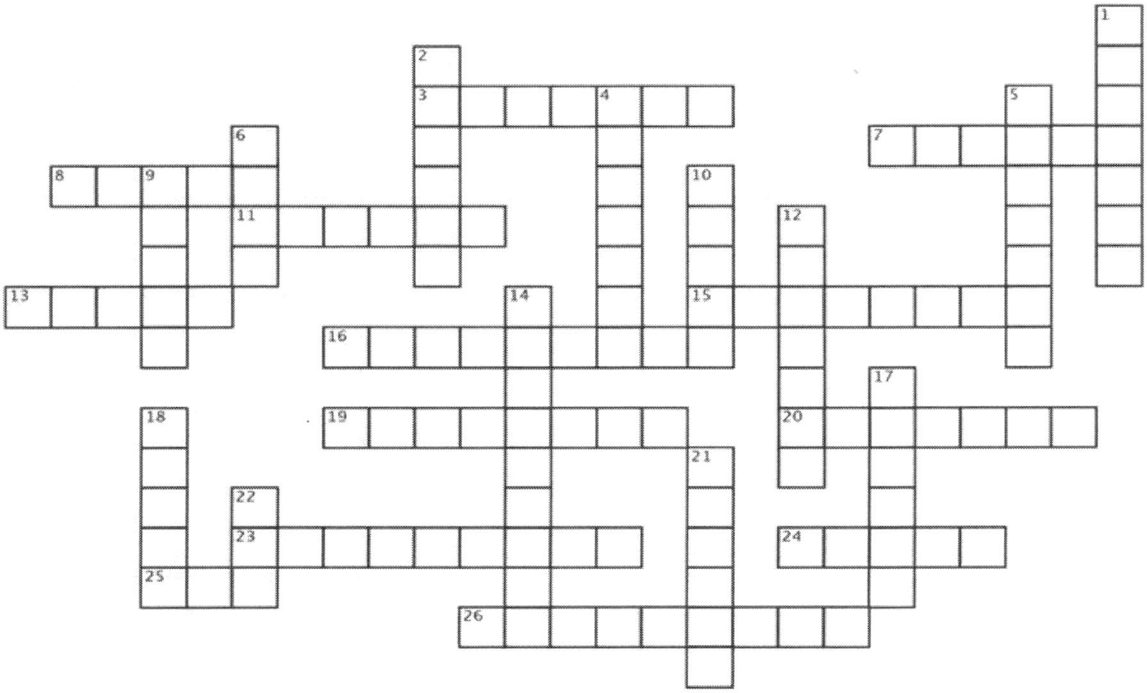

abhorrent bar chide debonair err frail glut haughty immerse jargon lofty malign abscond obscure parity ravage slander transpose unison vague amity ambiguous carcass hoist perpetual surmount

Across

3. to leave quickly
7. destroy or ruin
8. weak
11. together or at once
13. of considerable height
15. to overcome something
16. disgusting or hateful
19. stylish and charming
20. speaking falsely about someone
23. having more than one explanation
24. unclear or uncertain
25. to make a mistake
26. a state of being without change

Down

1. cover completely
2. specialized words
4. relatively unknown
5. arrogant
6. too much of something
9. friendly relations between two people
10. raise with a mechanical device
12. the remains of a dead animal
14. to change an arrangement
17. speak badly about
18. to scold
21. the equivalent of something
22. forbid or prevent

HOPEFULLY, THAT WASN'T TOO DIFFICULT. LET'S SEE HOW YOU DID!

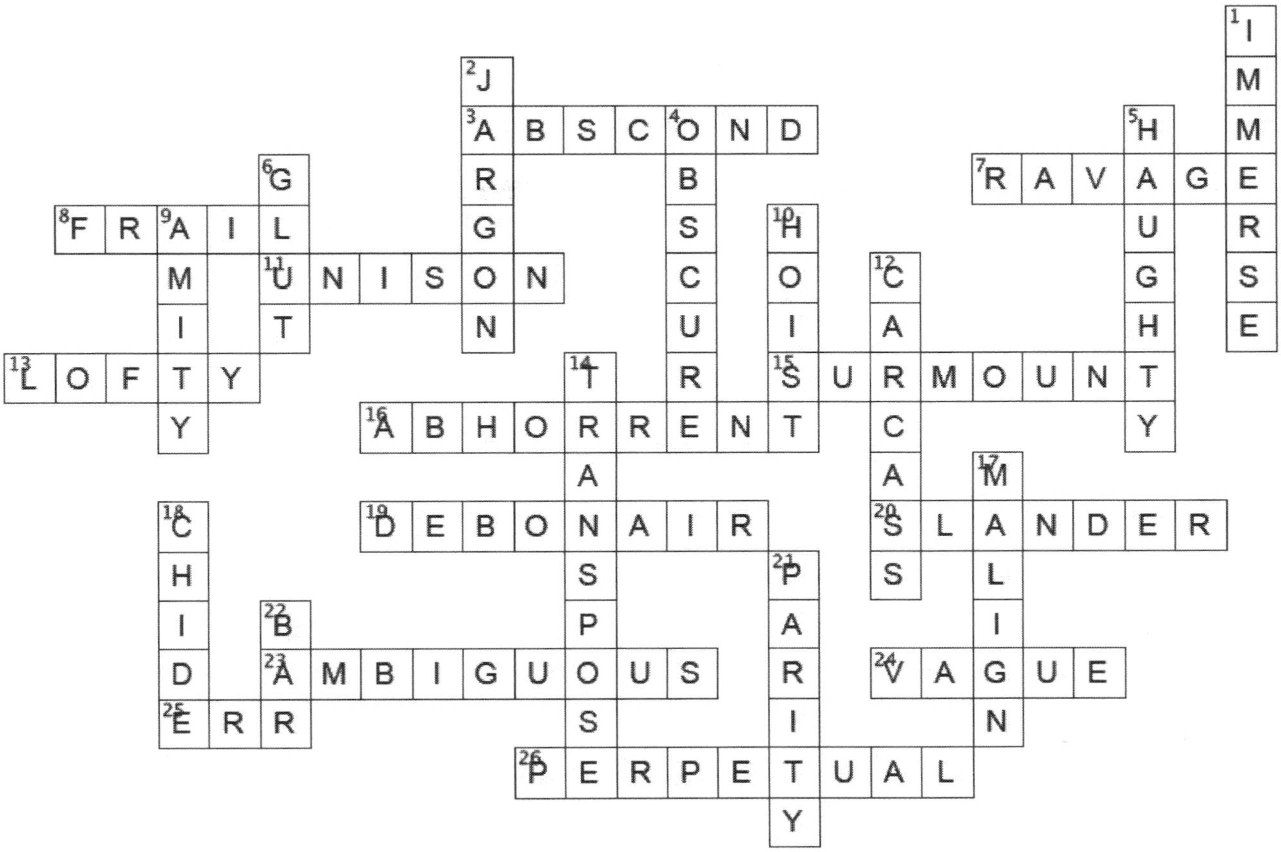

abhorrent bar chide debonair err frail glut haughty immerse jargon lofty malign abscond obscure parity ravage slander transpose unison vague amity ambiguous carcass hoist perpetual surmount

Across

3. to leave quickly [ABSCOND]
7. destroy or ruin [RAVAGE]
8. weak [FRAIL]
11. together or at once [UNISON]
13. of considerable height [LOFTY]
15. to overcome something [SURMOUNT]
16. disgusting or hateful [ABHORRENT]
19. stylish and charming [DEBONAIR]
20. speaking falsely about someone [SLANDER]
23. having more than one explanation [AMBIGUOUS]
24. unclear or uncertain [VAGUE]
25. to make a mistake [ERR]
26. a state of being without change [PERPETUAL]

Down

1. cover completely [IMMERSE]
2. specialized words[JARGON]
4. relatively unknown [OBSCURE]
5. Arrogant [HAUGHTY]
6. too much of something[GLUT]
9. friendly relations between two people [AMITY]
10. raise with a mechanical device [HOIST]
12. the remains of a dead animal [CARCASS]
14. to change an arrangement [TRANSPOSE]
17. speak badly about [MALIGN]
18. to scold [CHIDE]
21. the equivalent of something [PARITY]
22. forbid or prevent [BAR]

CRITICAL READING

INFERENCES AND HOW TO MAKE THEM AND USE THEM

INFERENCE QUESTIONS

Inference questions ask about ideas that are not directly stated, but rather are implied by the passage. They ask you to draw conclusions based on the information in the passage. Inference questions usually include words like "imply," "infer" or "conclude," or they may ask you what the author "would probably" think or do in a given situation based on what was stated in the passage.

With inference questions, it is important not to go too far beyond the scope of the passage. You are not expected to make any guesses. There is a single correct answer that is a logical, next-step conclusion from what is presented in the passage.

Let's take a look at some sample inference questions. Read through the following passages and use your inference skills to answer the questions. Remember that the inferences you make are not always obvious or directly stated in the passage.

SAMPLE 1

"Despite the fact that the practice is illegal in many states, some people set off their own fireworks at home each summer, especially on Independence Day. Most cities have public fireworks displays run by experienced professionals in a controlled environment, but many people still enjoy the thrill of setting off their own fireworks. However, this practice can be dangerous, and many people are injured each year from fireworks-related accidents. Having Independence Day fireworks in your own backyard is not worth the safety risk, especially when public fireworks displays are available in most areas."

THE AUTHOR OF THIS PASSAGE WOULD MOST LIKELY SUPPORT:

a) The complete legalization of fireworks nationwide
b) The reduction of public fireworks displays
c) More rigorous enforcement of restrictions on home fireworks
d) Promoting home fireworks use

ANSWER: C

In the passage, the author takes a negative tone toward home fireworks use, citing the fact that the practice is dangerous, illegal in some areas and unnecessary since many areas have safe public fireworks displays on holidays. Someone who is critical of home fireworks use would support strong enforcement of restrictions on their use.

SAMPLE 2

"A man took his car to the mechanic because the engine was overheating. The mechanic opened the hood to inspect the situation. He removed the radiator cap and could see that there was a sufficient amount of coolant in the radiator. He took the car for a drive and also noticed that the engine would overheat at a stoplight, but not on the highway."

ACCORDING TO THE PASSAGE, WHAT CAN YOU INFER ABOUT THE ENGINE?

a) The engine needs to be replaced
b) The radiator is leaking
c) The engine is operating normally
d) The radiator fan is broken

ANSWER: D

Although an overheating engine does indicate an abnormal condition, it does not necessarily indicate a catastrophic failure. Thus, the engine can be repaired instead of replaced. The radiator was full of coolant, so that eliminates the possibility of a leak. When a vehicle is moving, the airflow across the radiator cools the coolant. However, when a vehicle is stationary, the fan is responsible for cooling the coolant. If the fan is not working correctly, this would explain the overheating at a stoplight, but not on the highway.

ARITHMETIC REASONING

WORKING WITH SETS

All standardized math exams will touch on the basic statistical descriptions of sets of numbers: mean (the same as an average, for a set), median, mode and range. These are terms to know. Let's look at an example set and examine what each of these terms means:

Set of numbers: $42, 18, 21, 26, 22, 21$

MEAN/AVERAGE

The mean of a set of numbers is the average value of the set. The formula for finding the mean is:

$$\frac{\text{sum of the numbers in the set}}{\text{quantity of numbers in the set}} = mean$$

Use this formula to find the mean of the example set:

$$\frac{42 + 18 + 21 + 26 + 22 + 21}{6} = \frac{150}{6} = 25$$

You add together all the numbers that appear in the set, and then divide by the quantity of numbers in the set. The mean, or average, value in the set is 25. Notice that the mean is not necessarily a number that appears in the set, although it can be.

MEDIAN

The median of a set is the number that appears in the middle when the set is ordered from least to greatest. Therefore, the first step in finding the mean is to put the numbers in the correct order, if they are not already. You should always do this physically, on your scratch paper, to make sure that you don't leave any numbers out of the reordering. For the example set, that would be:

$$18, 21, 21, 22, 26, 42$$

Make sure you've included all the numbers in the order, even if there are duplicates. If a set with a lot of numbers, it's helpful to cross them off in the original set as you order them on your scratch paper. This helps ensure that you don't leave one out.

If there is an odd quantity of numbers in the set, the median will be the middle number. For example, if a set is comprised of nine numbers, the median will be the fifth number of the ordered set.
However, the example set has six numbers. Since no single number is in the exact middle, we average the two middle numbers to find the median:

$$\frac{21 + 22}{2} = 21.5$$

The median of this set is 21.5.

MODE

The mode of a set of numbers is the number that appears most often. Speakers of French will find this easy to remember: mode is the French word for style. The number that appears the most is "in style" for this particular set.

The example set has one number that appears more than once: 21. Therefore, 21 is the mode. Sometimes, it's easiest to see this after the set is ordered, when duplicate numbers appear next to one another.
If a set has two numbers that equally appear most often, such as two $21s$ and two $22s$, then both 21 and 22 are the mode. We don't average them together, as we do to find the median. Therefore, the mode is the only descriptor of a set that must always be a number in the set. Since there are two modes, the set would be described as "bimodal."

RANGE

The range of a set of numbers is the distance between the highest and lowest values. Once you've reordered a set, these values are easy to identify. Simply subtract the two values to get the range:

$$highest\ value\ -\ lowest\ value\ =\ range$$

For the example set, this would be:

$$42\ -\ 18\ = 24$$

The range of the set is 24.

Sets can include negative numbers, decimals, fractions, duplicates, etc. They may also appear in table form. Let's look at another example set to see what kinds of tricky questions you may encounter.

MONTH	RAINFALL (INCHES)
AUGUST	0.8
SEPTEMBER	1.3
OCTOBER	2.1
NOVEMBER	1.3
DECEMBER	3.7

What is the average rainfall for the months September, October, November and December?

SOLUTION:

Notice the first trick in this question – you are asked for the average of only four months, not all five listed in the table. This introduces two possible sources of error – you could add all five months' rainfall and/or divide by five when calculating the average. To find the average of only the four months stated in the question, the solution is:

$$\frac{1.3 + 2.1 + 1.3 + 3.7}{4} = 2.1\ inches$$

Here's another question for the same data table, but it uses a different approach to averaging:
The average monthly rainfall from July through December was 1.7 inches. What was the rainfall, in inches, in July?

SOLUTION:

This question gives you the average and asks you to find the missing rainfall value. This is a common way to make a mean/average problem a little tricky for the average (mean) test-taker. You can solve these types of questions by applying the basic equation for finding the mean:

$$\frac{\text{sum of the numbers in the set}}{\text{quantity of numbers in the set}} = mean$$

Next, fill in all the known values:

$$\frac{July + 0.8 + 1.3 + 2.1 + 1.3 + 3.7}{6} = 1.7$$

Solve algebraically:

$$July + 0.8 + 1.3 + 2.1 + 1.3 + 3.7 = 1.7 * 6$$
$$July = (1.7 * 6) - 0.8 - 1.3 - 2.1 - 1.3 - 3.7\, July = 1\ inch$$

Now, try to solve this question:
What is the difference between the mode and the median of the rainfalls for August through December?

SOLUTION:

Simply find the mode and median values. Remember, the first step is to order the set:

$$0.8, 1.3, 1.3, 2.1, 3.7$$

The mode is 1.3 because that is the only number that appears more than once.

The median is 1.3 because, of the five numbers in the set, 1.3 is the third (middle) number.

Therefore, the difference between the mode and the median is:

$$1.3 - 1.3 = 0$$

MATHEMATICS KNOWLEDGE

PROBABILITY

Every probability is a ratio as described below.

$$Probability = \frac{Total\ number\ of\ desired\ events}{Total\ number\ of\ possible\ outcomes}$$

The simplest example of this type of ratio is found when tossing a coin. There are always two total outcomes, heads and tails, so the probability of either a head or a tail is always 1/2 for that coin. Similarly, if you tossed that same coin 14 times, you would expect to see it land 7 times with the head showing and 7 times with the tail showing. Because these events are totally random, flipping the coin 14 times will not always provide an equal number of outcomes in a group of trials. So we say that the number of heads in a trial of 14 is the "expected value" of 7. Similarly, 7 would be the "expected value" for tails.

A common misconception is that there "has to be" a certain outcome based on the number of outcomes that have already occurred. In the repeated trial of an event, each outcome is its own trial and is not influenced by the previous trial or trials.

The other common type of probability problem is with dice, where each of six faces of a cube has its own number from 1 to 6. Each of these numbers has the probability of 1/6 for a single roll of the die. If we formulate a table of outcomes for two dice, thrown together, the details are slightly different. In this table, the individual numbers are shown across the top and vertically along the side. The entries in the table represent the total of the two dice.

	1	2	3	4	5	6	CUBE A
1	2	3	4	5	6	7	
2	3	4	5	6	7	8	
3	4	5	6	7	8	9	
4	5	6	7	8	9	10	
5	6	7	8	9	10	11	
6	7	8	9	10	11	12	
CUBE B							

A look at the table shows that there are 36 possible outcomes when two dice are thrown together $(6 * 6)$. The individual probabilities are shown below.

P (1) =	0		(never appears)
P (2) =	1/36	does not simplify	(appears once)
P (3) =	2/36	simplifies to 1/18	(appears twice)
P (4) =	3/36	simplifies to 1/12	(appears three times)
P (5) =	4/36	simplifies to 1/9	(appears four times)
P (6) =	5/36	does not simplify	(appears five times)
P (7) =	6/36	simplifies to 1/6	(appears six times)
P (8) =	5/36	does not simplify	(appears five times)
P (9) =	4/36	simplifies to 1/9	(appears four times)
P (10) =	3/36	simplifies to 1/12	(appears three times)
P (11) =	2/36	simplifies to 1/18	(appears twice)
P (12) =	1/36	does not simplify	(appears once)
P (13) =	0		(never occurs)

The symmetry of the table helps us visualize the probability ratios for the individual outcomes. By the definition of probability, any number larger than 13 will never appear in the table so the probability has to be zero. The probability of any impossible outcome always has to be zero. By the same reasoning, any event that must happen will have a probability of one. So, the probability of rolling a number from 2 to 12 is one.

If you are finding the probability of two events happening, the individual probabilities are added. For example, the probability of rolling a ten or eleven is the same as the probability of rolling an eight. The number eight appears in the table the same number of times as the combined total of appearances of ten or eleven.

The formulation of ratios for probabilities is simplest when using fractions. Often, the expression of a probability answer will be in a percent or a decimal. A coin from the first example would have the following probabilities P (heads) = 50% or .5 or 0.5.

Formulating probabilities from a word problem can always be structured around the ratio defined at the beginning of this section. However, the words can mislead or misdirect problem-solving efforts.
For example, a problem that describes a class distribution may often be stated as the number of boys and the number of girls. The probability of selecting a boy in a random sample is defined as the number of boys divided by the TOTAL number of boys AND girls. This is simple to see, but problems can be worded to mislead you into selecting the incorrect answer or to lead to the wrong conclusion when calculating an answer.

Another way that probability problems can be misleading is when multiple choices are used when simplified ratios are required. For example, if a class is made up of 6 girls and 10 boys, the probability of randomly selecting a girl from the classroom is $6/16$ or $3/8$. The misleading multiple choices that may be listed would often include 60%, (6/10) or 50% (since there are two outcomes; boys and girls). Reading a probability problem carefully is extremely important in both formulating the probability ratio and in making sure that the correct ratio is selected in the correct form. If the probability ratio for the example is formulated as $6/16$, the simplified form of $3/8$ is the only correct answer.

RATIOS AND PROPORTIONS

Ratios and fractions are synonymous when discussing numerical values. The ratios or fractions always imply division of the numerator by the denominator. In this section, the discussion is directed toward how words appear in ratio problems and how those words should be interpreted.

A commonly used ratio is contained in the term "miles per hour", usually abbreviated by mph. When the term "miles per hour" is interpreted numerically, it is the ratio of the total number of miles traveled divided by the number of hours traveled. The key word in this commonly used term is "per". It literally means for each hour of travel; a specific number of miles will be traveled. It has the same implication when the term is "gallons per hour" (how fast a tub is filled or a lawn is watered) or "tons per year" (how much ore is mined in one year).

Another way that ratios can appear is when a phrase defines a ratio as one value to another. A commonly used comparison is usually the ratio of "men to women" or "boys to girls". When this terminology is used, the first term is in the numerator, and the second term is in the denominator by convention. There is an inherent problem when this terminology is used as illustrated by the example below:
In a classroom setting, the ratio of girls to boys is 3 to 4 (or $3:4$ in strictly mathematical terms). How many boys are there in the classroom if the total number of students is 28?

There are two ways that this word problem may be easily solved. If the ratio of (girls/boys) is $3/4$, the actual numbers may be $3/4$ or $6/8$ or $9/12$ or $12/16$ and so forth. These fractions are all equivalent fractions since they all simplify to the value of 0.75. The equivalent fractions are easily determined as the ratios of multiples of the numerator and denominator of the original fraction.

There is only one fraction where the numerator and denominator add to 28, and that is the ratio $12/16$. Therefore, the solution is the classroom has 16 boys and 12 girls.

Notice that the words specify which group (boys or girls) is the numerator and denominator in the original problem and in the solution. When choosing multiple choice answers, make sure that the correct answer is chosen based upon the wording in the original problem. Most often, the correct ratio and its reciprocal are in the answer choices. For example, if the sample problem appeared on the exam, the multiple-choice answers would most likely include 16 boys and 12 girls AND 12 boys and 16 girls. But 16 boys and 12 girls is the correct answer choice.

BREAK TIME (15 MINS)

PERFORM AN ENJOYABLE ACTIVITY TO DISTRACT YOU FROM STUDYING.
READ SOMETHING LIGHT, GO FOR A WALK – WHATEVER YOU DO, TRY TO GET YOUR MIND OFF THE MATERIAL FOR A LITTLE WHILE.

MODULE 4

DAY, LOCATION, MUSIC

1

MONDAY, OCTOBER 12

COFFEE SHOP ON MAIN STREET

MY FAVORITE BAND

2

3

GENERAL HUMAN ANATOMY

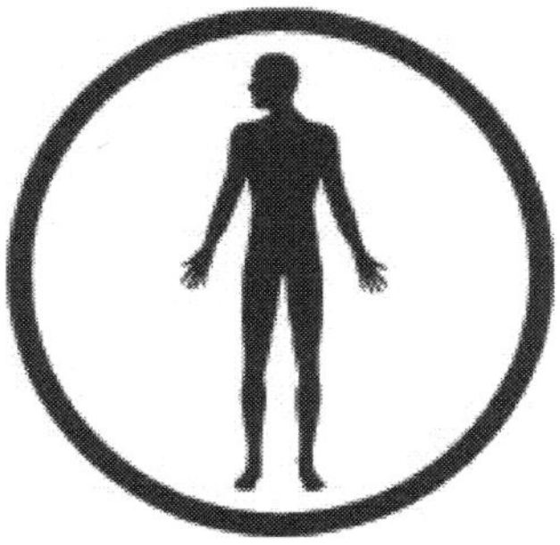

Cell Biology

The cell is the fundamental living unit of all organisms. Tissues are a group of cells with the same function. Tissues are grouped into organs, which carry out a single task. A group of organs that work together to perform coordinated functions are called organ systems. When many cells are organized to create a multicellular organism, the individual cells are usually specialized to serve specific functions within the organism. The broadest category of these functions is summarized below.

Basic Cell Parts

Organelles

The lowest hierarchical level is the organelles within a cell. Each organelle has a specific function that combines to complete a larger function of the individual cell.

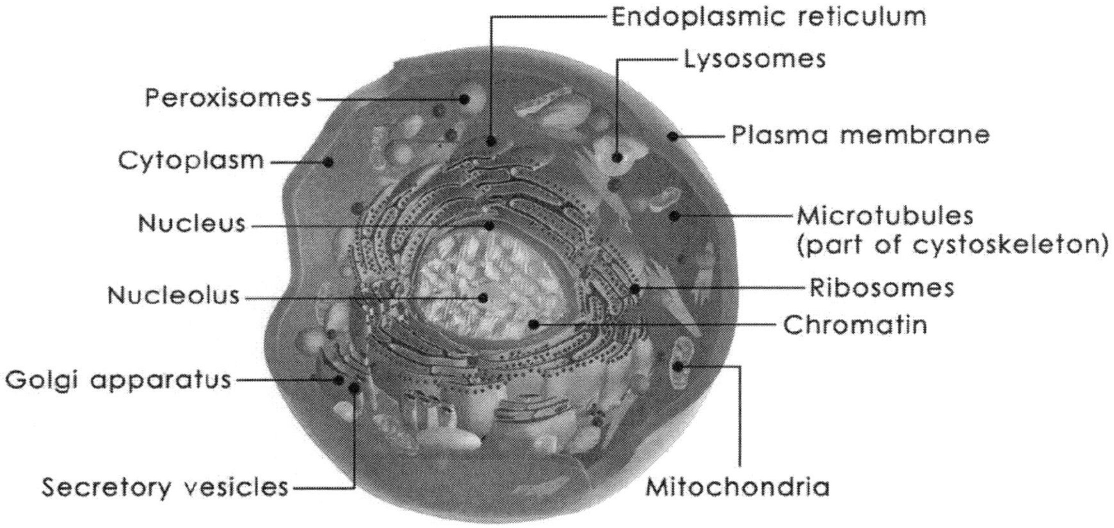

Cell Membrane

All cells have a cell membrane that separates the internal contents of the cell from the cell's external environment. This membrane is a bilayer of long, linear phospholipid molecules hydrocarbon chains that are attached as chain pairs to a phosphate group at one end of the molecule. The phosphate "heads" of molecules face outward in the outer layer of the membrane bilayer and inward in the inner layer; thus, forming the exterior and interior surfaces of the cell membrane. The hydrocarbon chains or "tails" of the molecule aligned and face inward toward the center of the bilayer.

Cytoskeleton

All human cells contain a cytoskeleton, a structural system that provides mechanical support and numerous other intracellular functions.

Cytoplasm

All cells contain cytoplasm. Cytoplasm consists of the material enclosed within a cell membrane except the material enclosed within the membrane of the cell nucleus (the nuclear membrane). The contents of the nucleus are called the nucleoplasm. Cytoplasm includes all the cell organelles and the cytosol which is the gel-like aqueous (watery) solution the fills the interior of the cell. The cytosol consists primarily of water but also contains countless other dissolved chemicals and proteins.

Flagella and Cilia

Flagella and cilia are extensions or attachments of cell membranes. Flagella are long whip-like energetically driven structures that can generate locomotion of a cell. Cilia are hair-like extensions of the cell membrane. The primary function of cilia is locomotion with independent movement ability of either the cell itself or fluids on the cell surface.

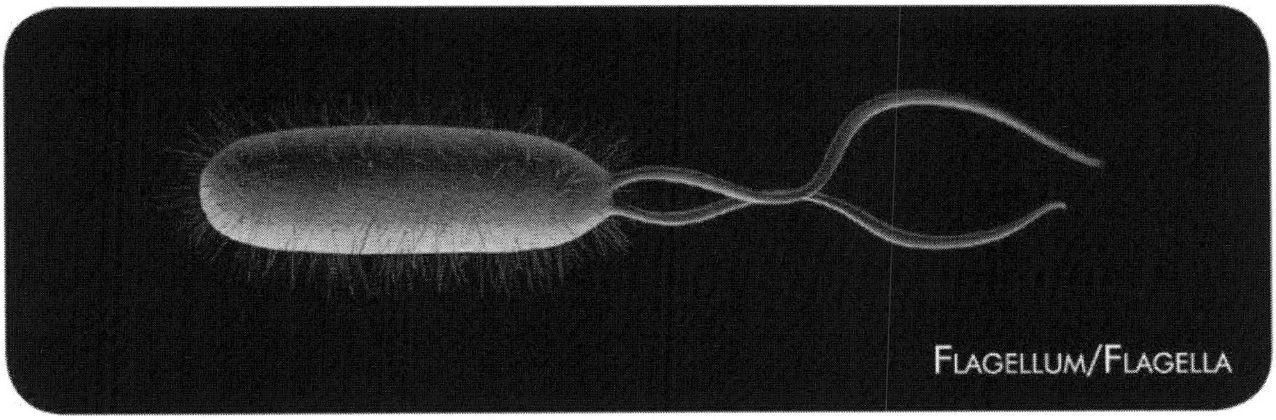

The Nucleus

Nearly all human cells contain a nucleus (mature red blood cells are a notable exception). The nucleus is a membrane-bound structure that contains the DNA of a cell and the nucleolus. The nucleolus is a structure where ribosomes are constructed. There are membrane pores in the nuclear membrane that allow various small molecules to enter - primarily building blocks of DNA and RNA molecules. Nuclear pores also allow messenger RNA (mRNA) molecules and ribosomes to exit from the nucleus into the cell cytoplasm.

Mitochondria

Mitochondria and chloroplasts are complex organelles that possess with both an inner and outer encapsulating membrane. Mitochondria contain enzymes that extract chemical energy from nutrients - usually glucose molecules - and convert the energy into potential energy stored in high energy molecules - usually ATP or NADH.

Nucleic Acids, Enzymes and Other Proteins

All cells contain nucleic acids - DNA and RNA molecules. These are the genetic information molecules of the cell. All cells have proteins that can replicate DNA within the cell. All cells have enzymes that can convert an energy source - sunlight or chemicals obtained from the outside environments - into high energy molecules that can drive other chemical reactions within a cell.

Ribosomes

All cells contain ribosomes. Ribosomes are small spherical complexes of proteins and RNA that can read messenger RNA transcripts and assemble the proteins coded for in the mRNA. The ribosomes assemble these proteins from individual amino acids that are dissolved in the cell cytosol.

Endoplasmic Reticulum

Rough and smooth endoplasmic reticulum (ER) are a convoluted network of membrane passageways that is connected to the cell nucleus and then continues extensively into the cell cytoplasm. Smooth ER is involved in synthesis of lipid compounds and the transport and packaging of various compounds produced by the cell. Smooth ER functions in close coordination with the Golgi apparatus. Rough ER (RER) is so called because ribosomes are distributed in the RER membranes, giving a granular or rough appearance to the RER membranes. Cells that produce large amounts of proteins for transport outside of the cell contain prominent amounts of RER.

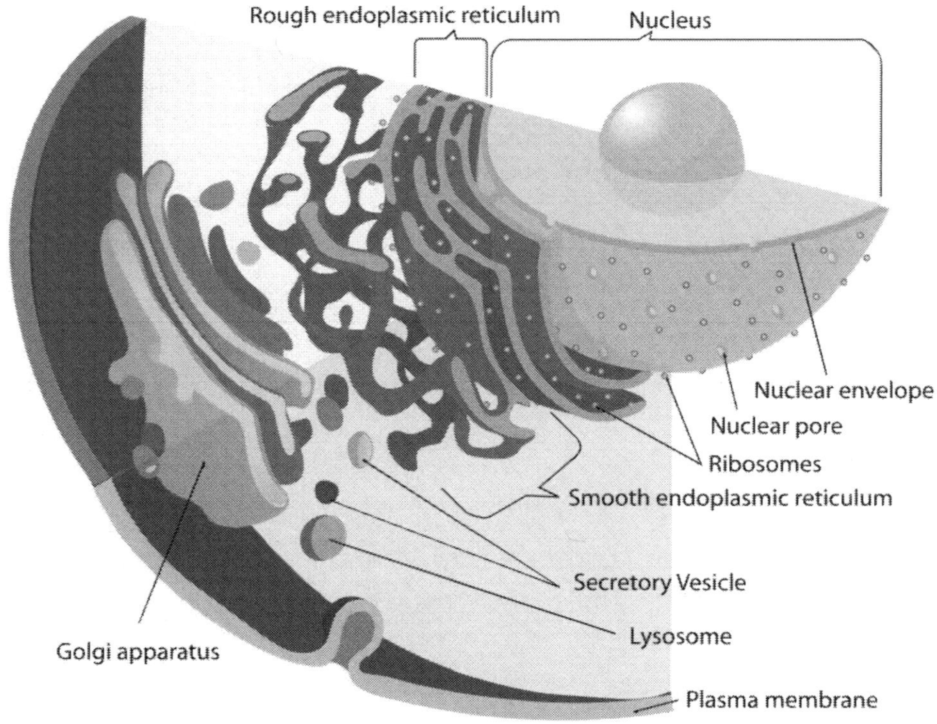

The Golgi Apparatus (the Golgi)

The Golgi is a highly folded series of membrane compartments that resembles a stack of pancakes. The Golgi functions with the smooth ER to process, package and transport a wide variety of products synthesized with the cell. Most often these products are packaged into secretory vesicles that are subsequently carried to the cell membrane and then secreted out of the cell into the external environment. In some types of cells, these vesicles remain inside the cell and are involved in intracellular digestion of phagocytized substances.

Centrosomes

Centrosomes are structures in eukaryotic cells that assemble and organize microtubule structures. These are required for a wide variety of purposes within the cell. They are for example central elements in the construction of flagella in human sperm cells and in the construction of the spindle apparatus during mitosis and meiosis stages of cell division.

Anatomical Positions and Planes

The anatomy of the human body and the discrete structures within the human body are described in part by their spatial orientations and relationships. The terms used to describe the relative positions of anatomical structures to one another are also used to describe specific regions of individual anatomical structures. Most of the terms are best understood as pairs of opposing directions or relative locations. The standard anatomical position is with the body standing up straight and eyes facing forward, the arms at the side of the body with palms facing forward and fingers pointed down, and feet parallel.

Dorsal vs. Ventral: Dorsal means towards the back of the body, and ventral means towards the front of the body. The ventral surfaces of the arms are the surfaces that face upward when the arms are extended straight out with palms facing upward.

Anterior vs. Posterior: These terms are to a large extent analogous to the terms dorsal and ventral, but they are usually the terms preferentially used to describe relative positions. It is common to describe one structure as being “anterior to” or “posterior to” another structure rather than to state, “dorsal to” or “ventral to.” Notable anatomical regions identified with these terms include the anterior and posterior pituitary (sub-regions of the pituitary gland) and the coronary arteries (arteries that supply oxygenated blood to the muscle tissue of the heart): the left anterior descending coronary artery, for example.

Lateral vs. Medial: Lateral means "to the side" or "the side(s) of." Medial means "toward the center" or "closer to the midline." Lateral and medial are often used in combination with other positional terms to produce a more precisely-defined location such as dorsolateral, ventromedial, anterolateral, etc. The ventromedial hypothalamus is a notable region described in this manner.

Inferior vs. Superior: Superior means "above," "over," or "towards the top of the head." Inferior means "below," "underneath," or "towards the feet." These terms can be combined with other positional terms to identify more precise and discrete anatomical regions, such as the anterior-superior ischial spine region of the pelvis.

Rostral vs. Caudal: This pair of descriptive terms is somewhat analogous to the terms superior and inferior. Rostral means "towards the head or cranium," and caudal means "towards the pelvis or the base of the spine." These terms are comparatively rarely used. They are most often used in reference to the regions between the head and pelvis and are not used to describe the appendages (arms and legs).

Superficial vs. Deep: Superficial means "shallow," "towards the surface of," or "closer to the skin." Deep means "closer to the center of" or "farther from the surface of." When describing relative positions of two or more anatomical structures or locations, the superficial structure or location is closer to the external surface of the body compared to the deep structure or location.

Proximal vs. Distal: Proximal means "close" or "nearer to" and distal means "distant," "further away from," or "towards the end of." The reference point that is used to define what is proximal or distal varies depending on what is being described. In the broadest sense, proximal is closer to the center of mass of the body within the deep chest or abdomen. Distal is nearer to the tips of the toes, fingers, or the top of the head.

Prone vs. Supine: This term pair defines two general positions of the entire human body. The supine position is when one is lying flat on one's back and the arms and legs are extended (straight, not bent at a joint such as the knee or elbow). The palms of the hands are facing upward, and the heels of the feet are in contact with the ground.

The prone position is the reverse of the supine position, occurring when one is lying flat and face down, with the palms of the hands and the tops of the feet in contact with the ground. In the supine position, the ventral anatomical surfaces of the body are facing upward. The reverse is true for the prone position where the dorsal surfaces of the body are facing upward (except for the upper arms, where the lateral surfaces face upward).

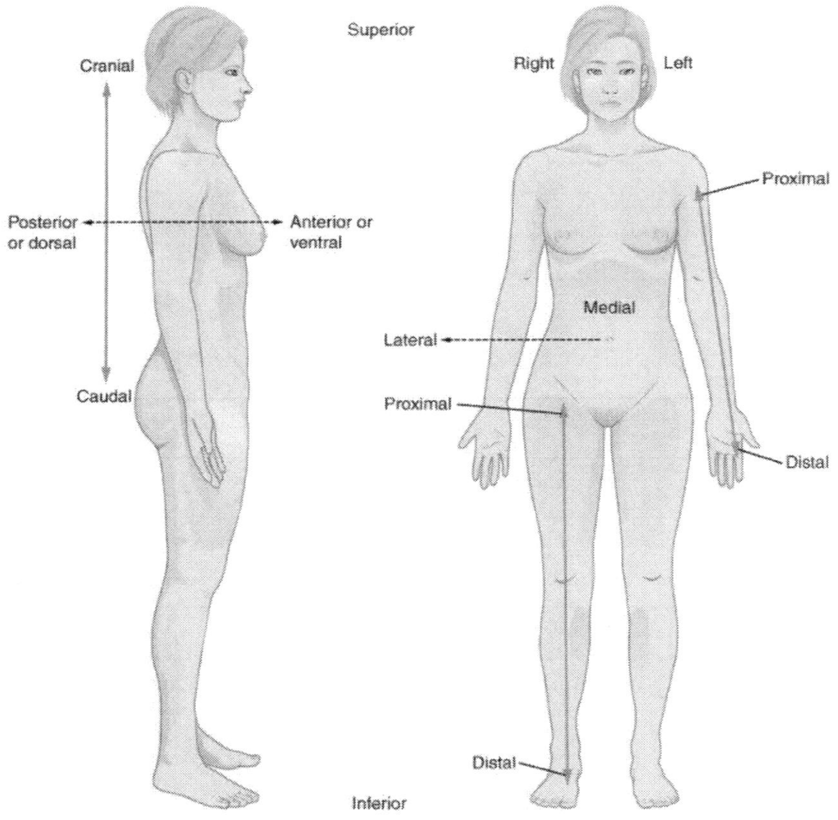

Cross Sections

The anatomy of the body can be visually displayed as cross sections, either of the entire body or of body structures, (the heart or the brain, for example). These sections are defined in relation to a human body that is in an upright standing position. There are three primary types of cross-sectional views: the transverse, the sagittal, and the coronal cross-sectional views.

Transverse sections are the views represented as if the body has been sliced cleanly in two on the horizontal plane – a mid-transverse view will divide the upper at about the waistline of a typical individual. Cross-sections of the body may occur at any higher or lower horizontal height, either moving toward the top of the head or toward the soles of the feet.

Sagittal sections divide the body into a left and a right side. The mid-sagittal section will divide the body into equal right and left sides.

Coronal sections are identical to sagittal sections except that the dissection plane is rotated by 90 degrees. Resulting in a transection of the body that creates a front, ventral, or anterior section and a back, dorsal, or posterior section. A mid-coronal section divides the body into front and back sections at the midline of the body. Any sagittal section of the body may be obtained by moving the dissection plane parallel and lateral to the midsagittal section. Any coronal section of the body may be obtained by moving the dissection plane parallel and lateral to the mid-coronal section.

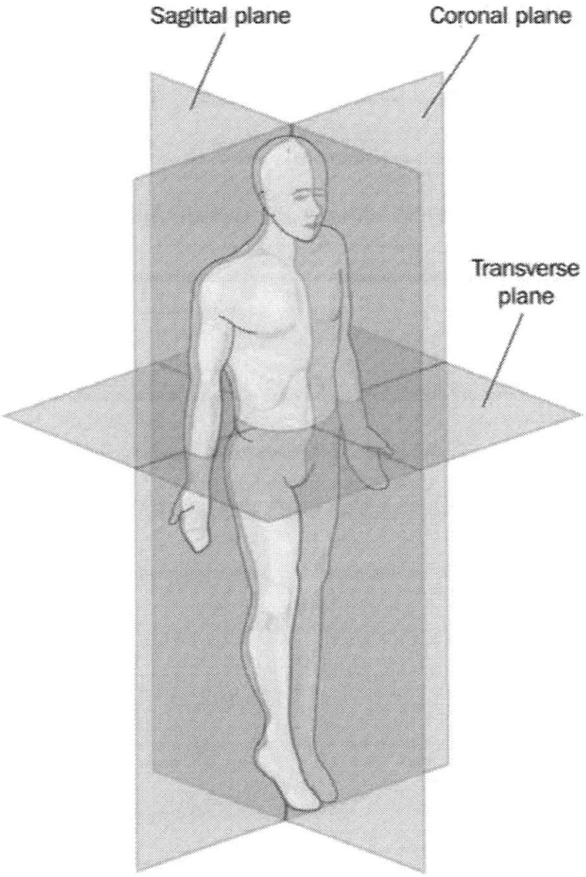

Direction of Motions of the Parts of the Human Body

Nearly all voluntary movements of the human body occur through muscle contractions that result in motions of bones at joints that are designed for body movement. Notable exceptions are facial expression movements and the motion of the diaphragm during breathing.

Generally, these motions refer to movement of the arms and legs (the appendages), but considerable numbers and types of movements occur along the skull-spine and spine-pelvis axis. The appendages are capable of quite complex motions, particularly at the shoulder, wrist, and ankle regions.

Flexion vs. Extension: At a joint, the adjacent ends of bones may be able to move such that the joint angle between the bones increases (opens) or decreases (closes), in a simple hinge-like fashion, usually within a maximum range of 180 degrees. This simple, hinge-like joint motion notably occurs at the elbow and knee joints, but most joints can produce this motion.

Extension is the increase in the angle of the joint (opening or extending out). Flexion is the opposite or reverse of extension. Flexion at a joint cause the bones at the joint to move in a manner that causes the joint angle to decrease (close or bend inward).

Abduction vs. Adduction: This type of motion is almost always in reference to motion of the upper arms at the shoulder joints and the upper legs at the hip joints. Abduction results in movement of the arms or legs outward or away from the midlines of the body. Adduction is the reverse of the motion of abduction, the movement of arms or legs towards the midlines of the body.

The Skeletal System

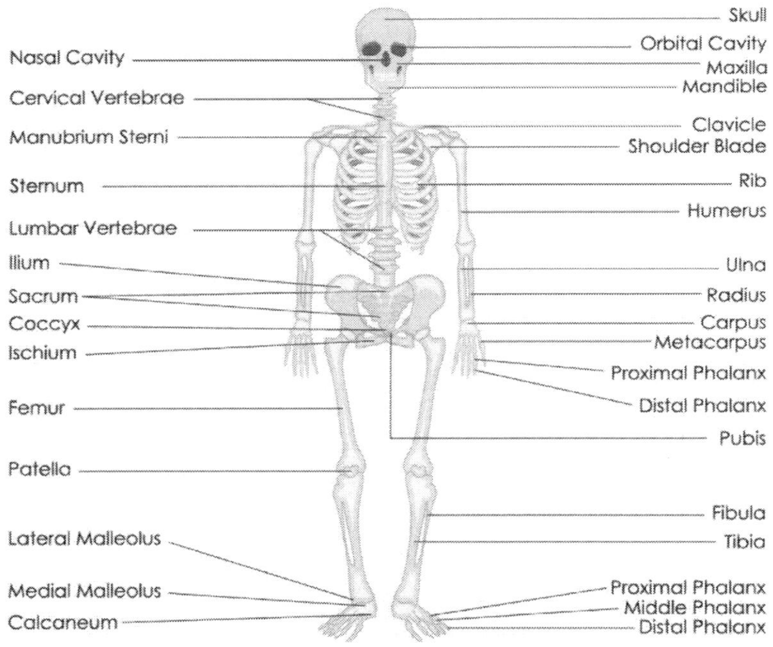

HUMAN SKELETON

Functions of the Skeletal System

Functions of the skeletal system include:

- Allows the muscles to pull for movement
- Provides articulation and structure
- Protection of organs
- Synthesize blood and immune cells
- Store calcium, phosphate, and lipids
- Bone synthesize and breakdown
- Metabolic needs

The Axial Skeleton

The axial skeleton consists of the bones of the skull and spinal column, the ribs, and the sternum.

The Spine

The spine consists of individual bones known as vertebrae arranged linearly to form a continuous, flexible, bony column. There are 5 regional spinal segments: the cervical, thoracic, and lumbar spinal segments, the sacrum, and the coccyx. The cervical segment begins with the vertebra that articulates with the base of the skull (this vertebra has a specific name – the atlas). There are seven cervical vertebrae, the vertebra found in the neck.

The thoracic spinal segment begins with the $8th$ vertebra. There are 12 thoracic vertebrae. They are notable in that they articulate laterally with the 12 pairs of ribs that are important structural components of the chest or thoracic walls. The lumbar vertebrae begin with the $19th$ vertebra; there are 5 lumbar vertebrae.
The final lumbar vertebra connects to the sacrum (which is actually 5 or 6 fused vertebrae). The sacrum is fused medially to the other bones of the hip, and together they form the bony pelvis. At the most distal end of the sacrum are four small partially-fused vertebrae that together are referred to as the coccyx. The terminal vertebra of the coccyx represents the caudal end of the spine.

The Vertebral Canal

The vertebral canal contains the spinal cord of the central nervous system. The spinal cord begins as the distal extension of the brainstem and enters the vertebral canal through the foramen magnum – a large opening in the posterior base of the skull.

The spinal cord does not extend for the entire length of the vertebral canal. The dorsal and ventral spinal nerve roots that combine to form the 31 sets of spinal nerves of the somatic or voluntary nervous system emerge from the spinal cord.

The Skull

The skull consists of the tightly-fused bones that contains the brain, pituitary gland, and facial bones, including the upper jaw bones – the maxillae – and the lower jaw – the mandible. The mandible is the only moveable bone of the skull. The inner surfaces of the bones that form the cranial cavity which correspond to the adjacent underlying regions of the cerebral cortex of the brain – the frontal bone, parietal bone, temporal bone, and occipital bone.

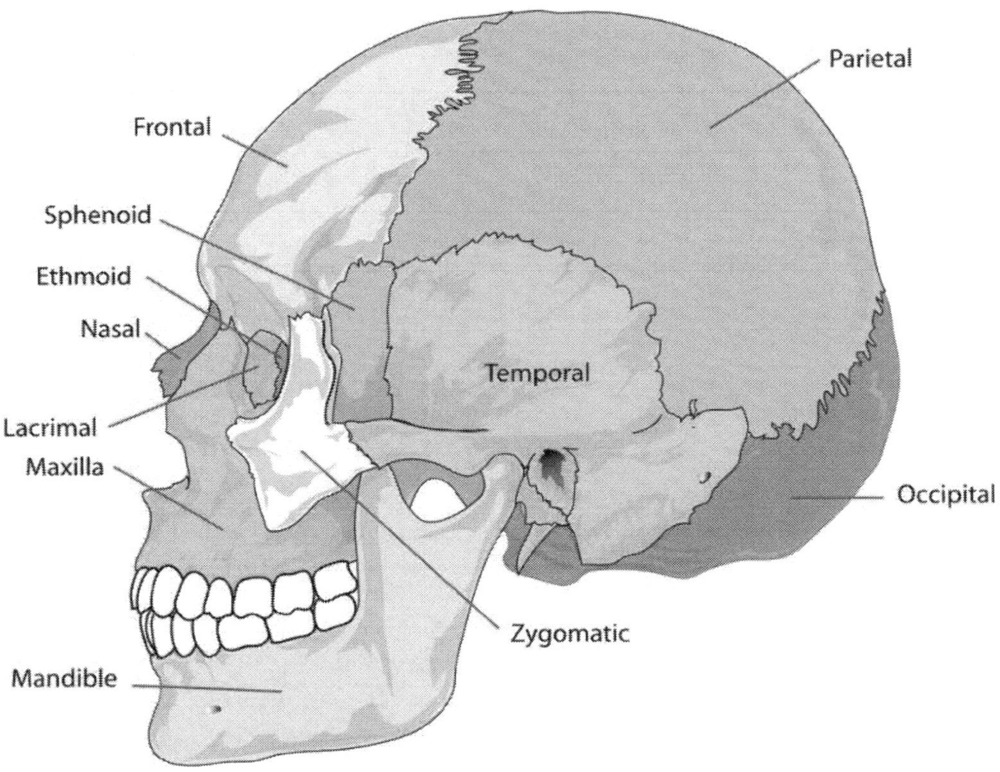

The Thoracic Skeleton

The thoracic (the chest and upper back) skeleton is comprised of the thoracic vertebrae, 12 sets of ribs, the sternum (breastbone), and the medial sections of the clavicles (collarbones). The ribs connect to the lateral surfaces of the thoracic vertebrae then extend laterally to form the dorsal thorax. The sternum located in the midline of the anterior (ventral) wall of the thorax. The thoracic skeleton creates a cage-like structural framework. When the associated muscles and connective tissues are added to this framework, an interior thoracic cavity is created. This cavity will contain the heart, lungs, and several other important anatomical structures. The floor of the thoracic cavity will be formed by a single dome-shaped sheet of muscle – the diaphragm.

The Appendicular Skeleton

The upper appendicular (attached) skeleton consists of the bones of the shoulder girdles, arms, wrists, hands, and fingers.

The distal end of the long bone of the upper arm – the humerus – forms the elbow joint with the proximal ends of the two lower arm bones – the radius and the ulna. The distal ends of the radius and the ulna articulate with several of the wrist bones – the carpals – to form the complex wrist joint. The carpals articulate with the metacarpal bones of the hand. The distal ends of the metacarpals articulate with the bones of the fingers – the phalanges.

The lower appendicular skeleton consists of the bones of the pelvis (except for the sacrum, which is part of the axial skeleton,) and the bones of the legs, ankles, feet, and toes.

The proximal end or "head" of the femur fits into a semicircular depression of the inferolateral borders in the bones of the pelvis. Along with associated muscles and connective tissues, these form the ball and socket joint of the hip. The distal end of the femur articulates with the proximal ends of the tibia and fibula at the knee joint. The distal ends of the tibia and fibula articulate with several tarsal bones to form the complex ankle joint. Tarsal bones in the ankle region articulate with proximal ends of metatarsal bones in the foot. Distal ends of metatarsal bones articulate with the bones of the toes – the phalanges.

Body Cavities

There are two major cavities of the human body – the dorsal and the ventral body cavities. These cavities are almost completely sealed off from the external environment by surrounding bone or muscle and other connective tissue. The dorsal body cavity consists of the cranial cavity and the spinal canal and contains the brain and spinal cord. The ventral cavity is enclosed by thoracic muscles, ribs, sternum, thoracic vertebrae, abdominal wall muscles, and the inner surface bones and associated muscles of the pelvis. The ventral cavity is divided into an upper cavity by a transverse dome-shaped muscle – the diaphragm. Major contents of the thoracic cavity are the heart and lungs. Major contents of the abdominal and pelvic cavity are the intestines, associated digestive organs – liver, gallbladder and pancreas - the urinary bladder and, in females, the uterus and ovaries.

Relationship Between the Skeletal System with the Neuromuscular System

The Formation of Bone

The cells that produce the extracellular matrix of bone tissue are chondrocytes, fibroblasts, and osteoblasts. Osteoblasts secret substances that form the first stage in the production of the extracellular matrix of mature bone. Endochondral ossification begins with various physiological processes that progressively break down and reabsorb the cartilage version bone while osteoblasts simultaneously invade the collagen matrix. Osteons are the structural subunits that form bone. Osteons are cylindrical columns that are tightly packed together in parallel arrangement in bone and often extend for the entire length of individual bones. An interconnected network provides pathways for the flow of oxygen and nutrients to all regions of the bone. The width of the osteon increases as osteoclasts form additional concentric layer of bone. A small percentage of osteoclasts become trapped within the extracellular matrix and then differentiate into osteocytes.

Bone marrow are cavities within bone that contain loose connective matrix and hematopoietic activity and a high content of adipocytes. Bones have an outer membrane, the periosteum that contains numerous nerve fibers and pain fibers. Osteoblasts and osteoclasts can precisely remodel a bone or a region of bone. Osteoclasts decompose bone activities and osteoblasts perform bone formation activities. At regions where osteoblast activity exceeds osteoclast activity, the bone thickens, and where the reverse is true, bone reabsorbs and thins.

Types of Bones

Bone Classification by Shape

The bones of the human body can be classified by shape into one of five general categories – long bones, short bones, flat bones, irregular bones, and sesamoid bones.

Long Bones

The longest section of long bones is the bone shaft or diaphysis. The ends of long bones are called epiphyses. The major bones of the upper and lower arms and legs – the humerus, femur, radius, ulna, tibia, and fibula are long bones. The phalanges (finger and toe bones) and the clavicles (collar bones) are also long bones. Most long bones have medullary cavities and are a major site of erythropoiesis.

Short Bones

Short bones have variable shapes, often cuboidal with dimensions of length, width, and height that are roughly equivalent. Examples of short bones include the tarsus bones in the foot and carpal bones in the hand.

Irregular Bones

Irregular bones have nonsymmetrical shapes and include bones of the skull, elbow, pelvis, knee, spinal vertebrae, and bones of the middle ear.

Flat Bones and Sesamoid Bones

Flat bones are thin with a high surface area. They have an outer layer of cortical bone and a thin central layer of trabecular bone. Most of the bones of the cranium are flat bones. Flat bones have a primary protective function – protection of the brain in particular – and have little if any role in erythropoiesis. Sesamoid bones are formed with muscle tendons. They have a mechanical function related to the amount of leverage that a muscle can generate on an attached bone. Most sesamoid bones are relatively small, a notable exception is the patella, which is located anterior to the synovial joint of the knee.

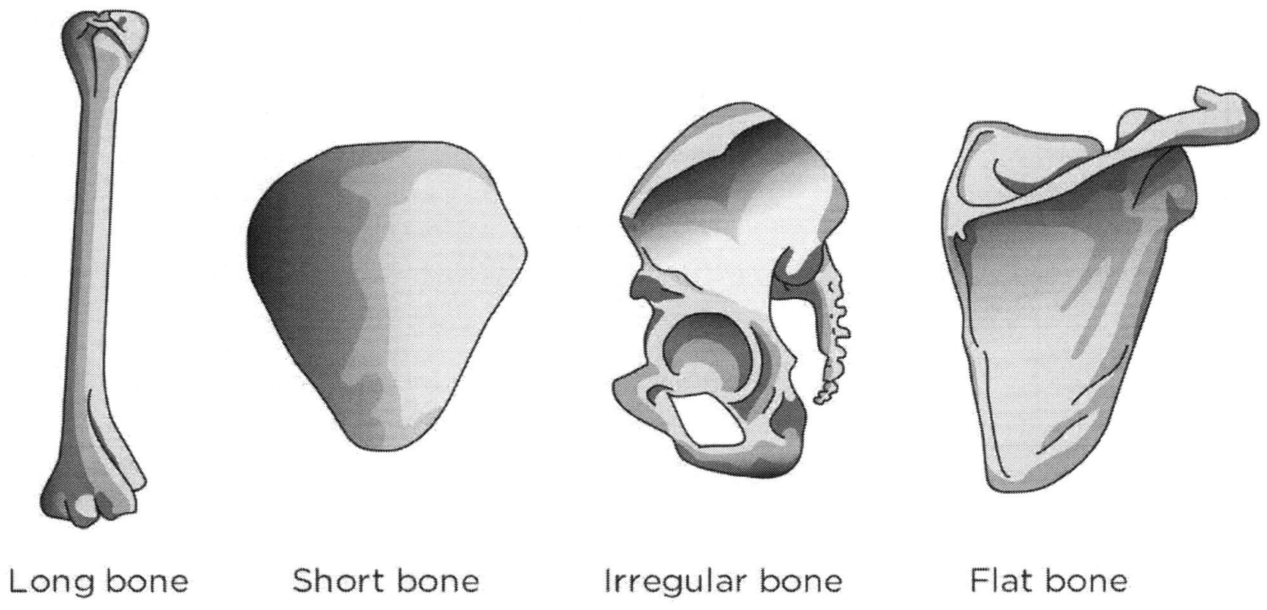

Bone and Joint Disorders

There are numerous diseases and other pathological conditions of bones and joints that are notable for their frequency or severity in humans. Joint disorders are so common there is a medical specialty – rheumatology – that focuses exclusively on the diagnosis and treatment of these conditions.

Disorders of the Synovial Joints

The two most important synovial joint disorders are rheumatoid arthritis and osteoarthritis. Rheumatoid arthritis is an autoimmune disorder that attacks synovial joints, resulting in progressive, painful disfigurement, and loss of function of joints throughout the body.

Osteoarthritis is a result of the wear and tear damage to articular cartilage in synovial joints. The mechanical forces acting on joints over decades of physical activity eventually wear away the cartilage in synovial joints, resulting in the loss of the protection the cartilage provides to underlying bone. The unprotected articulating bones grind against each other and cause severe pain and eventually loss of function. Most middle-aged to elderly males have some degree of osteoarthritis. The condition is most serious when the knee and hip joints are involved. Damage due to osteoarthritis is the number one reason for hip and knee replacements in the U.S.

Disorders of the Bone

Osteoporosis is the most common serious bone disorder and most commonly occurs in postmenopausal women. The condition is a loss of bone density and disruption of bone structure primarily due to inadequate calcium content. Persons with osteoporosis are at greatly increased risk of bone fractures, most seriously fractures of pelvic bones or the femur.

Osteogenesis Imperfecta (brittle bone disease) is an autosomal dominant genetic disorder caused by defects in the enzymes involved in collagen production. The result is brittle bones that fracture easily.

The Integumentary System

The integumentary system of the human body – or simply the integument – is a multilayered sheath of tissues and associated cells and extracellular structural and functional components that completely encloses the interior of the body. The integumentary system includes the skin, nails, and hair. The most superficial layer of the integumentary system is exposed to the external environment and forms the external surface of the body. Two of the most general primary functions of the integumentary system are to provide a physical containment of the internal body contents and to provide a physical and biochemical barrier to elements of the external environment. There are several secondary functions of the integumentary system as well. Most of these functions as a group that can be categorized as homeostatic functions in the sense that they all provide mechanisms to maintain a controlled and stable, yet adaptable internal environment that is distinctly separate from the external environment.

Functions of the Integumentary System

Defensive Barrier Functions

The external surface of the integumentary layer in humans is relatively impermeable to water and atmospheric gases. This feature prevents the loss of water (dehydration) and soluble substances from the body. The surface layer of the integument is resistant to radiation damage by ultraviolet wavelength light, which is a component of sunlight. The surface layer of the integument is also resistant to penetration by potentially harmful toxic chemicals and infectious biological agents such as viruses, bacteria, fungi, and other eukaryotic unicellular and multi-cellular parasites. Therefore, the integument provides a critical role as the first line of defense in the body's immune system.

Thermoregulation

Another important homeostatic function of the integument is thermoregulation, which allows the body to maintain a constant optimum internal temperature range. The lowest layer of the integument – the hypodermis – contains adipose tissue that has poor thermal conduction and therefore acts as an insulator to protect against excessive heat transfer between the internal regions of the body and the external environment.

Sweat and Evaporative Heat Loss

The insulation capacity of the integument is a passive form of thermoregulation. The integument possesses sweat glands, which transport an aqueous solution (sweat) to the surface of the skin by neural and hormonal signal regulation. The evaporation of sweat from the skin surface absorbs heat energy from the body as it undergoes a phase change, thereby lowering the internal body temperature when it exceeds the optimum internal temperature range.

Vasoconstriction and Dilation

The integument is also highly vascularized, and the dense capillaries near the skin surface can constrict or dilate in response to local conditions and in response to neural and hormonal signals. When the internal body temperature is too high, superficial blood vessels dilate and heat energy radiates to the environment or be removed via sweat evaporation. Conversely when internal body temperature is too low, superficial blood vessels constrict and decrease the loss of heat from the body via the bloodstream.

Somatosensory Functions

The middle layers of the skin are richly innervated and contain several types of sensory cells that are distributed throughout the entire volume of these integumentary layers. The sensory receptors are designed to provide nearly all the specific types of sensory information including sensations of pain, heat, cold, light touch, pressure, and vibration.

Excretory Functions

Alcohol and several metabolic waste products including urea and several types of organic acids are excreted from the bloodstream onto the skin surfaces. Excess body water and electrolytes may be excreted in the form of sweat. The excretion of these substances through the skin is simply a result of the forces of diffusion. They are not regulated excretory process of the body.

Vitamin D Synthesis

The integument has metabolic functions, most notably in the synthesis of vitamin D where ultraviolet radiation travels into the skin.

Layers of the Integument

The integument consists of a dermal or cutaneous layer and a subcutaneous or hypodermal layer. The dermal layer consists of two sub layers - the dermis and the epidermis.

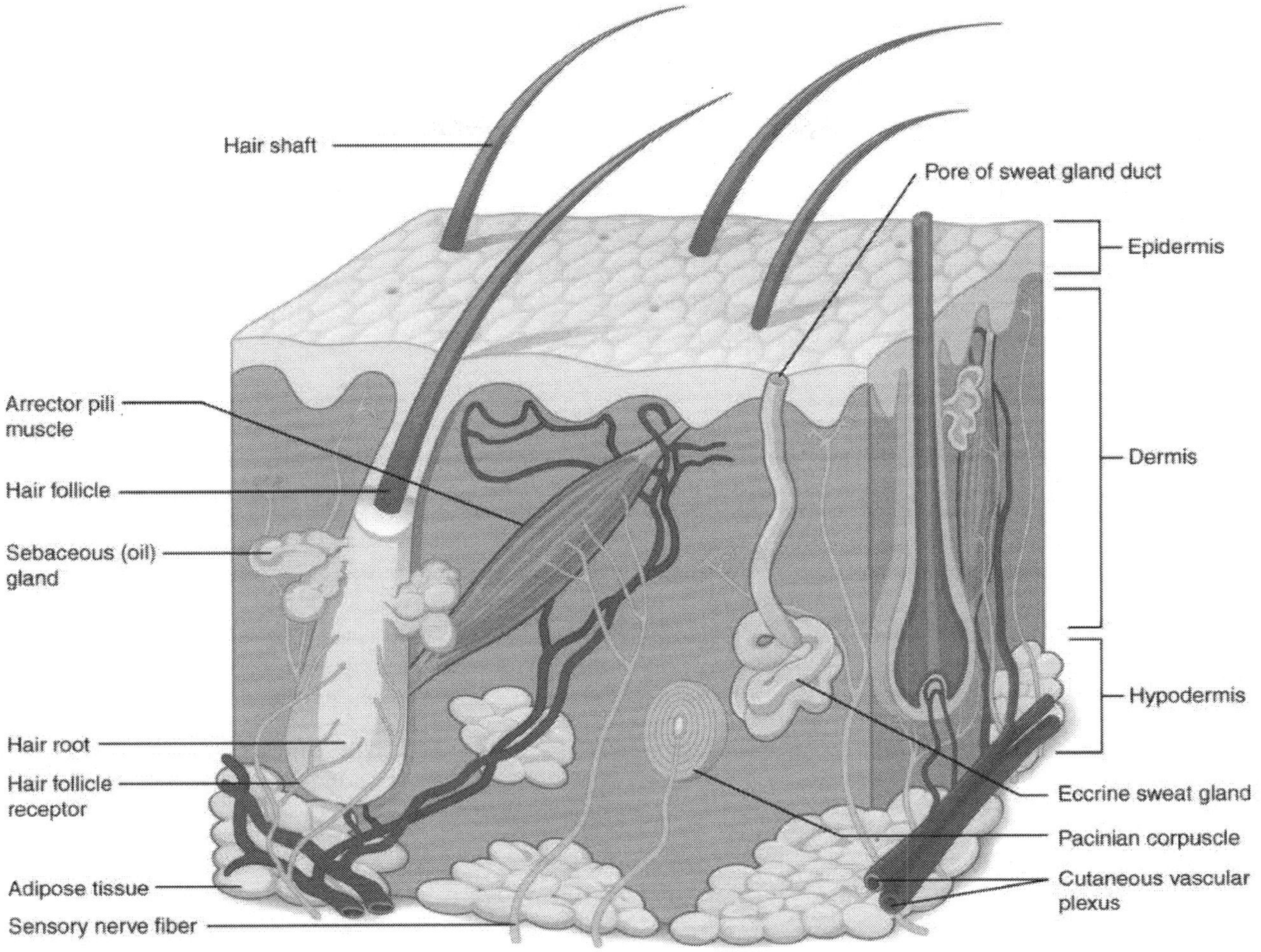

The Hypodermis (Subcutaneous Layer)

The lowermost or deepest layer of the integument is the hypodermis or the subcutaneous layer that consists primarily of loose adipose connective tissue, blood vessels, lymphatic vessels, and nerves. The hypodermis provides a transitional connective zone between the overlying dermal layer and the adjacent underlying body contents, usually outer skeletal muscle layers, but in some areas bony structures - particularly over the knee and elbow joints and the anterior surfaces of the lower leg (the shins).

The Dermis

The dermis is the middle layer of the three major integument layers. It is composed of three primary cell types, fibroblasts, macrophages, and adipocytes. The dermis consists of two sublayers, the reticular layer and the papillary layer.

The Dermal Reticular Layer

The roots of hair follicles, sweat glands, sebaceous glands, and sensory receptor cells are also implanted within the reticular layer of the dermis.

The Dermal Papillary Layer

The second sub layer of the dermis – the papillary layer – is immediately superficial to the reticular layer. The papillary layer consists of areolar connective tissue that allow substances to readily diffuse through the tissue.

The Epidermis

The most superficial layer of the integument is the epidermis. The epidermis has no direct blood supply and depends on diffusion for the supplies of oxygen and nutrients and for transport of CO_2 and other waste products. The epidermis begins immediately adjacent to the superficial surface of the papillary layer of the dermis. The two layers are separated by a basement membrane, a common feature of almost all epithelial tissues and serves as an attachment surface for the lowermost layers of epithelial cells. The basement membrane has several additional functions including immune system functions and cellular repair functions.

Glands of the Integument

The integument contains a variety of glands, most notably sebaceous, sudoriferous, and ceruminous glands. Exocrine glands secrete substances through a glandular duct (tube) onto the surface of epithelial tissue, either on the surface of the skin or the luminal surface of an epithelial-lined hollow organ such as the small intestine. In contrast, endocrine glands secrete substances directly into the bloodstream or lymphatic system.

Sebaceous (Oil) Glands

Sebaceous or oil glands are widely distributed within the integument, except the soles of the feet and the palms of the hands. Sebaceous glands have ducts that most commonly communicate with the hair follicles, but a small percentage open directly onto the external epidermal surface. Sebaceous glands synthesize and secrete a substance called sebum, an oily or waxy substance that provides an oily medium which contributes to the composition of the sweat layer on the surface of the skin. The oily component of sweat extends the cooling effects of evaporative sweating and prevents dehydration by increasing the adherence of the sweat layer to the surface of the skin. Sebum strongly inhibits the growth of potentially harmful microorganisms.

Sudoriferous Glands

Ceruminous Glands

Respiratory System

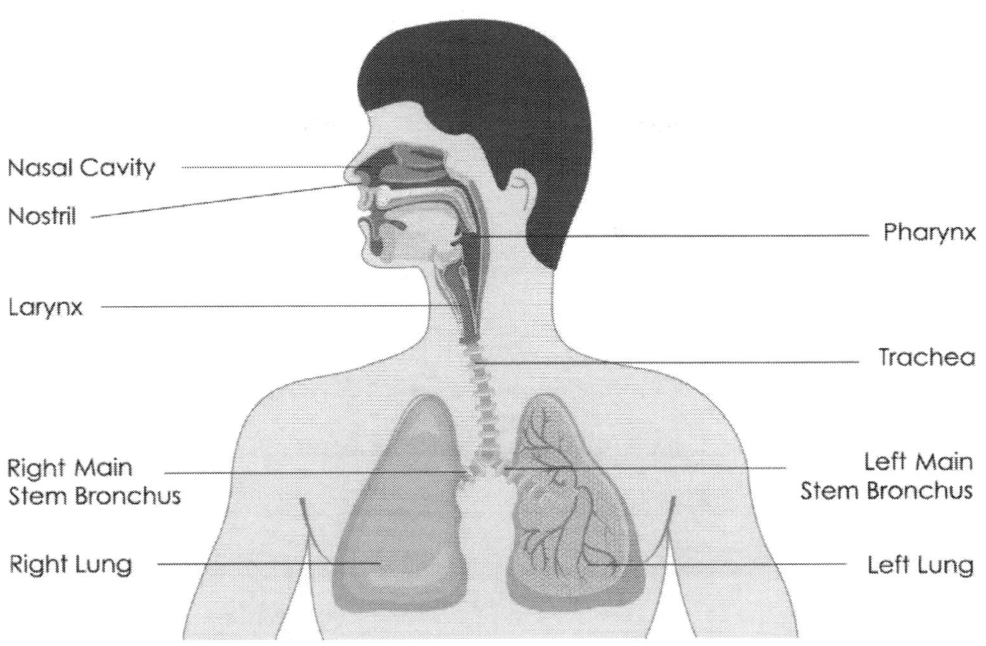

RESPIRATORY SYSTEM

The Respiratory Tract

The initial segment of the respiratory tract is the trachea. The tracheal tube consists of rings of cartilage and descends through the anterior region of the neck. The trachea continues to the base of the neck where it enters the thoracic cavity. At about the mid-sternum level, the trachea bifurcates into a left and right main-stem bronchus. The right and left main-stem bronchi then enter their respective right and left lungs. The main-stem bronchi undergo numerous subsequent branching into smaller and smaller and increasingly numerous air passages. This results in a dense tree-like network of airways that infiltrate the entirety of the lung tissues. The thinnest terminal branches of this respiratory airway tree are called bronchioles. At the terminal ends of the bronchioles, grape-like clusters of spherical air sacs called alveoli serve as the site of oxygen and carbon dioxide exchange between the blood contained in capillaries that encircle the alveoli and inspired air in the alveoli. The transport of gases across the body-airway interface in the lungs is greatly increased by segmentally increasing the surface area of the airways – at the level of alveoli, the diffusional surface area is approximately the area of a tennis court.

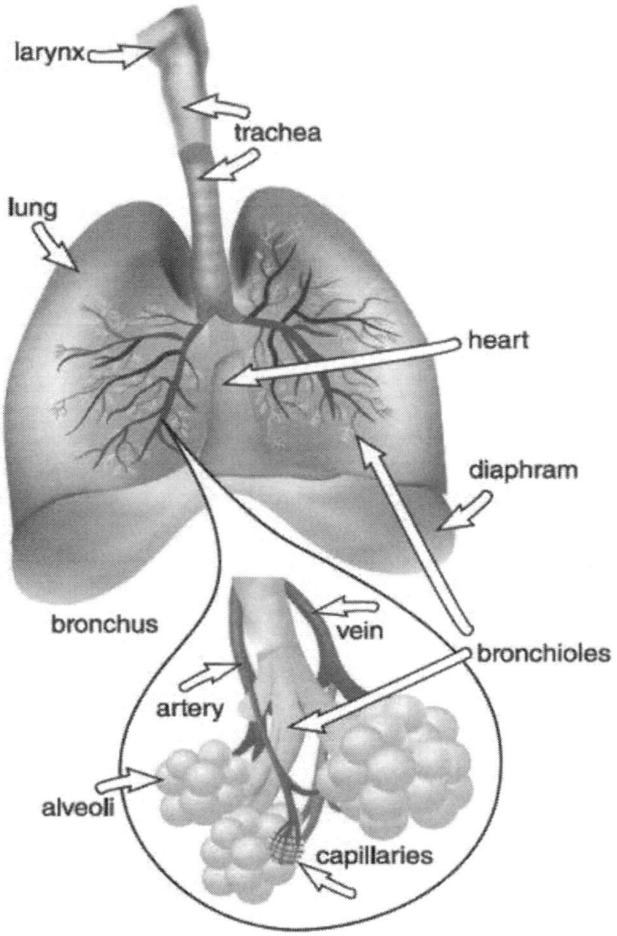

The Respiratory System

Along with the respiratory tract anatomy that has already been described, the respiratory system is composed of the lungs, internal spaces of the thoracic cavity, and the muscular diaphragm that forms the floor of the thoracic cavity. The lungs are composed of separate lobes, three on the left and two on the right. The heart is positioned between the left and right lungs and is directly adjacent to the medial surfaces of the lower lobe of the left lung. Individual secondary bronchi branch off the main-stem bronchi and enter the lobes of the lung. The diaphragm is a dome-shaped muscle that is convex into the thoracic cavity. The nasal sinuses also serve a role in the respiratory system. These located in cavities within the facial and occipital bones of the skull.

Respiratory Physiology

The primary functions of the respiratory system are to deliver oxygen from the air to the bloodstream and to remove carbon dioxide from the bloodstream into air in the lungs and then out of the body during expiration (exhalation). The primary tissues and structures of the respiratory system are the respiratory airway – trachea, bronchi, and alveoli, the lung tissue, and the diaphragm. Breathing is usually involuntary, but it can be under voluntary control for short periods of time.

Nervous System Control of Respiration

The basal breathing rate is driven by the medulla oblongata. Peripheral sensory receptors in major arteries and veins and within the brain itself monitor oxygen and pH levels and report this information to the hypothalamus and the medulla. Breathing depth and rate is modified as necessary to maintain optimum levels of oxygen and blood pH.

Cilia

The epithelial cells lining the bronchial airways secrete mucous and have numerous densely packed cilia on their membranes that are in constant coordinated motion to propel mucus and inhaled particulate matter out of the lungs through the trachea.

Inspiration

Lung tissue expands during the inspiratory phase of the breathing cycle. Lung tissue is elastic, and the expansion that occurs during inspiration dynamically stretches lung tissue. This process requires energy in the form of muscular work that is done by the diaphragm to increase the volume of the thoracic cavity and to decrease the pressure in the thoracic cavity.

Expiration

When the diaphragm relaxes, the elastic tissue in the lung relaxes to its normal level of relaxation. Air pressure within the lung then increases and exceeds that of the outside air. Air within the airways is then driven out of the lungs by the differences in pressure inside and outside of the lung. This term for this portion of the breathing cycle is expiration. Expiration – in contrast to inspiration – is a passive process that does not require energy utilization by the body. Pulmonary surfactant prevents alveolar collapse during expiration.

Gas Exchange – Diffusion

At the microscopic level, gas exchange between the bloodstream and the alveolar air is driven by diffusion. The blood arriving at the capillaries surrounding the alveoli is pulmonary arterial blood – which is deoxygenated blood. The oxygen concentrations in this blood are much lower and the carbon dioxide concentrations are much higher in this capillary blood than the air contained in nearby alveolar air sacs.

Common Disorders of the Respiratory System

Asthma

Pneumonia

Influenza

TB

Cystic Fibrosis

The Gastrointestinal System

Digestive System Physiology

The function of the digestive system is to bring macronutrients, micronutrients, electrolytes, and water into the body. The macronutrients are carbohydrates, fats, and proteins. Electrolytes are dissolved in body fluids. The micronutrients are vitamins and trace minerals. The digestive system also functions best when the diet includes indigestible plant fiber, which is composed primarily of cellulose.

The Digestive Tract

The digestive process begins in the mouth with the mechanical pulping of solids through the act of chewing. During this process, the enzymes salivary amylase and lipase – which is synthesized by cells of the salivary glands – is mixed into the food mass, where it begins to break down any starches and lipids that may be present in the food mass.

The digestive tract, beginning as the esophagus, follows along the same path as the trachea. A specialized hinged plate structure – the epiglottis – can drop across the top of the trachea during swallowing. This prevents ingested solids and liquids from entering the trachea. At the bifurcation of the trachea, the esophagus continues inferiorly to the base of the thoracic cavity, where it passes through an opening in the muscular diaphragm and enters the abdomen. Just after entering the abdomen, the esophagus connects to the stomach. Peristalsis helps move the bolus toward the stomach. A muscular sphincter – the gastroesophageal (GE) sphincter – seals the passage of the digestive tract at the junction of the esophagus and the stomach. The GE sphincter opens only during the passage of ingested material from the esophagus into the stomach.

At the distal end of the stomach, the digestive tract continues as the small intestine. The region of the small intestine that accepts the contents of the stomach is the duodenum. Another muscular sphincter – the pyloric sphincter – seals the passageway between the stomach and the duodenum. The sphincter will open at appropriate intervals to allow stomach contents to pass into the duodenum. Also, substances produced by the liver and the pancreas that are involved in the digestive process are secreted into the duodenum through the common bile duct. The digestive process continues as nutrients and water continue through the small intestine, beginning at the duodenum then through two subsequent segments of the small intestines, the jejunum and then the ileum. The ileum connects to the first segment of the large intestine – the cecum.

At this point, all the nutrients and most of the water passing through the digestive tract have been absorbed. Indigestible bulk material continues to pass through the sequential segments of the large intestine, beginning with the cecum, and next the ascending, then the transverse, and then the descending colon. Most of the remaining water in the material within the large intestine is absorbed, and feces are formed during this stage of the journey through the digestive tract. The feces pass into the terminal segments of the large intestine – the sigmoid colon and the rectum – and then pass out of the body via defection through the anal sphincter.

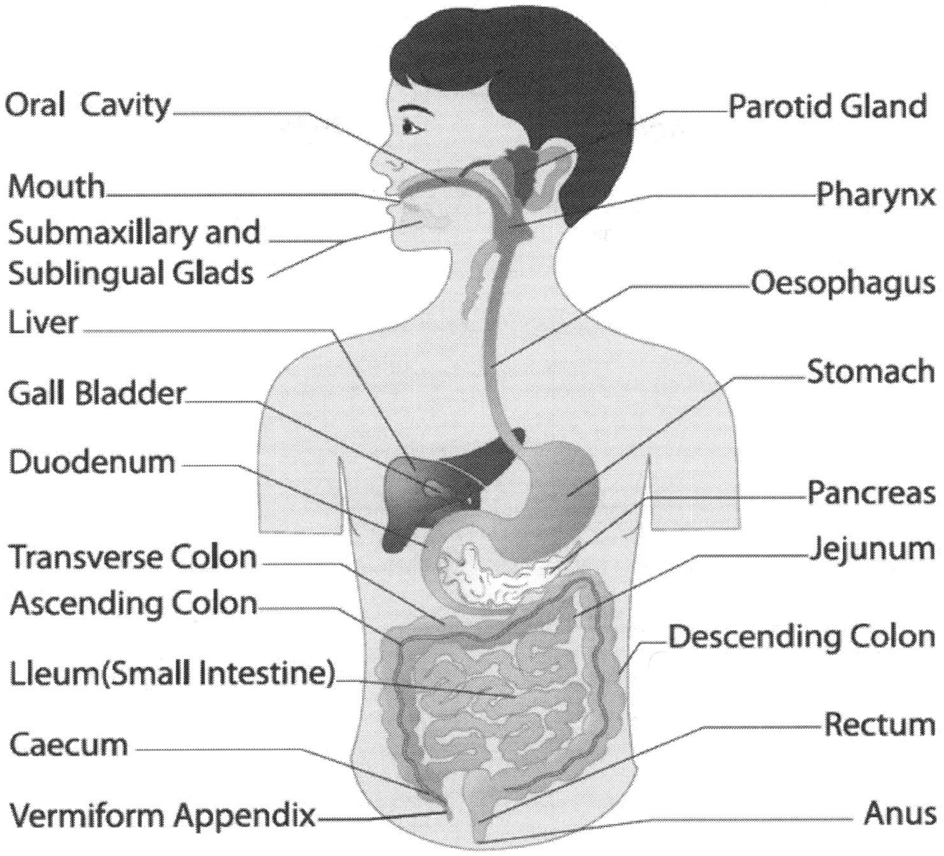

The Digestive System

Along with the digestive tract anatomy that has already been described, the digestive system also consists of the liver, the gallbladder, the pancreas, and a specialized regional venous circulatory system – the hepatic portal circulatory system – that carries blood from capillary beds in the intestines to capillary beds located in the liver. The liver is located on the right upper quadrant of the abdominal cavity, directly below the inferior surface of the diaphragm.

The gallbladder is connected to the liver and is nestled between liver lobes at the inferior surface of the liver. The pancreas located in the left upper quadrant of the abdomen, partially retroperitoneal (buried) in the dorsal abdominal wall.

The Stomach

The stomach protects its inner wall lining from acidic injury by secreting large amounts of mucous onto the inner surface of the gastric lumen. The stomach creates this acidic environment by synthesizing and secreting hydrochloric acid. This highly acidic fluid by itself causes widespread chemical breakdown of proteins and carbohydrates, but the stomach also synthesizes and secretes a powerful proteolytic (protein cutting) enzyme called pepsin. Pepsin is the first enzyme that engages in the enzymatic breakdown of all proteins.

Chyme

The stomach also engages is a considerable amount of mechanical digestion. The stomach walls are thick and constructed of several heavy muscle layers. This allows the stomach to generate powerful contractions that reduce food boluses into slurry of water and partially digested lipids, proteins, and carbohydrates referred to as chyme.

Intrinsic Factor

Another notable substance secreted by the stomach is intrinsic factor. Intrinsic factor is a substance that the small intestinal epithelial cells require for the absorption of vitamin B_{12}.

The Small Intestine

At a time determined by the demands of the body, the stomach will release its contents into the adjacent distal segment of the digestive tract, the duodenum of the small intestine. The duodenum is the first of three continuous segments of the small intestine. The second segment is the jejunum, and the third and final segment is the ileum.

Villi, Microvilli and the Brush Border

The total surface area of the small intestine is approximately 250 square meters (interestingly, this is about the same area as the surface area of the alveoli in the lungs).

In the small intestines, surface area is increased first by the intestinal villi – finger-like projections of the inner surface of the intestines into the intestinal lumen. Next, the outer surfaces of villi are covered in microscopic finger-like extensions called microvilli. The microvilli layer forms the brush border of the intestinal epithelial cell lining. The brush border is where the absorption of water and nutrients from the intestinal lumen and into the body occurs.

Anatomical Sites and Details of Absorption

Amino acids from the enzymatic breakdown of proteins and fats that have been reduced to fatty acids are absorbed through the brush borders of intestinal epithelial cells. The sugars present in the intestine often require further breakdown by enzymes (disaccharidases) located in the brush border prior to absorption. Amino acids and sugars are transported out of the epithelial cell and are absorbed by nearby capillaries. Absorbed fatty acids within the epithelial cells are processed into specialized particles and are then transported out of the cell and into lacteals – lymphatic vessel structures located in the core of villi. Water is absorbed from the intestine by passive diffusion.

Majority of nutrients are absorbed through the jejunum. Vitamin B_{12}, and bile salts – components of bile – are absorbed in the terminal ileum. Over 50 percent of ingested water is absorbed in the small intestine. The remainder of intestinal water is absorbed through the large intestine. There are no other significant digestive events other than fecal formation and defecation through the anal sphincter that occur in the large intestine.

The Duodenum

The duodenum contains cells that synthesize and secrete the hormones secretin and cholecystokinin (CCK). Prior to the release of the stomach contents into the duodenum, these hormones are secreted into the bloodstream. The absorption of dietary iron occurs exclusively in the duodenum.

Bile

When CCK arrives at the gallbladder, it stimulates the release of bile that is stored in the gallbladder into the gallbladder duct. The gallbladder duct connects to the common bile duct; bile travels from the gall bladder duct into the common bile duct and then empties into the lumen of the duodenum. Bile that enters the duodenum will be used to emulsify fats that are present in the digestive contents of the stomach once these contents are delivered into the duodenum.

Pancreatic Enzymes and Bicarbonate Ion

Secretin stimulates the pancreas to release a volume of bicarbonate-ion-rich solution into the lumen of the duodenum. The bicarbonate solution is a moderately-strong basic solution which serves a critical role in the digestive tract, namely the neutralization of the highly acidic stomach contents as they are delivered into the duodenum.

The Liver

Nutrients from the small intestine are carried in the blood to the liver through the hepatic portal duct. Liver enzymes deaminate amino acids, production of urea by converting ammonia, detoxification of harmful molecules from the bloodstream, and store glucose as glycogen and release into the bloodstream when needed.

Detoxification and Drug Metabolism

The liver receives the venous blood that from the intestines via the hepatic portal circulatory system. Liver cells can carry out thousands of complex chemical reactions that are responsible for majority of the catabolic chemical functions of the body. This includes the detoxification of harmful molecules in the bloodstream, the processing of drugs that are present in the bloodstream, and conversion of waste products produced by the turnover of cells – red blood cells in particular – and other organic debris that is generated by the continual metabolic activities of the cells of the body. All the cells in the body are subject to damage and lethal injury, and all the cells of the body are generating waste products from the metabolic activities that are occurring within the cells on a continual basis.

Cholesterol Metabolism

The degradation of cholesterol and related molecules is accomplished by the liver through the conversion of these molecules into bile acids. These are further processed into bile and secreted to the gall bladder and then to the duodenum. In addition to emulsification of fat, bile is also required for the uptake of the fat-soluble vitamins A, D, E, and K. Excess body cholesterol is removed from the body in bile acids that remain in the feces.

Nitrogenous Wastes and Production of Urea

Of significance are the nitrogen containing (nitrogenous) waste products resulting from protein and nucleic acid degradation. These waste products are highly toxic to cells, and the liver converts these nitrogenous waste products into the molecule urea, which is a small, highly water-soluble, nontoxic nitrogen-containing molecule. Urea is easily filtered out of the bloodstream and transferred into urine by the kidneys. Urine is subsequently excreted from the body during urination.

Carbohydrate Metabolism

The liver regulates glucose levels in the blood by absorbing excess glucose from the bloodstream and then converting this excess glucose into long highly branched molecular chains of glucose. This glucose polymer molecule is called glycogen. Glycogen is stored in liver cells. If the level of glucose in the bloodstream falls below normal levels, the liver cells can rapidly convert glycogen back into glucose and release this glucose into the bloodstream thereby restoring low blood glucose levels to normal levels. When glycogen reserves are exhausted, the liver can synthesize new glucose molecules from proteins and lipids. This process is termed gluconeogenesis.

Lipoprotein Synthesis

Liver cells also receive fats and cholesterol absorbed through the small intestine and process these fats and cholesterol molecules into lipoprotein particles, most notably the HDL and LDL lipoprotein-cholesterol complex particles. These particles are then released into the bloodstream by the liver cells.

Water Distribution

An additional important role of the liver is the production of the protein albumin. This protein is synthesized by liver cells and subsequently secreted into the bloodstream. Albumin molecules remain in the bloodstream and act as osmotic particles that favor retention of water within the bloodstream. This is a critical role that maintains the proper balance of water distribution between the intravascular spaces and the extravascular compartment of the body.

The Neuromuscular System

The nervous system can be anatomically divided into the central nervous system and the peripheral nervous systems.

The Central Nervous System

The central nervous system, as previously noted, consists of the brain – located in the cranial cavity – and the spinal cord – located in the vertebral canal of the spine.

The Peripheral Nervous System

All elements of the nervous system – neurons, nerves (axons of neurons), sensory cells, effector cells (muscle cells and glands), and supporting cells and structures – that are not located either inside of the skull or the spinal column – are classified as elements of the peripheral nervous system. All the neurological activity in the body is ultimately under the control of central nervous system, and all the neurons in the peripheral nervous system have nerve pathways that connect to the brain.

There are two broad divisions of the peripheral nervous system: 1) the voluntary or somatic nervous system and 2) the involuntary or autonomic nervous system.

The Somatic (Voluntary) Nervous System

The cranial nerves and spinal nerves carry sensory information from sensory receptor cells located throughout the body to the brain, and they carry instructions – in the form of electrical impulses – from the brain to effector cells located throughout the body. In most cases the effector cells are skeletal muscle cells or glands – endocrine glands and exocrine glands.

The sensory information provided by the peripheral nervous system is integrated with other conscious thought processes and allow one to make a voluntary decision to carry out physical actions. These decisions are translated into actions beginning with the generation and transmission of electrical signals through the somatic nerves to skeletal muscles. Skeletal muscles relax and contract in a fashion that results in the desired body movements.

Somatic Ganglia

Collections of neuron cell bodies not located in the central nervous system are classified as ganglia. Neurons in the dorsal ganglia contribute the sensory nerve fibers to spinal nerves. In ventral regions of the vertebrae, ventral root ganglia neurons contribute the nerve fibers that send signals to effector cells. These types of nerves are called motor nerves.

The Autonomic (Involuntary) Nervous System

Most of the neural regulatory activity of the body is not under voluntary control. The central nervous system regulates majority of the body's functions through the involuntary or autonomic nervous system. The two divisions of the autonomic nervous system are the sympathetic and the parasympathetic nervous systems. These are commonly described as – for the sympathetic division – the "fight or flight" nervous system and – for the parasympathetic division – as the "rest and digest" nervous system.

The Sympathetic Nervous System

Sympathetic nerves release neurotransmitters to cardiac muscle and smooth muscle located in bronchial walls, intestinal tract walls, and the walls of blood vessels that generate rapid response to environmental circumstances that require aggressive and highly energetic responses (fight or flight responses). The sympathetic effects in such circumstances include increased force of heart contractions, increased heart rate, increased blood pressure, redirection of blood flow from the intestines to the skeletal muscles, suppression of peristalsis, and dilation of the bronchial airways.

The Parasympathetic Nervous System

The parasympathetic nervous system innervates most of the same glands, cardiac muscle, and smooth muscle cells as the sympathetic system. The effects of the parasympathetic system are the opposite of the sympathetic effects in most cases. The parasympathetic system predominates during periods when the body requires rest, regeneration, and digestion of food. Perhaps most importantly, the body requires a continuously adjusting balance between the sympathetic and parasympathetic states. This is referred to as the autonomic tone of the body and it is essential for the continuous optimal performance of all body systems.

Neurophysiology

Neurons

Neurons are electrically excitable cells, such as muscle cells. All cells in the body maintain concentration levels of ions inside of the cell that are different than the ion concentrations outside of the cell. This causes a voltage difference across the cell membrane – the action potential.

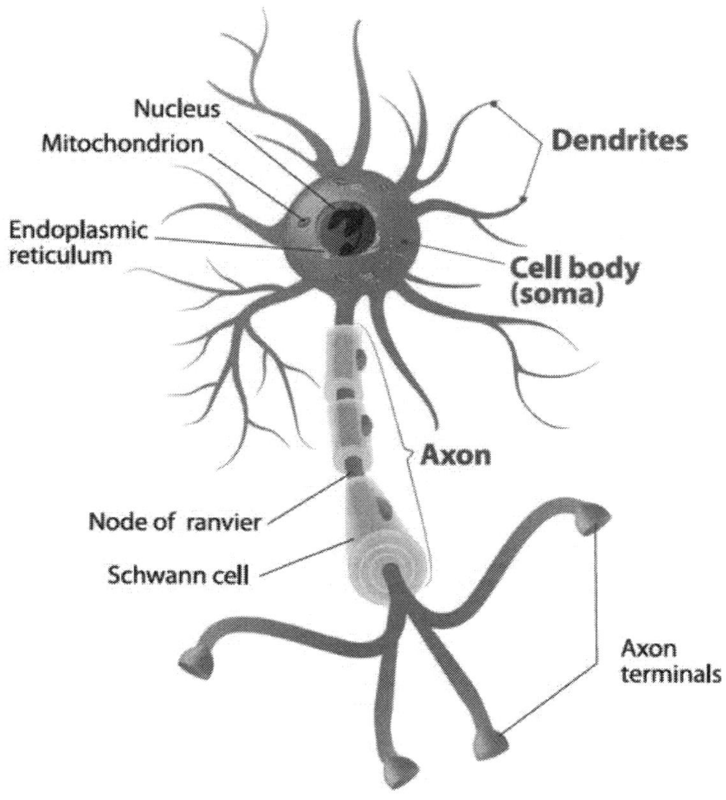

Axons, Dendrites and Synapses

The neuron has, in most cases, a very long membrane extension that looks like a tail called the axon. The nerves of the body are composed of these neuron axons. Action potentials generated by the neuron at the base of the axon travel along the axon to its terminal end.

At the end of the axon there is usually a dendrite – a branch-like extension of another neuron. The action potential in the first neuron axon causes the release of neurotransmitters – small molecules that diffuse across the gap between the axon and the dendrite of the second neuron. The neurotransmitter molecules bind to receptors on the second neuron's dendritic membrane. This can cause the second neuron to generate its own action potential, which again travels down the second neuron's axon. By this method, electrical impulses can be transmitted from one neuron to another. The location where the diffusion of neurotransmitters between two neurons occurs is called a synapse.

General Functions of the Neuromuscular System

Sensory Functions

The function of the nervous system is to monitor, regulate and coordinate all other body functions and to adapt to the external environment as needed.

The nervous system collects an enormous amount of information about the internal conditions of the body and about the outside environment. This collection process begins with sensory receptor cells. Sensory receptor cells are specialized to detect many types of stimuli and they report this information to the brain through electrical signals that they generate and then transmit to the brain via sensory nerves.

Motor Functions

When a conscious decision is made to carry out voluntary movements, the electrical signals to do so are first generated by neurons in the somatic motor cortex. These signals are then transmitted ultimately to voluntary skeletal muscles via the peripheral somatic nerves.

Notice that the peripheral somatic nerves transmit sensory information to the brain and instructions in the form of electrical signals from the brain to the muscles of the body. They are not purely sensory nerves or purely motor nerves; they are therefore designated as mixed nerves.

The motor cortex signals to initiate movement, and the myriad of involuntary movements that occur continuously in the body require huge amounts of processing at lower brain levels before they can be expressed as actual signals to the muscles.

Integrative Functions

An integrative function bridges the sensory and motor functions. These integrative functions involve cognitive awareness and intellectual and emotional thought processes that generate organized strategies of actions and complex behaviors that when operating properly, enhance one's ability to survive in a complex society.

These integrative processes are deeply connected to processing that occurs in the frontal cortices and also depend on continuous input from regions of the brain crucial to maintaining homeostasis, and to regions that are central in memory processing and those involved in generating primitive drives such as hunger, thirst, and nurturing behaviors and basic emotions such as anger, fear, and happiness.

Skeletal Muscles

Most of the skeletal structure of the body is covered by layers of muscles. Major skeletal muscle groups include the upper arm muscles (the biceps and triceps), the deltoid muscles of the shoulders, the large muscles of the anterior chest (the pectoralis major muscles) the large lateral muscles of the back (the latissimus dorsi), the large muscles of the pelvis (hips), the gluteal muscles, the anterior muscles of the upper leg (the quadriceps), the large muscles of the posterior upper leg (the hamstrings), and the largest muscle of the lower leg – the gastrocnemius (calf) muscles.

Neuromuscular Disorders

Muscle Strain

Muscle Sprain

Muscular Dystrophy

The Endocrine System

The endocrine system is the system that synthesizes and secretes hormones directly into the bloodstream or the lymphatic system. Hormones exert a vast array of effects on the body. The endocrine system includes purely endocrine glands, whose sole function is the synthesis and secretion of hormones, and other tissues and organs that, in addition to their primary or co-functions, also synthesize and secrete hormones.

Functions of the Endocrine System

The endocrine system secretes hormones that regulate many body functions, including:

- Production of blood
- Control of appetite
- Reproduction
- Brain function
- Regulation of the sleep cycle
- Sodium homeostasis
- Growth
- Sexual development
- Response to stress and injury

The Hypothalamus and the Pituitary Gland

The hypothalamus and the pituitary gland are closely related anatomically. Together these two structures serve as master controllers of the endocrine system through the secretion of hormones that regulate the levels of other hormones. The hypothalamus is a region of the brain, but it also synthesizes and secretes many critically important hormones.

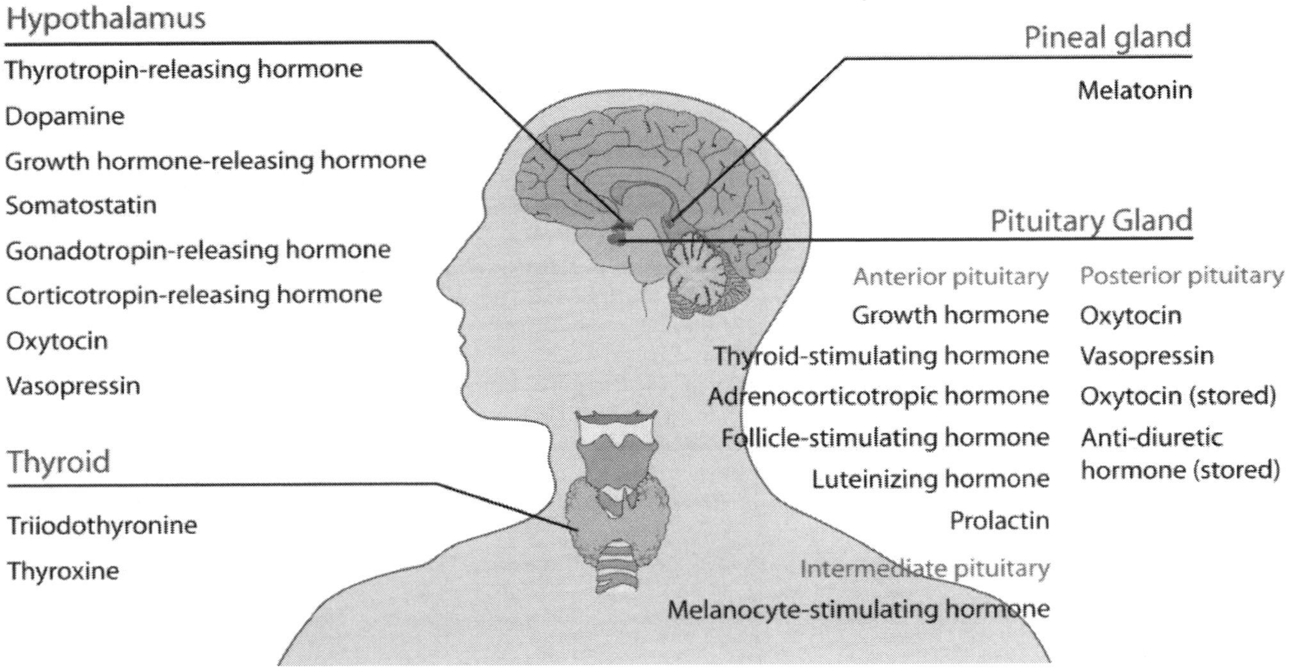

The Hypothalamic Hormones

As we have discussed, the hypothalamus is a critical brain region for the maintenance of homeostasis within the body. A primary mode of this regulation of homeostasis by the hypothalamus is through the release of hypothalamic hormones. Primary hormones secreted by the hypothalamus include:

Thyrotropin-Releasing Hormone (TRH)
This hormone acts on the anterior segment of the pituitary gland and stimulates the release of thyroid-stimulating hormone (TSH).

Corticotropin-Releasing Hormone
This hormone also acts on the anterior segment of the pituitary gland and stimulates the release of adrenocorticotropin hormone (ACTH).

Growth Hormone-Releasing Hormone (GHRH)
This hormone stimulates the release of growth hormone (GH) from the anterior segment of the pituitary gland.

Somatostatin
(Also known as growth-hormone-inhibiting hormone - GHIH) - This hormone inhibits the release of growth hormone (GH) and follicle-stimulating hormone from the anterior segment of the pituitary gland.

The Posterior Pituitary Gland Hormones
The pituitary gland is attached to the inferior portion of the hypothalamus by a connective stalk. The pituitary secretes a wide variety of hormones. An important anatomical feature of the pituitary gland is that the posterior pituitary synthesizes only two hormones – oxytocin and vasopressin (also known as antidiuretic hormone - ADH) – and all other pituitary hormones are synthesized by the anterior pituitary.

Oxytocin
Oxytocin triggers the milk letdown reflex in nursing mothers.

Vasopressin (or ADH)
Vasopressin is a very important hormone that regulates blood pressure and the fluid balance of the body. The blood pressure effects are partially accomplished by ADH effects on smooth muscle in the walls of blood vessels. ADH causes smooth muscle contraction in blood vessel walls, which in turn constricts blood vessel passageways. This results in an increase in blood pressure.

The other actions of ADH are on the microscopic filtering units of the kidney – the nephrons. ADH decreases the loss of water from the body by causing the nephrons to reabsorb water from fluids that have been filtered out of the bloodstream and are in the process of passing out of the kidney filtering system and into the bladder.

Anterior Pituitary Gland Hormones
The hormones secreted by the anterior pituitary are described below.

Adrenocorticotropic Hormone (ACTH)
ACTH is secreted continuously but at increased levels when the body is under physical or psychological stress and when blood glucose is too low. ACTH stimulates the cortex of the adrenal gland to release the corticosteroid hormone cortisol.

Thyroid-Stimulating Hormone (TSH)

TSH stimulates the thyroid gland to release thyroid hormones. Thyroid hormones are the primary hormones that establish the overall metabolic rates of the body.

Luteinizing Hormone (LH) and Follicle-Stimulating Hormone (FSH)

LH and FSH are critical in the differentiation of cells to produce both male and female gametes and are the primary regulators of the female menstrual cycle.

Prolactin (PRL)

Prolactin stimulates glandular growth of mammary glands and subsequent production of milk in breastfeeding females.

Growth Hormone (GH)

The levels of GH during childhood determines the maximum lean body mass and height that individuals attain by the time they complete this type of growth. This completion of growth is the physiological definition of adulthood.

Melanocyte-Stimulating Hormone (MSH)

The levels of MSH, particularly during prenatal (before birth) development determines the darkness of skin color and is the basis for racial differences in skin color.

The Pineal Gland

The pineal gland is located within the midbrain and is essentially at the anatomical center of the brain. The pineal gland produces melatonin, which regulates sleep patterns and circadian rhythms.

The Thyroid and Parathyroid Glands

The thyroid glands are located superficial and to either side of the midline of the tracheal cartilage – many anatomists classify the thyroid as a single gland with left and right lobes. The parathyroid glands are notable for being, in a sense, glands within glands. There are usually four parathyroid glands buried deeply in the thyroid gland, usually two per lobe. The parathyroid glands secrete parathyroid hormone (PTH).

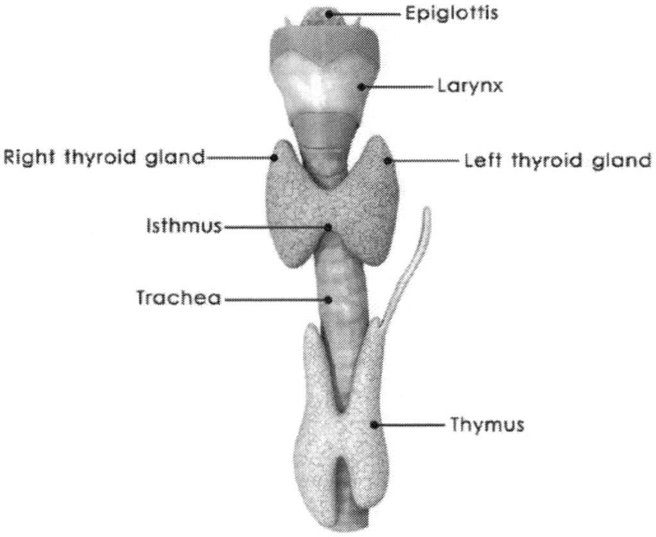

The thyroid gland produces and releases two types of thyroid hormone, thyroxine (T_4) and triiodothyronine (T_3), and the hormone calcitonin.

T_3 and T_4

Iodine atoms are included in the structure of the thyroid hormone, and iodine deficiency leads to hypothyroidism and enlargement of the thyroid gland (a goiter). The release of thyroid hormone is triggered by the pituitary hormone TSH. T_3 is more potent than T_4 but both hormones have the same effects. Thyroid hormones directly affect nearly every cell in the body, and the overall effect is to increase the basal (baseline) metabolic activity of the body.

Calcitonin and Parathyroid Hormone (PTH)

PTH is synthesized and secreted by the parathyroid glands. PTH – along with the hormone calcitonin – is vitally important in the regulation of blood levels of calcium ion.

The Thymus Gland

The thymus gland helps develop an early immune system.

The Pancreas

The pancreas is not a purely endocrine gland; it also has critical exocrine gland function as a part of the digestive system, but its endocrine function is even more important. The pancreas located in the upper right quadrant of the abdomen, in a partially retroperitoneal position, immediately below the diaphragm and posterior to the stomach.

The Pancreatic Hormones – Glucagon and Insulin

In addition to its exocrine function in the synthesis and release of digestive hormones and bicarbonate ions, the pancreas, in its endocrine gland role, synthesizes and releases two hormones, glucagon and insulin. Both hormones are vital to maintaining proper levels of blood glucose. Insulin also is essential to most cells for the uptake of glucose into the cell. Insulin is produced by pancreatic islet cells. In type 1 diabetes, islet cells are attacked and destroyed by the body's own immune system. A total lack of insulin is fatal within hours to days.

The Adrenal Glands

The adrenal glands rest upon the superior surface of the kidneys, one gland per kidney. The anatomical structure of the adrenal gland is significant in that the adrenal cortex (the surrounding outer layer) synthesizes the corticosteroid hormones, including cortisol and aldosterone, and the adrenal medulla (the central region) synthesizes epinephrine, norepinephrine, and dopamine.

The Adrenal Cortical (Steroid) Hormones – Cortisol and Aldosterone

The adrenal cortical hormones are steroid hormones. Steroid hormones are molecules that are modified versions of the cholesterol molecule.

Since the steroid hormones are based on a lipid type molecule – cholesterol – they are fat-soluble, rather than water-soluble. Steroid hormones are secreted into lymphatic vessels rather than blood vessels. The principle cortical hormones are the glucocorticoid steroid hormone cortisol and mineral corticosteroid hormone aldosterone. The adrenal cortex also produces the precursor molecules that are transformed by the gonads into the male hormone, testosterone, and the female sex hormone, estrogen.

Cortisol

Cortisol release is stimulated by the pituitary hormone ACTH. Cortisol has a wide range of actions including regulating the metabolism of fats, proteins, and carbohydrates. Cortisol also plays an important role in the immune system – generally, this involves suppression of the immune response. Cortisol also is involved in the regulation of glucose levels. Cortisol stimulates the liver to synthesize new glucose molecules by a process termed gluconeogenesis. Baseline levels of cortisol are essential to life. An absence of cortisol is fatal within weeks to months.

Aldosterone

Aldosterone is a critical hormone in the regulation of blood pressure and electrolyte concentrations in the body. This regulation mechanism is highly complex and involves several other hormones in what is termed the renin-aldosterone-angiotensin hormone axis.

The Gonads

The gonads have two important co-functions: the production of male or female gametes and the synthesis of sex hormones. The gonads in males are the testicles and are located externally within the testicular pouches. The gonads in females are the ovaries, which are located lateral to and at the level of the superior region of the uterus, one ovary one the left and one on the right. The distal entry into either the left or right fallopian tube is closely adjacent to the left or right ovary. The fallopian tubes provide a passageway into the uterine cavity. The uterus is a midline pelvic organ that is posterior to the urinary bladder and anterior to the rectum.

The Gonadal Hormones – Testosterone and Estrogen

The gonadal hormones – testosterone and estrogen – are synthesized in the testes in males and in the ovaries in females. The sex hormones are synthesized from cholesterol-based precursors that are produced in the adrenal cortex. During the prenatal stage, testosterone is responsible for the development of male external genitalia. During adolescence, the sex hormones are responsible for the development of secondary sexual characteristics – pubic hair, testicular maturation, and breast development. Estrogen also appears to provide protection from coronary artery disease and osteoporosis in premenopausal females.

Endocrine System Disorders

Diabetes

Insulin is a hormone produced by the pancreas that helps blood glucose, from eating, into the cells to be used as energy. Diabetes is a chronic disorder that occurs if the pancreas does not produce enough or fails to produce insulin to regulate blood sugar. Type I diabetes occurs when the pancreas fails completely to produce insulin. Patients are insulin-dependent and must administer artificial insulin daily. Pancreas can produce insulin in type II diabetes, but the body effectively responds to insulin.

Gigantism

Gigantism is caused if the pituitary gland produces too much growth hormone (GH) or somatotropin in children. The main symptom of gigantism is a large body stature with increased height compared to peers and enlargement of muscles and organs. The abnormal growth affects height Acromegaly results if a pituitary tumor secretes an excessive amount of GH after the bone growth plates fuse during childhood. Enlargement of the extremities, hands, and feet are the most prominent features. Other symptoms are associated with acromegaly, such as changes in facial features, skin changes, and joint disorders, such as arthritis.

Hyperthyroidism

The thyroid gland produces too much thyroid hormone, T_4. Hyperthyroidism increases metabolism causing unintentional weight loss and a rapid or irregular heartbeat.

The Cardiovascular System

The anatomy of the cardiovascular circulatory system begins with the heart, which is located at the base of the thoracic cavity directly superior to the diaphragm and centered slightly to the left of the midline of the sternum. The heart consists of muscular walls that enclose four chambers – the thin-walled right and left atria and the thick-walled right and left ventricles. The right and left ventricles share a common medial wall – the interventricular septum – as do the right and left atria – the interatrial septum. The right atrium is directly superior to the right ventricle and the left atrium is directly superior to the left ventricle. The atria and ventricles are separated by a common septum – the atrioventricular septum – which forms the bases or floors of the atria and the ceilings of each atrium's underling ventricles.

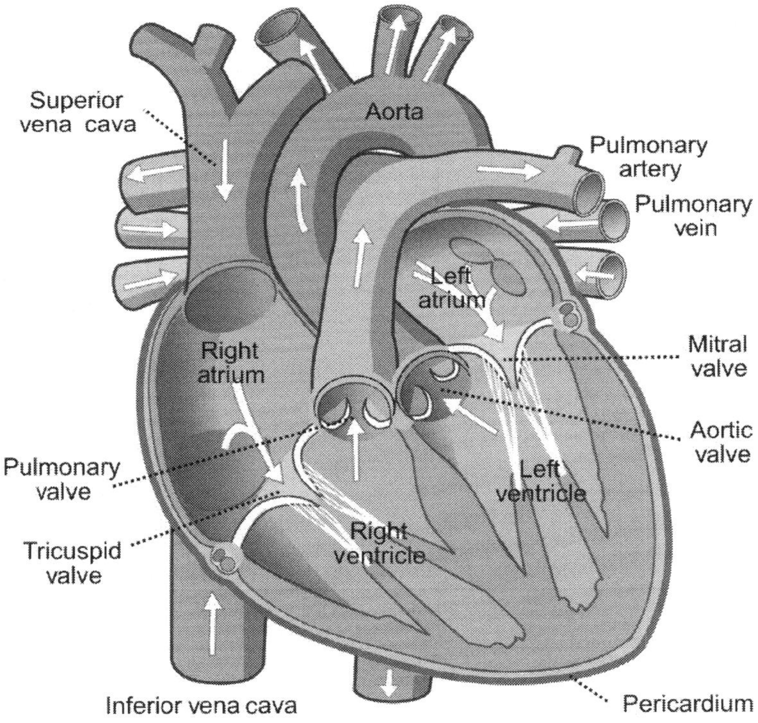

Cardiovascular Blood Flow

Deoxygenated blood from all other regions arrives at the heart from the body via veins. The smaller veins eventually pass blood through to either the superior or inferior vena cava – the largest veins of the body. The superior and inferior vena cava empty into the right atrium. Blood then passes from the right atrium through a three-leaflet valve – the tricuspid valve – into the right ventricle. Subsequently, this blood is pumped out of the right ventricle through a two-leaflet valve – the pulmonic valve – into the main pulmonary artery. Blood in the main pulmonary artery continues to either the left or right pulmonary arteries, which then enter either the left or right lung.

Pulmonary Blood Flow

The pulmonary arteries branch into increasingly smaller and more numerous arteries. The smallest terminal arterial branches are the arterioles. From the arterioles, blood passes into capillaries – one-cell thick walled vessels. Blood passing through these capillaries exchange oxygen from inspired air in alveolar airspaces. Carbon dioxide diffuses out of the blood in the capillaries and into the alveolar airspaces. This carbon dioxide it is then expelled from the body through respiratory airways during exhalation (expiration).

The capillary blood, now oxygenated, passes to venules, then to larger veins, and finally returns to the heart via the main pulmonary veins. The main pulmonary veins (usually there are four of these) empty into the left atrium. Blood from the left atrium passes into the left ventricle through a two-leaflet valve – the mitral valve. The blood is then pumped out of the heart from the left ventricle through a two-leaflet valve – the aortic valve – into the aorta.

The aorta is the largest artery in the body. From the aorta, oxygenated blood is delivered through a network of branching arterial trees to all regions of the body. Oxygen and nutrients are transferred to tissues and carbon dioxide and other waste products are absorbed at capillary beds. Capillary blood, now deoxygenated, returns to the heart through networks of veins as already described.

An important anatomical concept in the cardiovascular system is that blood that is pumped out of the heart, either via the left or the right ventricle. It always first enters a main artery, then travels to sequentially smaller arteries then to the smallest arteries – arterioles – and then into capillaries. From capillaries, this blood next travels to the smallest veins – venules – and then to larger veins.

Cardiovascular (Circulatory) Physiology

The primary functions of the cardiovascular system are:
1) to deliver oxygen from the lungs to all the cells of the body along with water, electrolytes, glucose, and other essential substances.
2) to transport waste products to the organs responsible for detoxifying and excreting waste products from the body.

Carbon dioxide is delivered to the lungs and other wastes are delivered either directly to the kidneys or indirectly to the kidneys through the liver. To accomplish these functions, the circulatory vessels must maintain a large, driving blood pressure differential between the arterial side of the heart (the left heart) and the venous side of the heart (the right heart).

The Sinoatrial (SA) Node

The heart must contract in a precisely synchronized fashion to cause blood to be pumped in the proper manner and direction throughout the circulatory system. The atria must begin to contract from top to the base of the atrioventricular septum. This squeezes blood toward the tricuspid and atrial valves. Next the ventricles must contract beginning at the base of the ventricles and progressing toward the pulmonic and aortic valves.

This coordinated contraction pattern begins with the sinoatrial node tissue located in the wall of the right ventricle. This tissue has an intrinsic (inbuilt) ability to generate electrical signal at a rate on average of 60-80 signals per minute. For this reason, the sinoatrial node is referred to as the pacemaker of the heart. The electrical signals generated at the SA node are conducted through the cardiac muscle of the atria with a geometrical progression that automatically produces the desired contraction pattern of the atria.

The Cycle of Heart Contractions

The heart has two cycles of contractions, systole and diastole. Systole represents contraction of the heart muscle and diastole is the relaxation of the heart muscle. The ventricles contract causing ventricular systole causing the mitral and tricuspid valves to close, making the "lub" sound of "lub-dub." Blood is being pushed out during atrial systole causing the ventricles to empty. The semilunar valves in the aorta and the pulmonary arteries close, making the "dub" sound and preventing blood from go back into the ventricles.

The Composition of Blood

The functions of blood include:

- Transport oxygen and nutrients to the lungs and tissues
- Create blood clots to prevent excess blood loss
- Carries cells and antibodies during an immune response
- Transports waste products to the kidneys and liver to filter the blood
- Body temperature regulation

Blood has four main components, plasma, red blood cells (RBCs), white blood cells (leukocytes), and platelets (thrombocytes).

Plasma

Plasma is the main liquid component of blood and composed of a mixture of water, sugar, fat, protein, and salts. The main function of plasma is to transport blood cells with nutrients, waste products, antibodies, clotting proteins, hormones, and proteins that main fluid balance.

RBCs

Red blood cells (RBCs) are the most abundant blood cell, accounting for about 40-45% of the volume of blood. RBCs have a biconcave disk with a flattened center without a nucleus which allows them to change shape and squeeze into numerous blood vessels. The hormone erythropoietin produced in the kidneys maintains the production of RBCs. The lifespan of RBCs is 120 days, the entire volume of red blood cells in the body must be recycled every four months. The waste products of RBC degradation include large amounts of fragmented cell membrane, DNA, RNA, hemoglobin, and products resulting from chemically degradation of hemoglobin, and other cell proteins. RBCs contain a protein called hemoglobin which transports oxygen throughout the body and returns carbon dioxide from the body to the lungs for exhalation. Hemoglobin is also bound to the RBC and gives the cell its red color. The hematocrit percentage represents the amount of whole blood volume composed of RBCs.

WBCs

White blood cells (leukocytes) have a vital role in immunity by protecting the body from infection. WBCs only account for 1 percent of total blood volume. The most common type of WBC is the neutrophil and responsible for the rapid response to areas of injury or immunologic deficit. Neutrophils account for 55-70% of the total WBC count. The bone marrow continuously replaces the neutrophils each day. Lymphocytes are another critical type of WBC. T-lymphocytes regulate the functions of other immune cells and directly attacks various infected cells and tumors. B-lymphocytes produce antibodies that specifically target bacteria, viruses, and other foreign material.

Platelets (Thrombocytes)

Platelets are small fragments of cells that produce coagulation, creating a fibrin clot. Fibrin creates a covering on the wound to prevent blood leaking out, develops new tissues, and promotes healing.

The Genitourinary System

The genitourinary system consists of the kidneys, renal arteries and veins (renal is an adjective meaning "related to the kidney" or "of the kidney"), ureters, urinary bladder, and urethra. The kidneys are bean-shaped and are located within the walls of the abdomen in a dorsolateral position, retroperitoneal position, on either side of the lumbar spine.

The renal arteries carry blood to the kidney, where it eventually arrives at capillaries surrounding microscopic filtering units called nephrons. Blood filtration occurs at these sites. Filtered blood from nephrons moves through venous networks and emerges from the kidneys within the renal vein. Filtered products from the nephrons pass through tubules that empty into a central collecting cavity in the kidney known as the renal pelvis.

The ureters (one per kidney) are thin tubes connecting the renal pelvis to the urinary bladder. The ureters transport the kidneys' filtered liquid wastes – urine – from the renal pelvis to the urinary bladder. The urinary bladder is a distensible (inflatable) bag-like structure that located in the central anterior pelvic region of the abdominal and pelvic cavity.

The bladder stores urine until it is released through another tube – the urethra. The urethra carries the urine outside of the body, exiting at the meatus (outer opening) of the glans penis in males and immediately anterior the entrance of the vagina in women.

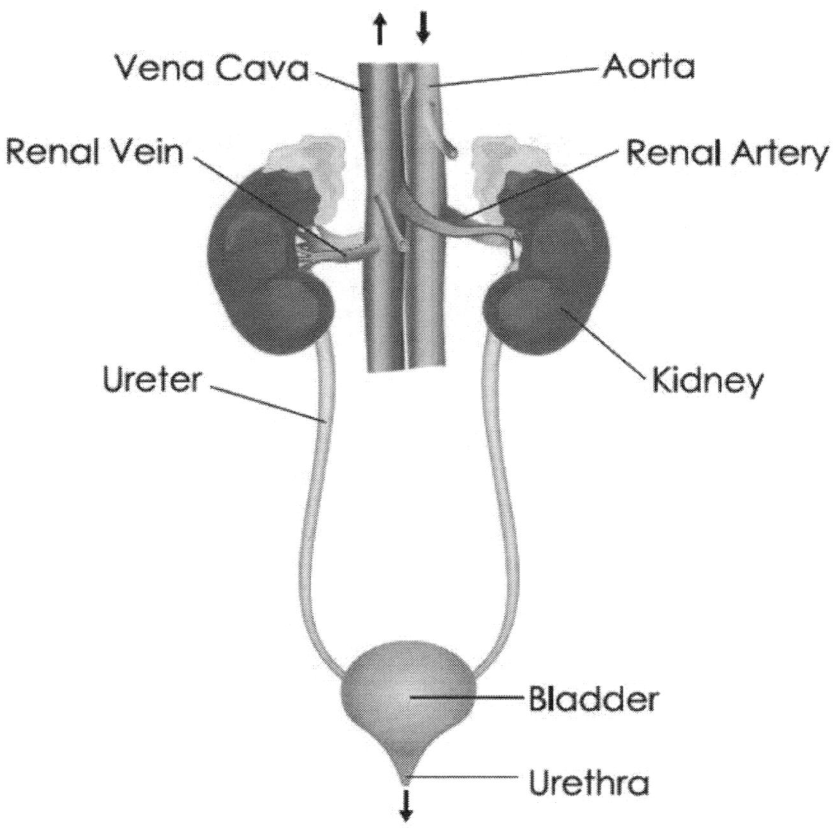

The Kidneys

The kidneys have several critical functions in the human body. Obviously, the kidneys produce urine, but this is only the final stage of kidney function. The production of urine and its transport to the urinary bladder is the excretory function of the kidneys.

Additionally, the kidneys play a crucial role in maintaining an optimal pH of body fluids and in maintaining an optimum blood pressure. The kidney removes soluble waste products from the body, most notably urea, bilirubin, organic acids including uric acid, and ammonia. The solid tissue of the kidneys is divided into two anatomical regions. The outer region is the renal cortex, and the inner region is the renal medulla.

Renal Functions

The functions of the kidney include:

- Blood filtration
- Urine formation
- Excrete waste products
- Maintain an optimum blood pH
- Water and salt homeostasis
- Blood pressure regulation
- Produce the active form of vitamin D

Renal Microscopic Anatomy

The functional unit of the kidney is a microscopic structure called a nephron. There are approximately one million nephrons in the human kidney. The nephron consists of two subunits – a tuft or tangled cluster of capillary loops called a glomerulus, and a one-to-two cell thick-walled renal tubule. The renal tubule consists of four segments. These are Bowman's capsule, the proximal convoluted renal tubule, the loop of Henle, and the distal convoluted renal tubule.

If total body water volume falls below a critical level, there is insufficient blood volume in the circulatory system to maintain a minimum survivable blood pressure. This occurs when the heart is contracting as strongly and rapidly as possible, the blood vessels are at maximum tone, and the kidney is concentrating urine at the highest possible level. When sodium ion concentrations fall below optimum levels (hyponatremia), the volume of water within blood vessels decrease and can be inadequate to maintain a minimum blood pressure even when there is a normal or even excessive volume of total body water. The kidney's response to this is to reabsorb the maximum possible amount of sodium ion from fluids that are filtered by the kidney. The kidney produces a hormone, renin, maintains blood pressure by reabsorbing water and salt.

The Renin-Aldosterone-Angiotensin Hormone System

The kidney can directly detect the sodium ion concentration of plasma within renal arterioles. A response of the kidney to an undesirably low plasma sodium ion concentration (and to low blood pressure) is the release of the hormone renin. Renin in the bloodstream leads to the production of angiotensin II. Angiotensin II is the activated form of angiotensin hormone.

Angiotensin II has a direct effect on circulatory vessels, causing contraction of smooth muscle cells located in the walls of arteries and veins. This increases the force of the vessel walls on the blood within the vessels, resulting in increased blood pressure. Angiotensin II has a direct effect on the proximal tubules to increase sodium reabsorption. Angiotensin II is a potent vasoconstrictor and stimulates the release of aldosterone from the adrenal gland. Aldosterone causes the kidney to increase the reabsorption of sodium ion thereby helping to restore plasma ion concentrations to normal levels. Several other mechanisms can lead to the release of aldosterone.

The Immune System and the Lymphatic System

Generally, the body's immune system does not intentionally attack the body's own normal healthy cells. Intentional attacks are usually directed against abnormal cells of the body – particularly if they are infected with a cellular organism or virus or have mutated into a benign (nonmalignant) abnormal mass of cells (tumor) or a malignant form (cancer). Although infection and other ongoing immune events can be generalized or "spread out" throughout the body (usually viral or blood-borne disease), the immune system generally operates at distinct sites or locations. These can be sites of infections by a biological or viral agent, but many other processes can trigger localized immune responses.

Immune Responses

Immune responses describe activities of the immune system. Immune responses may be broadly categorized as innate (immune system) responses or adaptive (immune system) responses. They may also be broadly categorized as cell-mediated responses.

Barriers to Infection

Nonspecific barriers include physical, cellular, and soluble components that prevent pathogens from entering the body or multiplying. Physical barriers are the first line of defense in the human immune system is the body's exterior barriers to entry of foreign substances. This is the outer surface of the integumentary system – the skin, epithelial lining of the body's digestive system, mucus secretions, and conjunctival tissue of the eyes.

Internal barriers such as antimicrobial peptides initiate protection if the pathogen breaches the external barriers and enters the tissues or blood. Interferons prevent viral infection and the complement system binds antibodies to the invading pathogen.

Passive Mechanical Barriers

The outer layers of epidermis of the skin create a relatively impermeable physical barrier to nearly all substances, including water and atmospheric gases. Additionally, the flaking of the outermost layers of epidermis tends to prevent the accumulation of foreign substances on the outer skin surface.

Active Mechanical Barriers

Physical defenses that remove or decrease the amount of potentially harmful substances on body surfaces and in body cavities include flushing actions of tears on the corneas of the eyes and the outward transport of substances from the lungs and trachea by the coordinated rhythmic motions of cilia on the outer or apical surfaces of bronchial epithelial cells. This process begins with the secretion of mucous by specialized cells that are interspersed in the outer or apical layer of epithelial cells in the respiratory tract.

Chemical Barriers

The highly acidic environment within the stomach, as well as proteolytic (protein cutting) enzymes within the stomach and elsewhere within the remainder of the digestive tract also contribute to the destruction of potentially harmful agents (viruses, microorganisms, and toxic chemicals). Enzymes in saliva and tears also contain substances with antimicrobial properties

Secretory substances from the sweat and oil glands of the skin create a hostile environment for the growth of organisms on the skin surface. Organic acid molecules secreted onto the surface of the skin also create an unfavorably acidic environment for the growth of microorganisms.

The mucosal lining of the vaginal walls is also sufficiently acidic to suppress the growth of most foreign organisms (the yeast Candida albicans is a frequent exception).

Microbiological Colonization Barriers

A stable community of a variety of microorganisms within the GI tract also suppresses the ability of harmful microorganisms to survive within the GI tract. Stable beneficial colonization of the skin and the vaginal mucosa by microbiological communities also contribute to the barrier defenses at these regions of the body.

The Active Immune Systems

Traditionally, the elements of the non-barrier or active human immune system is described as consisting of two sub-systems – the innate immune system and the adaptive immune system. The innate immune system evolved in vertebrates (including humans) before the adaptive immune system and is theoretically capable of functioning without or independently of an adaptive immune system.

The Innate Immune System

The innate immune system responds to foreign agents in a general manner – it cannot precisely identity foreign agents based on the specific antigens that the agent presents to the immune system. The innate immune system functions in the same ways to any substance that it encounters and then recognizes as a foreign agent.

The activity of the innate immune system proceeds in a specific series of cellular and biochemical steps that are the same regardless of what stimulus is triggering the innate immune responses.

The Adaptive Immune System

The adaptive immune response can identify a specific infectious agent and, over time, becomes progressively more selective and effective in eradicating that agent from the body. The adaptive immune system is also able to remember a specific infectious agent (antigens) that triggered an initial or first-encounter adaptive immune response. Upon a subsequent identification of this agent in the body, the adaptive immune response is then able to mount a much more rapid and powerful immune response to that agent.

Antibodies and Antigens

The adaptive immune system can identify specific molecular features (antigens) that are possessed by a foreign agent and can generate specific molecules (antibodies) that bind to these specific antigens.

Antibody-Producing Cells

Antibodies are synthesized by B-cells and plasma cells. B-cells are a key cell type of the adaptive immune system. Plasma cells are derived from B-cells that have transformed after activation by an immunological event. Plasma cells synthesize and secrete specific antibodies into the surrounding regions of the body. These antibodies can diffuse into the local interstitial (extracellular) space surrounding the plasma cell. Many of these antibodies then enter the circulatory system and subsequently are widely distributed throughout the body. Antibodies are the primary components of the adaptive immune system.

B-Cells and Plasma Cells

B-Cells are lymphocytes. When an inactive B-cell is activated, it often undergoes several rounds of mitotic division to form a clonal population of identical B-cells. These B-cells can then differentiate (transform) into plasma cells. Plasma cells synthesize and secrete antibodies. B-cells and plasma cells – by most definitions – participate in adaptive immune system events. This is because B-cell and plasma cell activity ultimately results in the production and release of antibodies, and antibodies are not cells. Therefore, antibodies are agents of the immune system. Of course, plasma cells are required to produce antibodies, so this can be a point of confusion regarding the difference between cell-mediated and immune agents and events. Memory cells that can remember the antigen are produced if antigen levels subside or if plasma cells stop making antibodies.

Antibody-Antigen Specificity

Antibodies can tightly bind to (attack) a vast number of unique or specific small molecules and larger molecules which contain these molecules as subunits of their overall molecular structure. Small specific molecules and small specific regions of larger molecules that can be targeted by a specific antibody are called antigens ("anti" for "antibody" and "gen" for "genesis"). Antigens can trigger a direct attack by a specific antibody.

All antibodies that can specifically bind to an antigen are classified as complementary antibodies to that antigen. Conversely, all antigens that can be specifically bound to an antibody are complementary to that antibody.

Antigen-Presenting Cells (APCs)

Antigen-presenting cells (APCs) are a class of immune cells that mediate the cellular immune response by processing and presenting foreign antigens that they have acquired - usually by phagocytosis or endocytosis - from the extracellular environment for recognition by certain lymphocytes such as T-cells.

T-Cells

T-cells are the other major cell type of the adaptive immune system. T-cells, like B-cells, are lymphocytes. There are several important subtypes of T-cells. These are T-helper cells, cytotoxic T-cells, memory T-cells, and natural killer T-cells (these are not the same as natural killer cells).

T-Helper Cells

Ingested pathogens, products of pathogen and fragments of pathogens are digested within the antigen presenting cells and the antigen fragments resulting from this intracellular digestion are then transported to the cell membrane and presented on the cell surface. The T-helper cell that recognizes this complex has been pre-formed or primed to recognize only the specific foreign antigen presented on the cell.

Once the antigen presenting cell finds a complementary T-cell for its foreign antigens, the T-helper cell binds and activates the T-cell to initiate the processes that lead to the production of large amounts of antibodies that then circulate throughout the body in search of any cell or other substance that contains the foreign antigen. These antibodies are perfectly designed to bind to the specific foreign antigens whenever and wherever they encounter the antigens anywhere in the body. This is called the antigen-specific immune response.

Cytotoxic T-Cells

Cytokines are produced when a helper T-cell comes across a cytotoxic T-cell that recognizes a previous known antigen. These antigens are involved in identifying cells of the body that have been infected and are therefore targets of destruction by cytotoxic T-cells.

Natural Killer (NK) Cells

NK cells are the third major class of lymphocyte (the others being B-cells and T-cells). NK cells can attack virally infected and cancerous cells of the body ("abnormal-self" cells). NK cells can attack these cells without interacting with other cells or other substances of the adaptive immune system. For this reason, NK cells are members of the innate immune system. NK cells nevertheless often do interact with the adaptive immune system. Again, do not confuse NK cells with natural killer T-cells. NK T-cells cannot attack immunogenic agents without assistance from other elements of the adaptive or innate immune system.

PAMPs

Pathogen-associated molecular patterns (PAMPs) refer to a class of molecular structures that are shared by a wide range of immunogenic agents. These molecular structural patterns are typically present on the exterior surfaces of immunogenic agents, but they may also be elements of substances contained within these agents.

PAMPs are analogous to antigens. They can be recognized by cellular elements of the immune system without any participation of antibodies. Some complement proteins can bind to these molecular patterns and many immune cells have receptors that are designed to bind to theses molecular patterns. Antibodies may also recognize PAMPs as antigens (or recognize one or more molecular sub-regions of PAMPs and as more than one antigen).

Phagocytes

Although we have already discussed several types of cells with a primary phagocytic function in the immune system.

Phagocytes are a class of cell types that participate in immune responses and function as custodians by engulfing other undesirable substances that serve no purpose in the body. These include fragments of dead cells and other molecular remnants that are essentially "trash" such as protein or other macromolecular fragments. Phagocytic cells also participate in the formation and remodeling of structures within the body. Bone formation and remodeling by osteoclasts is a notable example.

Macrophages

Macrophages reside in locations throughout the body, where they patrol for substances that require removal from the body. Macrophages also patrol for immunogenic substances and are capable of presenting antigens from ingested immunogenic agents.

Dendritic Cells

Dendritic cells are phagocytic cells that are residents of tissues throughout the body, particularly at sites that are likely portals of entry for foreign immunogenic substances. Dendritic cells possess toll-like receptors on their cell membranes which can bind to pathogen-associated molecular patterns (PAMPs) that are present on or in a wide variety of foreign microorganisms. After recognizing and then phagocytizing a foreign immunogenic substance, dendritic cells are usually able to digest the substance and present the digested fragments as antigens on the outer cell membrane surfaces. Dendritic cells are also capable of migrating to lymph nodes and other lymphatic tissues where they can present antigen complexes to B-cells and T-cells.

The Complement System

The complement system is an important subsystem of the immune system. The system comprises at least 30 different individual complex proteins and other molecular factors that can be activated by a wide variety of foreign substances and by interactions with cells and antibodies and infectious microorganisms, especially bacteria. The complement system results in direct killing of an infectious cell as an innate immune response or a consequence of adaptive immune responses. Complement proteins directly enhance the effectiveness of phagocytosis of infectious cells by other cells of immune system. Activated complement protein fragments attached to the surface of an infectious cell's outer membrane promote the recognition and engulfment of infectious cells by phagocytic cells of the immune system.

Inflammation

Activated complement proteins also promote the inflammatory processes associated with innate immune responses. Either directly or indirectly, these proteins participate in the processes resulting in the four cardinal signs of inflammation – swelling, redness, warmth, and pain. Permeability of local blood vessels results in increased fluid leakage from the vessels into the intravascular spaces and localized swelling at an infection site. Blood vessels at the site also dilate, resulting in increased blood flow. This causes the increased temperature and redness associated with localized infection. These four components of the local inflammation immune response produce the fifth sign of inflammation – incapacitation or impairment of function of the cells, tissues, and/or organs at the infection site.

Passive Immunity

The immune protection through the passive introduction of antibodies, such as immediate treatment for a snakebite.

Active Immunity

The immune protection through the active introduction of antibodies, such as when the body produces antibodies in response to the presence of an antigen, such as during vaccination.

Autoimmune and Hyper-Immune Responses

Although the human immune responses are designed to deactivate dangerous foreign chemical agents such as venoms and other toxic substances and to combat infectious agents such as viruses, bacteria, and eukaryotic organisms – single cell fungi and protist (such as amoeba) and multicellular parasites – often immune responses are inappropriate and harmful – including fatal – human immune responses. Autoimmune responses (immune reactions that attack the body's own healthy cells and extracellular components) and hyper-immune responses (excessively-intense or disproportional responses to non-self-substances) are responsible for a large fraction of all human diseases.

Most commonly this damage caused by the immune system to the body occurs through the generation of the inflammatory response. The inflammatory response produces swelling of tissues and a variety of toxic chemicals and cell activity that cause damage to normal cells and non-cellular structures in the body.
This damage can be rapidly destructive and potentially fatal when the inflammatory response is particularly severe.

Inappropriate and prolonged generalized inflammatory states are proven or strongly suspected to be a primary cause of many common and severe human diseases.

The Lymphatic System

The immune system is a complex and widely distributed network of cells, organs, and other structures. The lymphatic system is a body-wide circulatory system that includes lymphatic vessels, lymph nodes, and lymphoid organs. The lymphatic vascular system is closely associated in both structure and distribution to the blood vessels of the cardiovascular system.

The lymphatic system functions include the removal of excess fluids and debris from the extracellular or interstitial compartments of the body (the area surrounding cells not including spaces inside blood vessels). The lymphatic system is also a major component of the immune system. Capillary-size lymphatic vessels are found throughout the body. They are terminal branches of the lymphatic vascular system. Lymphatic fluid moves from interstitial spaces into the lymphatic capillaries, then to progressively larger vessels and then to lymph nodes. Lymph nodes are nodular structures that contain numerous antigen-presenting cells capable of triggering the adaptive immune system. Lymph nodes are widely distributed throughout the body. Lymphatic fluid is filtered at lymph nodes and continue in vessels leaving the lymph nodes.

Lymph Nodes

For the TEAS, the anatomy of lymph nodes is significant in that the cortex of the lymph node is a site where T-cells accumulate and interact with B-cells and that the medulla of lymph nodes is one of the anatomical regions where the maturation of B-cells occurs.

The Reproductive System

The male and female human reproductive systems are responsible for the generation of human offspring. The first stage of this process begins with the production of male and female gametes. In males, the gamete is a sperm cell and in females, the gamete is a mature ovum.

The second stage of this process is fertilization, where male gametes are transported to the female reproductive system and a sperm cell fuses with an ovum to produce a zygote. The resultant zygote has a full set of 21 pairs of autosomes and two sex chromosomes – either an X and a Y chromosome or two X chromosomes. Zygotes with an X and a Y chromosome develop into male human offspring, and those with two X chromosomes develop into female offspring.

The synthesis and secretion of the sex hormones – testosterone in the male and estrogen in the female – also occurs in the gonads of the reproductive system.

The Male Reproductive System

The male reproductive system consists of the external male genitalia – the penis, the scrotum, and the testis, and the internal male genitalia – the distal segment of the urethra, the seminal vesicles, and the prostate gland, and bulbourethral glands. The penis consists of a central canal – the urethra – which also serves as the passageway for the delivery of urine from the bladder to the exterior of the body. The distal end of the penis forms the head or glans of the penis, which contains the external opening of the urethra – the meatus and surrounding tissue called the foreskin.

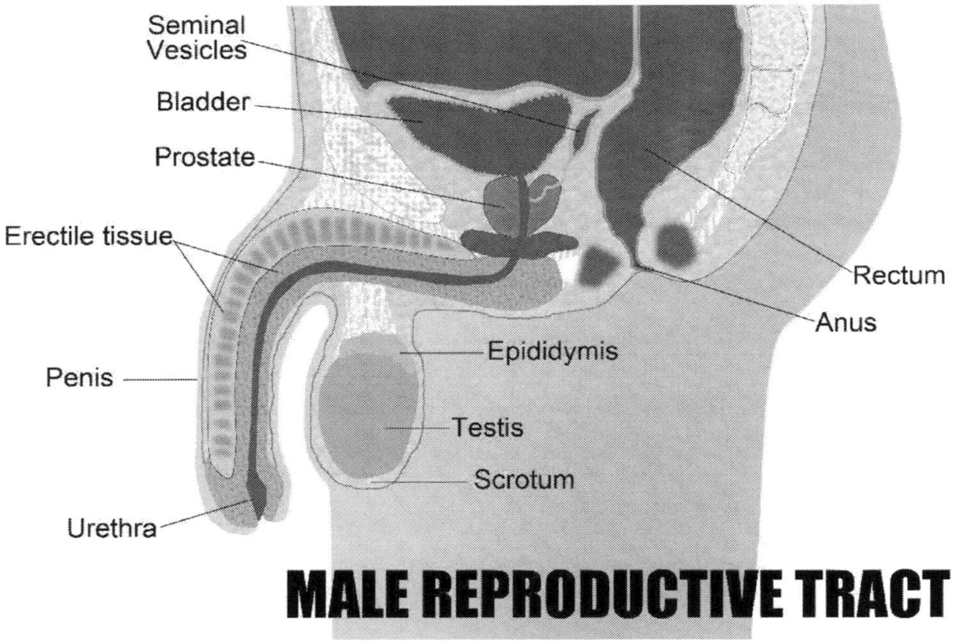

The scrotum is an external anatomical pouch or sack consisting of skin and smooth muscle. The scrotum is divided into two chambers. Each chamber contains a single testis along with the associated structures of the testis – the epididymis and the ductus deferens. The scrotum allows the testes to experience a slightly lower temperature environment than internal body temperature. This is necessary to allow the proper functioning of spermatogenesis (sperm production) that occurs within the testis. The testes are ovoid-shaped organs that are responsible for the first stages of the production of sperm cells. The prostate gland regulates the release of urine and secretes the semen structure that increases sperm motility and fertility.

Testosterone Production

A primary function of the male gonads – the testes – is the production of the male sex hormone testosterone. Testosterone is a steroid hormone whose synthesis and secretion are regulated by the hypothalamus through the release of gonadotrophin releasing hormone (GnRh), which regulates the synthesis and release of luteinizing hormone (LH) and follicle-stimulating hormone (FSH) by the anterior pituitary.

Both FSH and LH stimulate the testes to synthesize and release testosterone. Luteinizing hormone directly stimulates the production of testosterone. Testosterone production occurs in Leydig cells. Leydig cells are interstitial cells (located in loose connective tissue) that are located alongside the seminiferous tubules of the testis. Testosterone produced by the Leydig cells stimulates the sexual maturation of prepubescent males and during puberty stimulate the development of male secondary sexual characteristics. Secondary male sexual characteristics include the development of pubic and facial hair, an increase in muscle and bone mass, a deepening of the voice, and the maturation of the gonads and external male genitalia. After puberty, testosterone plays critical roles in the maturation of sperm cells.

The Female Reproductive System

The female reproductive system consists of the external and internal female genitalia. The functions of the female reproductive system are the production of female gametes, the support of the fertilization of the fusion of female and male gametes to create a human zygote, and the physical support, protection and nourishment of the development of the zygote to a mature human fetus and the subsequent delivery of the fetus to the outside world. The gonads of the female reproductive system are also responsible for the synthesis and release of the female sex hormone estrogen.

The Female Internal Reproductive System

The female internal reproductive system consists of five major components, the vagina, uterus, fallopian tubes, cervix, and the ovaries. In contrast to the male reproductive system, the female urethra does not communicate with any female reproductive structures and has no role in the female reproductive system.

FEMALE REPRODUCTIVE SYSTEM

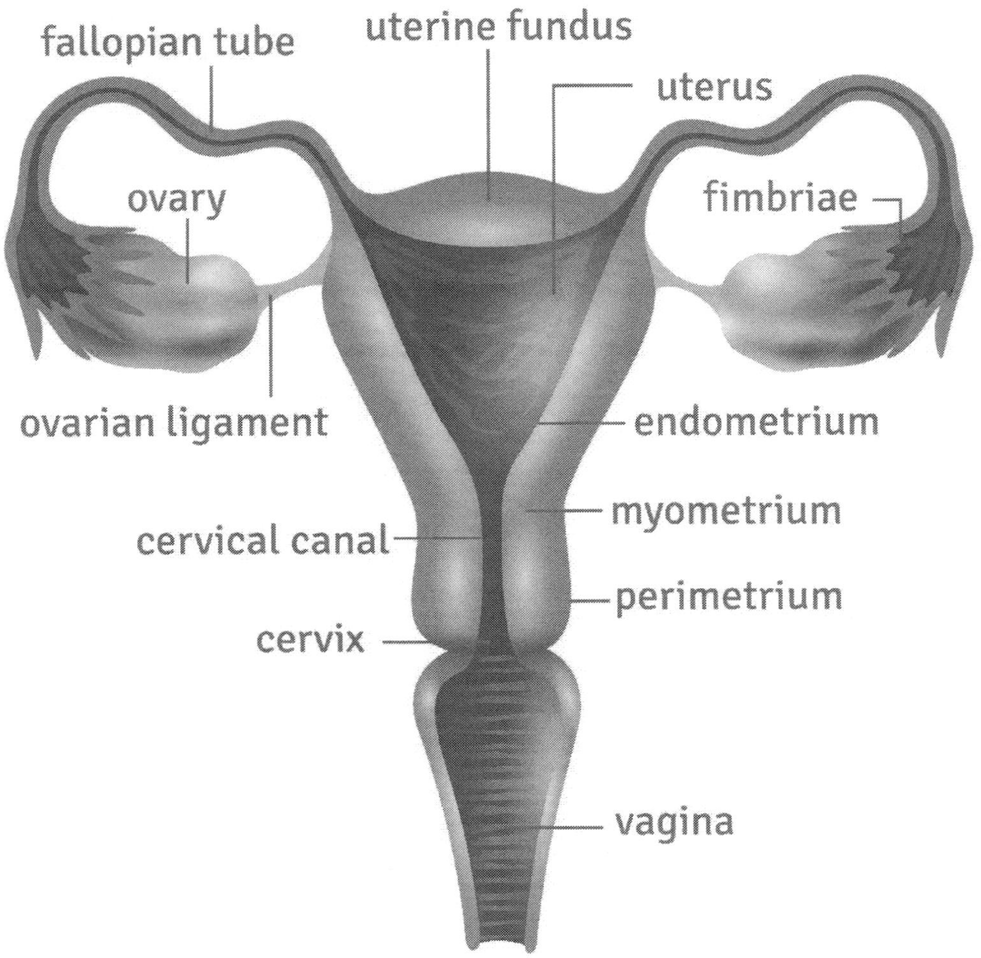

The Vagina

The vagina is an anatomical tube consisting of muscular and fibrous tissue. The lumen of the vagina begins at the vaginal orifice and extends internally to the pelvic cavity where it terminates at the cervix of the uterus. The cervix is the inferior portion of the uterus and protrudes into the lumen of the vagina. The walls of the vagina encircle the cervix, and the interior lining of the vaginal lumen is continuous with the external surfaces of the cervix.

The Uterus

The functions of the uterus are to serve as a site for the implantation of a developing embryo and to provide a continuous supportive, nurturing, and protective environment for the continued development of the embryo into a viable human fetus. When the fetus is sufficiently developed to survive outside of the uterus, the uterus undergoes a series of muscular contractions that expel the fetus from the internal uterine cavity through the cervical canal and into the lumen of the vagina.

The uterus is a pear-shaped muscular organ located in the pelvic cavity in a position immediately adjacent and dorsal to the urinary bladder and immediately adjacent and ventral to the rectum.

The endometrium undergoes an approximately once-per-month cycle of growth, degeneration and regeneration (menstrual cycle) that occurs in response to the variations in the levels of hormones that regulate the menstrual cycle.

The Fallopian Tubes

The fallopian tubes are a pair of structures that extend from the left and right side of the uterus and connects the ovaries to the uterus. During ovulation – when a mature follicle within the ovary ruptures and releases a mature ovum (female gamete) – the ovum is drawn into the fallopian tube by local peritoneal fluid currents generated by the motion of cilia within the fallopian tube. Once inside the tube, the ovum is carried by the same ciliary motions into the central cavity of the uterus. Fertilization of the ovum by a sperm cell (which sometimes occurs within the fallopian tubes) triggers a set of reactions that allows the developing embryo to implant within the wall of the endometrium of the uterus.

The Ovaries

The ovaries are the female gonads. There are two ovaries in females, one located to the distal end of the fallopian tube. In addition to their role as the primary estrogen producing glands the ovaries also are the organs that contain all a female's germ cells that will eventually mature and be released by the ovaries during ovulatory cycles.

Hormonal Regulation During the Menstrual Cycle

With the onset of puberty, the hypothalamus begins to release GnRH in a controlled fashion that varies throughout the menstrual cycle. For the first half of the cycle GnRh is released in increasing amounts. This triggers the anterior pituitary to release FSH and LH also in increasing amounts.

Ovulation and FSH and LH Peaks

As this process is occurring the ovaries are also producing increasing amounts of estrogen. This increasing estrogen level reaches a critical level at about day 15 of the menstrual cycle. The critical estrogen level feeds back to the hypothalamus and the pituitary resulting in a rapid spike in FSH and LH levels. In response, one of the developing secondary follicles randomly becomes dominant and further matures. The LH spike stimulates this dominant secondary follicle to rupture at the surface of the ovary. This event is called ovulation. The secondary oocyte of the ruptured follicle escapes and is drawn into the lumen of the fallopian tube.

Progesterone and the Corpus Luteum

The corpus luteum is a mast of cells within the ovary. The corpus luteum begins to produce the steroid hormone progesterone, which stimulates the endometrium of the uterus to continue to thicken in anticipation of the potential implantation of a fertilized ovum. If implantation occurs, the corpus luteum will persist and continue to produce progesterone to maintain the endometrium. If implantation does not occur, the corpus luteum degenerates, progesterone levels fall, and the blood vessels of the endometrium degenerate. The endometrial tissue then sloughs off and is expelled from the uterus during menstruation.

VOCABULARY

YOU COMPLETED A CROSSWORD PUZZLE FOR THE VOCABULARY CHAPTER IN MODULE 3. LET'S TRY ANOTHER ONE. BELOW IS A CROSSWORD PUZZLE TO HELP YOU LEARN SOME ADDITIONAL WORDS AND EXPAND YOUR VOCABULARY.

accost boggy canvass defy eccentric fidget hypocrite inertia jetty limber menagerie notary obliterate prestige reluctant spontaneous turmoil vestibule abdicate belligerent corrugated dilemma profane sublime thrift vagrant

Across

1. aggressively approach and speak to someone
5. flexible or supple
6. hostile and aggressive
9. unwilling or hesitant
10. moral or spiritual
11. a person authorized to perform legal formalities, usually relating to contracts or other documents
15. the mechanics principle where an object will remain in motion or at rest unless acted on by another force
17. a space adjacent to a main room or area
21. when a material is molded into a network of ridges and grooves
22. resist or refuse to obey
23. a difficult choice
24. a small pier at which boats can dock
25. deep respect and admiration

Down

2. to survey someone about his/her opinion
3. completely destroy
4. suddenly or instantly
7. somewhat strange or uncoventional
8. a great disturbance or uncertainty
12. irreverent or disrespectful
13. someone who claims to have certain principles or beliefs, but does not act in the same manner
14. a strange collection of items
16. to renounce or fail to carry out
17. a person without a settled home
18. very wet and muddy
19. a characteristic of being wise with money
20. wiggle or squirm about

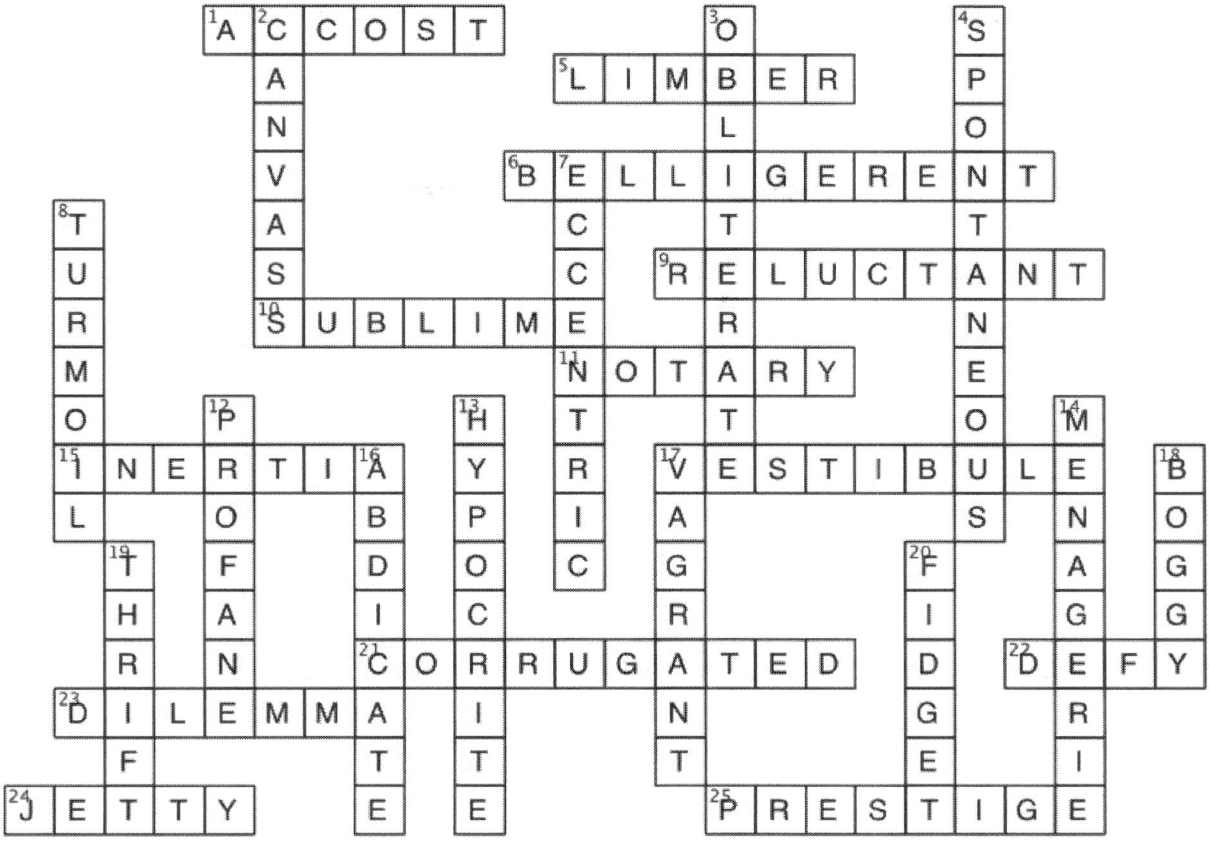

accost boggy canvass defy eccentric fidget hypocrite inertia jetty limber menagerie notary obliterate prestige reluctant spontaneous turmoil vestibule abdicate belligerent corrugated dilemma profane sublime thrift vagrant

Across

1. aggressively approach and speak to someone [ACCOST]
5. flexible or supple [LIMBER]
6. hostile and aggressive [BELLIGERENT]
9. unwilling or hesitant [RELUCTANT]
10. moral or spiritual [SUBLIME]
11. a person authorized to perform legal formalities, usually relating to contracts or other documents [NOTARY]
15. the mechanics principle where an object will remain in motion or at rest unless acted on by another force [INERTIA]
17. a space adjacent to a main room or area [VESTIBULE]
21. when a material is molded into a network of ridges and grooves [CORRUGATED]
22. resist or refuse to obey [DEFY]

Down

2. to survey someone about his/her opinion [CANVASS]
3. completely destroy [OBLITERATE]
4. suddenly or instantly [SPONTANEOUS]
7. somewhat strange or uncoventional [ECCENTRIC]
8. a great disturbance or uncertainty [TURMOIL]
12. irreverent or disrespectful [PROFANE]
13. someone who claims to have certain principles or beliefs, but does not act in the same manner [HYPOCRITE]
14. a strange collection of items [MENAGERIE]
16. to renounce or fail to carry out [ABDICATE]
17. a person without a settled home [VAGRANT]
18. very wet and muddy [BOGGY]
19. a characteristic of being wise with money [THRIFT]

CRITICAL READING

VOCABULARY-IN-CONTEXT

Vocabulary-in-Context questions ask you for the definition of a word as it is used within the context of the passage. The format of these questions is similar to that of Word Knowledge questions. You will be given a word and asked to select the closest meaning from a list of four choices. The difference, though, is that where Word Knowledge questions test straightforward vocabulary, the words chosen for Vocabulary-in-context questions are often words that can have more than one meaning. You will need to use context clues from the passage in order to figure out which meaning is correct.

It's also important to note that many questions on the exam will not always ask you to simply determine the meaning of a vocabulary word. Many times, instead of asking you for a synonym or definition of a vocabulary word, the question will ask you what the vocabulary word "most nearly means". For these types of questions, you'll need to use context clues and your existing vocabulary knowledge to determine which answer choice has a meaning that is closest to that of the vocabulary word.

To answer these questions, reread the sentence from the passage that the word is taken from. Come up with a prediction your own definition or synonym of what the word means as used in that sentence. Then, look at the answer choices and choose the one that best matches your prediction. If you do not see your prediction among the answer choices, read each of the answer choices as part of the sentence, replacing the original word, and choose the one that makes the most sense.

Let's look at some examples.

Some of the questions you'll encounter will ask you to fill in the blank in a sentence. For the questions below, select the word that fits best in the sentence.

1. The bolt was ___________. It took a lot of effort to loosen the fastener.

   A. Rusted
   B. Shiny
   C. Loose
   D. Strong

Answer: A.
Using the context clues in the sentence, you can assume that the missing word is somehow related to the phrase "loosen the fastener". Something about the bolt made it difficult to remove. You can immediately eliminate "shiny" since it is not related to the action of removing a fastener. Likewise, "loose" is not correct because if the bolt were loose, it wouldn't be difficult to remove it. "Strong" could possibly fit if there wasn't a better answer choice, but it's not typically used to describe how difficult a fastener is to remove. The word that best fits in the sentence is "rusted" because rust directly increases the difficulty of removing a fastener.

2. As the commanding officer's eyes widened and his face turned red, he proceeded to __________ the lance corporal.

   A. Tease
   B. Scold
   C. Compliment
   D. Correct

Answer: B.
Using the context clues in the sentence, you can assume that the missing word is somehow linked to widened eyes and a red face, which are associated with anger. You can immediately eliminate "tease" and "compliment" since those words connote lightheartedness and sincerity, not exactly similar to the demeanor described in the sentence. "Correct" could possibly fit if there wasn't a better answer choice, but it's not necessarily associated with widened eyes and a red face. The word that best fits in the sentence is "scold" because scolding connotes anger or irritation, which correlate with widened eyes and a red face.

Sure, those were fairly easy, but those are just one type of vocabulary-in-context questions you'll probably encounter on the exam. For the questions below, select the word that MOST NEARLY means the same as the underlined word.

1. The chairman of the board abandoned his position after a damaging scandal.

   A. Squandered
   B. Resigned
   C. Ignored
   D. Neglected

Answer: B.
All the answer choices connote negative characteristics of the position of chairman of the board, but only "resigned" most closely matches the underlined word. "Squandered" suggests a wasted opportunity. "Ignored" means deliberately taking no notice of. "Neglected" signifies a failure to pay attention to. "Resigned" indicates voluntarily leaving a job, which MOST nearly means the same as "abandoned", leaving permanently.

2. Sarah considered herself a <u>parsimonious</u> shopper. She loved finding great shopping deals.

A. Cheap
B. Frugal
C. Economical
D. Thrifty

Answer: A.
All the answer choices reflect the general meaning of "parsimonious", being careful with money, but only one choice has a negative association. "Frugal", "economical" and "thrifty" are all adjectives with a positive connotation, but "cheap" is usually used as a negative description.

Those were a bit more difficult, but let's try a few more. For the questions below, select the word that LEAST LIKELY means the same as the underlined word.

1. The evidence of the murder was <u>destroyed</u> before the trial.

A. Devastated
B. Obliterated
C. Ruined
D. Incinerated

Answer: D.
While all the answer choices can be used in place of "destroyed", "incinerated" suggests a specific type of damage: destruction by fire. Technically, "incinerated" is a logical answer, but the question isn't asking which choice is not logical. It's asking which choice LEAST likely means the underlined word. This was a tough one, but you should expect to see some questions like this on the exam.

2. While trying to negotiate a peace treaty, one side was being entirely <u>hostile</u> to the other.

A. Belligerent
B. Threatening
C. Averse
D. Combative

Answer: C.
While all the choices are mostly synonyms of "hostile", only one choice excludes a violent implication in its definition. "Averse" means strongly opposed to, but "belligerent", "threatening" and "combative" all suggest harm or death, as does "hostile".

Sometimes, you will need to read a passage before answering the questions. Let's look at some examples of those questions.

"American elections consist of citizens voting for their government representatives. Today, this includes members of the U.S. Senate, but this was not always the case. When the United States Constitution was first written, the people did not get to elect their senators directly. Instead, the senators were appointed by state legislators (who are elected directly by the people in their respective states). This changed in 1913, however, with the 17th Amendment to the Constitution. This amendment allows for the direct election of U.S. Senators by the citizenry. While this election process can make the senators more accountable to their constituents, since the citizens will decide whether a senator will keep his or her job at the next election, it diminishes the voice that state legislatures have in the federal government."

1. The word <u>constituents</u> in the passage most nearly means:
   A. Elements
   B. Employees
   C. Senators
   D. Voters

Answer: D.
By reading the choices back into the sentence, you can see that the best synonym for "constituents" is "voters". It is the voters who decide whether or not to reelect the senators. The word "constituents" on its own can have several meanings, including voters, elements, members, components and parts. In the context of this passage, however, "voters" is the best definition.

2. The word <u>amendment</u> in the passage most nearly means:
   A. Rule
   B. Principle
   C. Alteration
   D. Truth

Answer: C.
By reading the choices back into the sentence, you can see that the best synonym for "amendment" is "alteration". The passage states how the Constitution originally provided for senator selection. However, the passage explains the difference in process after the 17th amendment. Because "alteration" means "change", it is the best choice.

ARITHMETIC REASONING

SCIENTIFIC NOTATION

Scientific notation was originally developed as a simplified way for scientists to express extremely large or small numbers. In mathematics, scientific notation is used to easily compare large and small numbers. Let's take a look at how to translate a real number to its scientific notation equivalent.
Converting standard numbers to scientific notation is performed without calculation, although counting place values is still essential. For example:

The number 2,345,000 is equal to 2.345 * 1,000,000. By writing the value of 1,000,000 as 10^6 (10 multiplied by itself 6 times), the formulation of the scientific notation equivalent of the original number is completed: 2.345 * 10^6.

Similarly, small decimal numbers can be written using scientific notation as well. For example:
The number 0.00736 is equal to 7.36 * 0.001. By writing the value of 0.001 as 10^{-3} (1 divided by 10, three times), the formulation of the scientific notation equivalent of the original number is completed: 7.36 * 10^{-3}.

Instead of dividing (or multiplying) by 10, the translation to scientific notation can also be simplified by counting the number of places that the decimal point is transferred in the conversion process. In the first example above, when the scientific notation was written, it began with writing 2.345. This number was formulated by moving the decimal point six places to the left in the original number. Therefore, the exponent of 10 was 6 (10^6).

Similarly, in the second example, the decimal part of the scientific notation number, 7.36, was written by moving the decimal point three places to the right. Therefore, the exponent of 10 was -3 (10^{-3}).
Using this method, no calculation is required. The included benefit is that the "significance" of numbers is easily determined. Answering the question of the number of significant figures for the two examples is a simple matter when using scientific notation. The number of digits in the decimal part of the scientific notation is always the number of significant figures. 2,345,000 has four significant figures. 0.00736 has three. The zeros in these numbers are often referred to as "place holders" when converting to scientific notation.

Notice that the exponent is NOT determined by counting zeros, but by counting the number of decimal places that are moved when formulating the scientific notation. The decimal part in scientific notation always has only one digit to the left of the decimal point.

MATHEMATICS KNOWLEDGE

GEOMETRY

To tackle geometry questions on a mathematical reasoning test, there are a few formulas and rules that you need to know. This section takes you through those basic rules. It covers intersecting lines, triangles, squares and rectangles, and circles.

BASIC VOCABULARY

Vocabulary that is important to know for geometry questions includes the following:

Line Segment – A line is a set of all points between two endpoints. Lines have no area or width, only length.

Angle – An angle is the corner formed by two intersecting line segments, and it is measured in degrees. Degrees measurements show the magnitude of the "sweep" of the angle. In the figure below, angle x is shown as the measure between the two

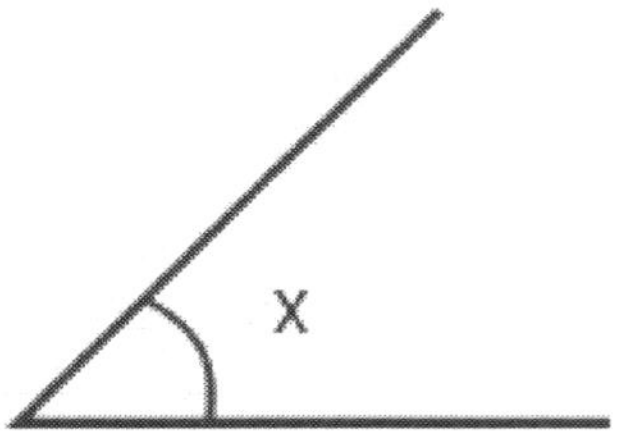

360° describes the angle measurement all the way around a full circle. Half of that, 180°, is the angle measurement across a straight line. Two lines at right angles to each other, called perpendicular lines, have an angle measurement of 90°.

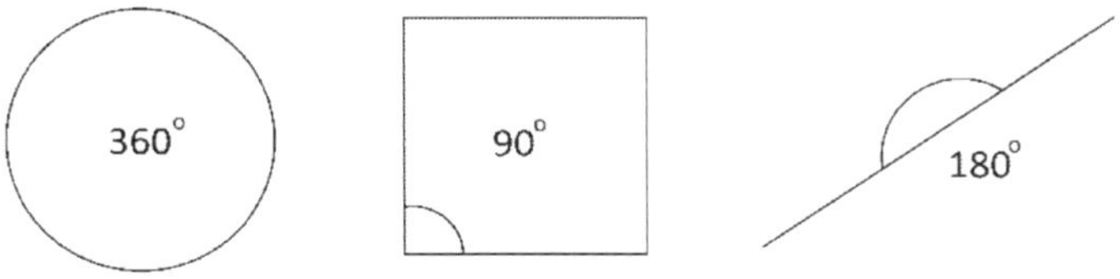

Area – The area is the measure of space inside a two-dimensional figure. It has units of length * length, or length^2. For example, rooms are described as being a number of square feet. Counties are described as being so many square miles. Each basic shape has a special formula for determining area.

Perimeter – The perimeter is the measure of the length around the outside of a figure.

Volume – For three-dimensional figures, the volume is the measure of space inside the figure. Volume has three dimensions: length * width * height. Because of this, it has units of length3 (cubic length). For example, you may have heard "cubic feet" used to describe the volume of something like a storage unit. This formula applies only to square and rectangular three-dimensional shapes. Other figures have their own formulas for determining volume.

INTERSECTING LINES

There are two important properties to know about pairs of intersecting lines:

1. They form angles that add up to 180° along the sides of each line.
2. They create two pairs of equal angles.

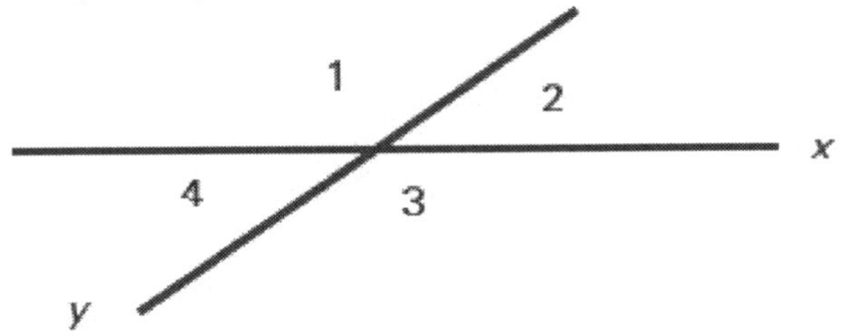

For example, in the diagram above, line x intersects line y, forming the four angles 1, 2, 3 and 4. Any two angles along one side of a line will add up to 180°:

Angle 1 + Angle 2 = 180°
Angle 2 + Angle 3 = 180°
Angle 3 + Angle 4 = 180°
Angle 4 + Angle 1 = 180°

All four of the angles added together would equal 360°:

Angle 1 + Angle 2 + Angle 3 + Angle 4 = 360°

The two angles DIAGONAL from each other must be equal. For the figure above, we know that:

Angle 1 = Angle 3
Angle 2 = Angle 4

This property is very useful: if you are given any one of the angles, you can immediately solve for the other three. If you are told that Angle 1 = 120°, then you know that Angle 2 = 180° - 120° = 60°. Since Angle 3 = Angle 1 and Angle 4 = Angle 2, you now know all four angles.

PARALLEL/PERPENDICULAR LINES

Parallel lines are lines that lie on the same 2-D plane (i.e., the page) and never intersect each other. The thing to remember about parallel lines is that if a line intersects two parallel lines, it will form a bunch of corresponding angles (like the ones discussed above). Also, you can never assume that two lines are parallel just from a diagram. You need to be told or given enough information that you can deduce it. Parallel lines have the same slope.

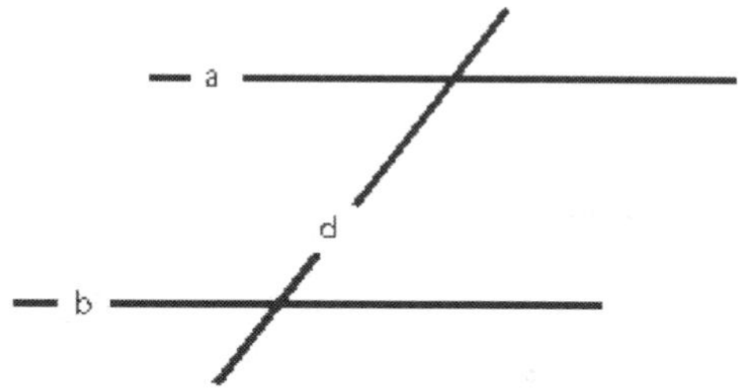

Lines a and b are parallel and are intersected by line d. In the diagram above, all four of the acute angles (the ones smaller than 90°) are equal to each other. All four of the obtuse angles (the ones greater than 90°) are equal to each other. Why? Because a line intersecting parallel lines forms equivalent angles. This is simply an expanded case of the intersecting lines concept discussed earlier.

SQUARES AND RECTANGLES

By definition, a square has four sides of equal length and four angles of 90°. A rectangle has two pairs of sides of equal length and four angles of 90°. This means that the sum of all four angles in a square or rectangle is 360°.

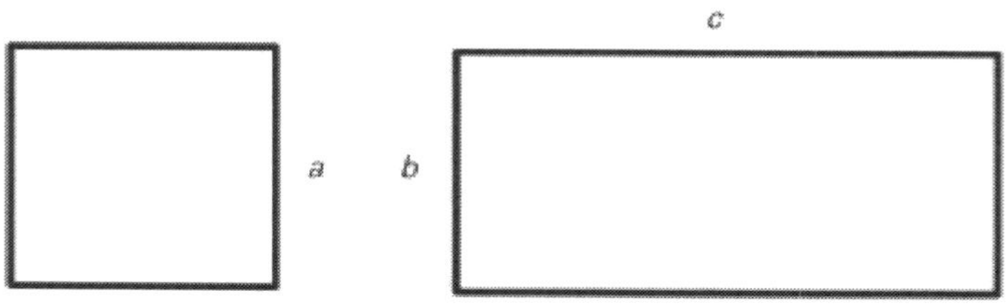

In the diagram above, the shape on the left is a square. So, if you are given the length of side a, you automatically know the length of every side. You already know the measure of every angle, because they are all 90° – the measure of right (perpendicular) angles.

The shape on the right is a rectangle. So, if you are given the length of side b, you know the length of the opposite side. However, you do not know the length of the longer two sides unless they are given.
The perimeter of a square is the sum of all four line segments. Since the line segments are equal, the equation is as follows:

Perimeter of a square = 4 * (side length)

The perimeter of the square above is 4a.

The perimeter of the rectangle is also the sum of its sides. However, since there are two pairs of equal length sides in a rectangle, the equation is as follows:

Perimeter of a rectangle = 2 * (long side length) + 2 * (short side length)

The perimeter of the rectangle above is 2b + 2c

The area of a square is its length times its width. Since length and width are the same for a square, the area is the length of one of its sides squared (that's where the term "squared" comes from) and the equation is as follows:

$$Area = a^2$$

For a rectangle, length times width is not equal to one side squared (it's not a square, so the sides are not all the same length). The equation for the area of a rectangle is as follows:

Area = b * c

TRIANGLES

A triangle is a polygon (closed shape) made of three-line segments. While the four angles in a square and rectangle always add up to 360°, the three angles in a triangle always add up to 180°. However, these angles are not always the same measure, as they are for squares and rectangles. Below are the different types of triangles:

EQUILATERAL
SIDES OF SAME LENGTH

ISOSCELES
TWO SIDES OF SAME LENGTH
TWO ANGLES OF SAME

RIGHT
ONE ANGLE OF 90°

The area of a triangle will always equal one half of the product of its base and its height. You can choose any side to be the base (the one at the bottom of the triangle is probably best), and the height of a triangle is the perpendicular line from the base to the opposite angle. The height is NOT the length of a side, unless the triangle is a right triangle. For example:

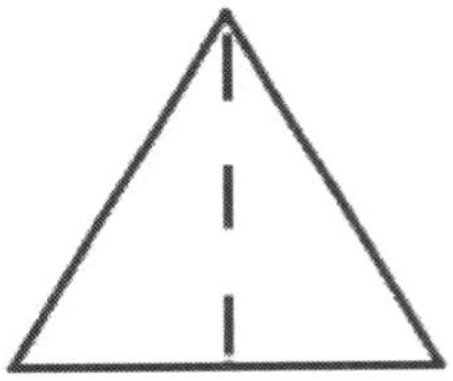

In this triangle, the bottom leg is the base, and the dotted line is the height. A = 1/2 (base * height)
Another important formula to know when working with triangles is the Pythagorean Theorem. This tells you how to relate the lengths of the sides of right triangles – the ones that include 90° angles.

In the diagram to right, you have right triangle ABC. You know it's a right triangle because it has a 90° angle – not because it looks like one. Never assume the measure of an angle without being given that information. Side c is called the hypotenuse, which is the longest side of a right triangle. Sides a, b and c are related to each other according to the Pythagorean Theorem:

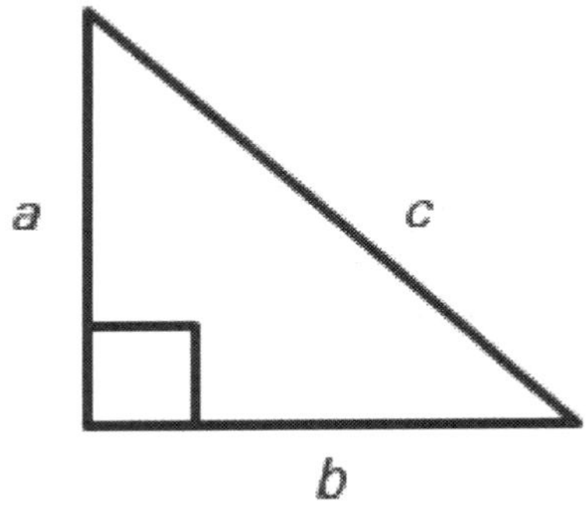

$$c^2 = a^2 + b^2$$

Regardless of how the sides of the right triangle are labeled, the length of the longest side squared is equal to the sum of the lengths of the two shorter sides, each squared. There will likely be a few problems that will require you to use this relationship to solve.

Here are some important details to remember about triangles:

- A triangle has three sides and three angles.
- ˜e angles of a triangle will always add up to 180°.
- A triangle is a "right triangle" if one of the angles is 90°.
- If a triangle is equilateral, all angles are 60°, and all sides are the same length.
- ˜e area of a triangle is one half times the base times the height.
- For right triangles, you can relate the lengths of the sides using the Pythagorean ˜eor em.

CIRCLES

A circle is a figure without sides. Instead, it has a circumference with a set of points equidistant from the center of the circle.

Here are some important details to remember about circles:

- ˜e measurement around the outside of a circle is called the circumference.
- ˜e line segment going from the center of the circle to the circumference is called the radius.
- ˜e line segment that goes across the entire circle, passing through the center, is the diameter.
- ˜e number of degr ees in the central angle of a circle is 360°.

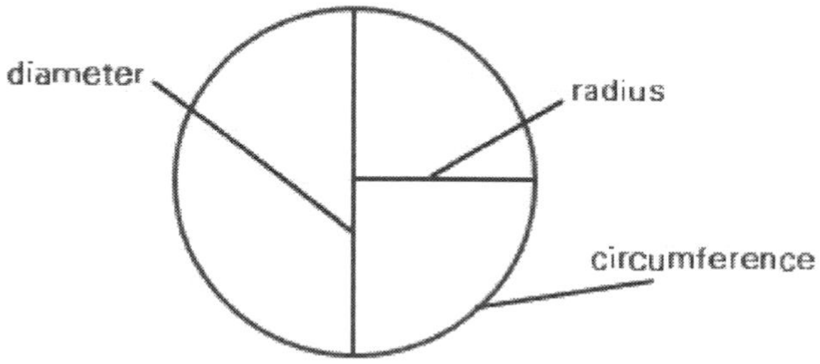

The circumference of a circle can be found using the following formula:

$$C = 2\pi r$$

In this formula, r is the radius (or the distance from the center of the circle to an outside point on the circle). If you are given the diameter, then you can find the circumference using this formula:

$$C = \pi d$$

The radius is twice the length of the diameter:

$$D = 2r$$

The area of a circle can be found using this formula:

$$A = \pi r^2$$

So, the area is equal to the radius squared times the constant π (pronounced pi). Sometimes, answer choices are given with π as a part of the value 2π , for example. When you see this, work out the problem without substituting the value of (approximately 3.14). You can, in fact, estimate that π is 3.14 or 22/7 in your calculations, but you'll end up with a decimal or fraction for your answer.

PRACTICE TEST 1

So, you think you're ready for Practice Test 1? Or maybe you just started, and you need to take the Pre-test. Either way, it's time to test what you know. Turn to the next page to begin.

MATHEMATICS

1. The number of students enrolled at Two Rivers Community College increased from 3,450 in 2010 to 3,864 in 2015. What was the percent increase?
   A. 9%
   B. 17%
   C. 12%
   D. 6%

---

2. Find the median in this series of numbers: 80, 78, 73, 69, 100.
   A. 69
   B. 73
   C. 78
   D. 80

---

3. Solve this equation: $\sqrt{11 * 44} =$
   A. 36
   B. 24
   C. 18
   D. 22

---

4. Amy drives her car until the gas gauge is down to 1/8 full, then she fills the tank to capacity by adding 14 gallons. What is the capacity of the gas tank?
   A. 16 gallons
   B. 18 gallons
   C. 20 gallons
   D. 22 gallons

---

5. Which of these numbers is largest?
   A. -345
   B. 42
   C. -17
   D. 3^4

---

6. Which of the following is a prime number?
   A. 81
   B. 49
   C. 59
   D. 77

---

7. The area of a triangle equals one-half the base times the height. Which of the following is the correct way to calculate the area of a triangle that has a base of 6 and a height of 9?
   A. $(6 + 9)/2$
   B. $\frac{1}{2}(6 + 9)$
   C. $2(6 * 9)$
   D. $\frac{(6)(9)}{2}$

8. Calculate the value of this expression: $2 + 6 * 3 * (3 * 4)^2 + 1$

   A. 2,595
   B. 5,185
   C. 3,456
   D. 6,464

9. If x ≥ 9, which of the following is a possible value of x?

   A. 2^3
   B. 9
   C. −34
   D. 8.5

10. Solve this equation: $-9 * -9 =$

    A. 18
    B. 0
    C. 81
    D. −81

11. Solve this equation: $x = a^2 * a^3$

    A. x = a
    B. x = a^5
    C. x = 1
    D. x = 0

12. Jean buys a textbook, a flash drive, a printer cartridge, and a ream of paper. The flash drive costs three times as much as the ream of paper. The textbook costs three times as much as the flash drive. The printer cartridge costs twice as much as the textbook. The ream of paper costs $10. How much does Jean spend altogether?

    A. $250
    B. $480
    C. $310
    D. $180

13. Which of the following is the smallest possible integer value of x in this equation: $x > 3^2 - 4$

    A. 3
    B. 5
    C. 6
    D. 7

14. In the graduating class at Emerson High School, 52% of the students are girls and 48% are boys. There are 350 students in the class. Among the girls, 98 plan to go to college. How many girls do not plan to go to college?

    A. 84
    B. 48
    C. 66
    D. 72

15. A cell phone on sale at 30% off costs $210. What was the original price of the phone?
   A. $240
   B. $273
   C. $300
   D. $320

16. Seven added to four-fifths of a number equals fifteen. What is the number?
   A. 10
   B. 15
   C. 20
   D. 25

17. If the sum of two numbers is 360, and their ratio is 7:3, what is the smaller number?
   A. 72
   B. 105
   C. 98
   D. 108

18. Alicia must have a score of 75% to pass a test of 80 questions. What is the greatest number of questions she can miss and still pass the test?
   A. 20
   B. 25
   C. 60
   D. 15

19. Carmen has a box that is 18 inches long, 12 inches wide, and 14 inches high. What is the volume of the box?
   A. 44 cubic inches
   B. 3,024 cubic inches
   C. 216 cubic inches
   D. 168 cubic inches

20. The lines in the diagram below are

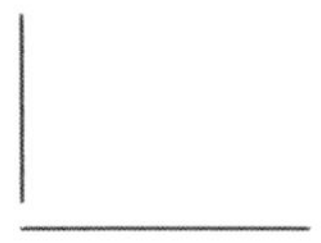

   A. Parallel
   B. Perpendicular
   C. Acute
   D. Obtuse

21. Find the area.

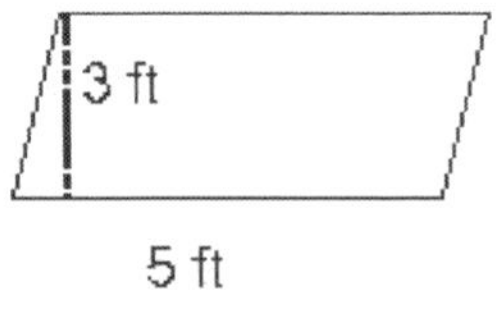

A. 16 square feet
B. 7.5 square feet
C. 15 square feet
D. 30 square feet

---

22. Which of these numbers is largest?
    A. 5/8
    B. 3/5
    C. 2/3
    D. 0.72

---

23. It took Charles four days to write a history paper. He wrote 5 pages on the first day, 4 pages on the second day, and 8 pages on the third day. If Charles ended up writing an average of 7 pages per day, how many pages did he write on the fourth day?
    A. 11
    B. 8
    C. 12
    D. 9

---

24. What is the approximate area of the portion of the square that is not covered by the circle?

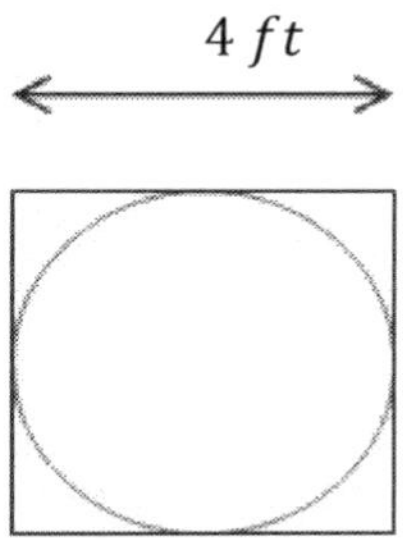

    A. 4.14 square feet
    B. 3.44 square feet
    C. 6.25 square feet
    D. 5.12 square feet

---

25. Which of the following is equivalent to the equation: $\frac{5}{mp} \div \frac{p}{4}$
    A. $\frac{5p}{4mp}$
    B. $\frac{20}{mp^2}$
    C. $\frac{20mp}{4p}$
    D. $\frac{4mp}{5p}$

---

26. Danvers is 8 miles due south of Carson and 6 miles due west of Baines. If a driver could drive in a straight line from Carson to Baines, how long would the trip be?
    A. 8 miles
    B. 10 miles
    C. 12 miles
    D. 14 miles

27. Lourdes rolls a pair of 6-sided dice. What is the probability that the result will equal 10?

A. $1/36$
B. $2/36$
C. $3/36$
D. $4/36$

28. Four friends plan to share equally the cost of a retirement gift. If one person drops out of the arrangement, the cost per person for the remaining three would increase by $12. What is the cost of the gift?

A. $144
B. $136
C. $180
D. $152

29. What is the factorial of 5?

A. 25
B. 5 and 1
C. 120
D. 125

30. Which digit is in the thousandths place in this number: 1,234.567

A. 1
B. 2
C. 6
D. 7

31. What is the mode in this set of numbers: 4, 5, 4, 8, 10, 4, 6, 7

A. 6
B. 4
C. 8
D. 7

32. Which of the following numbers is a perfect square?

A. 5
B. 15
C. 49
D. 50

33. Amanda makes $14 an hour as a bank teller, and Oscar makes $24 an hour as an auto mechanic. Both work eight hours a day, five days a week. Which of these equations can be used to calculate how much they make together in a five-day week?

A. $(14 + 24) * 8 * 5$
B. $\frac{14+24}{(8)(5)}$
C. $(14 + 24)(8 + 5)$
D. $14 + 24 * 8 * 5$

34. The population of Mariposa County in 2015 was 90% of its population in 2010. The population in 2010 was 145,000. What was the population in 2015?
    A. 160,000
    B. 142,000
    C. 120,500
    D. 130,500

35. What is the sum of 1/3 and 3/8?
    A. 3/24
    B. 4/11
    C. 17/24
    D. 15/16

36. In four years, Tom will be twice as old as Serena was three years ago. Tom is three years younger than Serena. How old are Tom and Serena now?
    A. Serena is 28, Tom is 25
    B. Serena is 7, Tom is 4
    C. Serena is 18, Tom is 15
    D. Serena is 21, Tom is 18

37. A rectangle's length is three times its width. The area of the rectangle is 48 square feet. How long are the sides?
    A. Length = 12, width = 4
    B. Length = 15, width = 5
    C. Length = 18, width = 6
    D. Length = 24, width = 8

38. Which of the following is the prime factorization of 24?
    A. 24 = 8 * 3
    B. 24 = 2 * 2 * 2 * 3
    C. 24 = 6 * 4
    D. 24 = 12 * 2

39. x is a positive integer. Dividing x by a positive number less than 1 will yield:
    A. A number greater than x
    B. A number less than x
    C. A negative number
    D. An irrational number

40. Solve this equation: $x = 8 - (-3)$
    A. x = 5
    B. x = −5
    C. x = 11
    D. x = −11

41. Which of the following statements is true?
    A. The square of a number is always less than the number.
    B. The square of a number may be either positive or negative.
    C. The square of a number is always a positive number.
    D. The square of a number is always greater than the number.

42. Marisol's score on a standardized test was ranked in the 78th percentile. If 660 students took the test, approximately how many students scored lower than Marisol?
    A. 582
    B. 515
    C. 612
    D. 486

43. Sam worked 40 hours at *d* dollars per hour and received a bonus of $50. His total earnings were $530. What was his hourly wage?
    A. $18
    B. $16
    C. $14
    D. $12

44. Solve for r in this equation: $p = 2r + 3$
    A. $r = 2p - 3$
    B. $r = p + 6$
    C. $r = \frac{p+3}{2}$
    D. $r = \frac{p-3}{2}$

45. What is the least common multiple of 8 and 10?
    A. 80
    B. 40
    C. 18
    D. 72

46. Solve this equation: $x = -12 \div -3$
    A. x = −4
    B. x = −15
    C. x = 9
    D. x = 4

47. Convert the improper fraction 17/6 to a mixed number.
    A. $2\frac{5}{6}$
    B. $3\frac{1}{6}$
    C. $\frac{6}{17}$
    D. $3\frac{5}{6}$

48. What value of q is a solution to this equation: 130 = q(−13)

A. 10

B. −10

C. 1

D. 10^2

49. Find the value of $a^2 + 6b$ when a = 3 and b = 0.5.

A. 12

B. 6

C. 9

D. 15

50. If the radius of the circle in this diagram is 4 inches, what is the perimeter of the square?

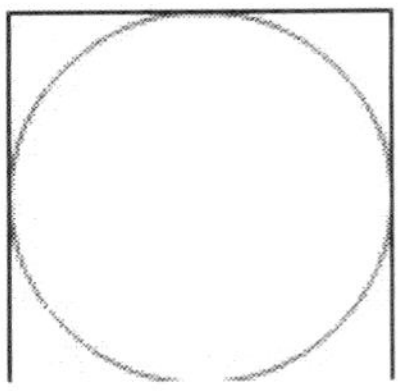

A. 24 inches

B. 32 inches

C. 64 inches

D. 96 inches

SCIENCE

1. Bronchial epithelial cell membranes possess which of the following?
   A. microvilli
   B. cilia
   C. flagella
   D. dendrites

---

2. Emulsification of fats requires ____ and occurs in the _____.
   Which of the following correctly completes the statement above?
   A. amylase; stomach;
   B. bile; stomach
   C. amylase; small intestine
   D. bile; small intestine

---

3. In immune functions involving T-helper cells, the T-helper cell most likely engages in which of the following?
   A. phagocytosis
   B. cell lysis
   C. circulating antibody production
   D. intercellular membrane binding

---

4. In a normal human, once blood is pumped out of the heart, which of the following statements is always true?
   A. It passes through capillaries before returning to the internal chambers of the heart
   B. It has been fully oxygenated
   C. It immediately enters the aorta
   D. It travels to the lungs before returning to the heart

---

5. Oxygen enters the circulatory system during
   A. inspiration only
   B. inspiration and the interval between inspiration and expiration only
   C. the interval between inspiration and expiration and during expiration only
   D. continuously throughout the entire respiratory cycle

---

6. The integrative functions of the nervous system require which of the following?
   A. sensory input
   B. hormonal regulation
   C. spinal cord reflexes
   D. effector cells

---

7. The duodenum releases which of the following biologically active proteins? Which of the following will open at appropriate intervals to allow stomach contents to pass into the duodenum?
   A. GE sphincter
   B. pyloric sphincter
   C. muscular sphincters
   D. gastroduodenal sphincter

8. Which of the following is NOT a capacity of the human innate immune system?
   A. phagocytosis of foreign cells
   B. stimulation of fever
   C. production of antibodies
   D. the release of and response to cytokines

---

9. Which of the following correctly describes the relative anatomical positional relationship between two anatomical structures in a normal human adult?
   A. The heart is ventral to the esophagus.
   B. The scapula is proximal to the vertebral column.
   C. The kidneys are medial to the abdominal aorta.
   D. The urinary bladder is rostral to the pancreas.

---

10. In humans, urea is produced in which of the following locations?
   A. the liver
   B. the kidney
   C. the pancreas
   D. red blood cells

---

11. In humans, which of the organs listed below does NOT receive supplies of both oxygenated and deoxygenated blood?
   A. the lungs
   B. the heart
   C. the liver
   D. the large intestine

---

12. In humans, which of the skeletal muscles listed below are more often than not under involuntary rather than voluntary control?
   A. the masseters
   B. the diaphragm
   C. the biceps
   D. the tongue

---

13. In humans, the majority (>50%) of water obtained through oral intake is absorbed into the body through which of the following?
   A. the oral mucosa and the esophagus
   B. the esophagus and the stomach
   C. the small intestines
   D. the large intestines

---

14. Which of the following cell types bind to PAMPs?
   A. plasma cells
   B. dendritic cells
   C. natural killer (NK) cells
   D. T-helper cells

15. In humans, which of the following is true regarding dietary intake of proteins?
   A. It does not occur in individuals who are strict vegetarians
   B. It must include a variety of proteins that consist of all 20 amino acids required for protein synthesis in the body
   C. Inadequate intake during childhood development can lead to the disease kwashiorkor.
   D. Breakdown begins when protein reaches the ileum of the small intestine.

16. Which hormone inhibits the release of follicle-stimulating hormone (FSH)?
   A. Somatostatin
   B. Luteinizing hormone (LH)
   C. Oxytocin
   D. Corticotropin-releasing hormone

17. What is the corresponding atomic weight if an atom has an atomic mass of 8 AMU?
   A. 8 AMU
   B. 8 grams
   C. Approximately the sum of the masses of the protons and neutrons
   D. Approximately the sum of all subatomic particles

18. For all biological nucleic acids, a nucleotide is composed of which of the following three components?
   A. a carboxylic acid, a nitrogenous base, and a pentose sugar
   B. an amino acid, a hexose sugar, and a nitrogenous base
   C. a phosphate group, a pentose sugar, and a nitrogenous base
   D. a phosphate group, a hexose sugar, and an amino acid

19. Where does the diffusion of oxygen from inhaled air to the bloodstream occur?
   A. bronchi
   B. lungs
   C. trachea
   D. alveoli

20. Which of the following cellular organelles do not possess an outer encapsulating organellar membrane?
   A. mitochondria
   B. ribosomes
   C. chloroplasts
   D. nuclei

21. Which of the following is true regarding the relationship between a complete segment of mRNA and the gene from which the mRNA segment was transcribed?

A. The mRNA segment base sequence is identical to the DNA gene base sequence
B. The mRNA segment base sequence is identical to the complementary DNA strand segment of the gene base sequence
C. The mRNA segment base sequence is identical to the complementary DNA strand segment of the gene base sequence except that adenine is substituted for thymine in the mRNA base sequence
D. The mRNA segment base sequence is identical to the complementary DNA strand segment of the gene base sequence except that uracil is substituted for thymine in the mRNA base sequence

---

22. Which pair of physical quantities is NOT a pair of SI units and comparable to British/English units?

A. Watts: Horsepower
B. Liters: Gallons
C. Newtons: Joule
D. All of the above are appropriate pairs

---

23. In a covalent bond, two atoms share electrons in order to fill their __________ as much as possible.

A. valence shells
B. electromagnetic fields
C. hydrocarbon molecules
D. isotope

---

24. What molecule is responsible for transmitting genetic information to a cell's ribosomes?

A. nucleosome proteins
B. mRNA
C. the sense strand of DNA
D. tRNA

---

25. What is the name for the testicles and ovaries of the male and female reproductive system?

A. gametes
B. gonads
C. offspring
D. GnRh

---

26. In human cells, which of the following statements correctly states a true principle of the processing of genetic information?

A. A single, unique sequence of genes codes for a single unique protein
B. A single, unique three-base codon will code for only one single, unique type of amino acid.
C. A single unique protein can only be coded for by a single, unique sequence of codons
D. A single unique protein can only be coded for by a single, unique sequence of DNA bases.

---

27. Where are the neurotransmitters in the peripheral nervous system released?

A. myelin sheath
B. synapse
C. sarcomere
D. ganglia

---

28. Using the common conversion factor between meters and feet, approximately how many miles would an 8K race be?

A. 4 miles
B. 4 ½ miles
C. 5 miles
D. 6 ½ miles

---

29. What is the electric charge of an atom with equal numbers of electrons and protons?

A. type 1 diabetes
B. neutrons = electrons
C. energy electric charge of zero
D. exactly one atomic mass unit

---

30. What cells mediate the cellular immune response by phagocytosis or endocytosis for recognition by T-cells.

A. antigen-presenting cells (APCs)
B. defensins
C. antibody-producing cells
D. -antigen affinity

---

31. An organized functional collection of adipose cells is considered to be which of the following

A. epithelial tissue
B. connective tissue
C. a syncytium
D. a gland

---

32. In chemical reactions where a catalyst participates, the catalyst-------of the reaction by ------ of the reaction

A. increases the efficiency of the reaction; increasing the activation energy
B. increases the efficiency of the reaction; decreasing the activation energy
C. increases the rate of the reaction; increasing the activation energy
D. increases the rate of the reaction; decreasing the activation energy

---

33. Which of the following is

A. $1s^2\ 2s^2\ 2p^6$
B. $1s^2\ 2s^2\ 3s^2\ 3p^4$
C. $2s^2\ 2p2\ 3s^2\ 3p^2\ 3d^2$
D. $6s^2\ 2p^2$

---

34. In biological chemical systems, an increase in the activity of an enzyme indicates that which of the following has occurred?

A. The enzyme has increased its optimum functional pH range
B. The enzyme has increased its optimum functional temperature range
C. The enzyme has increased its effect on the rate of a chemical reaction
D. The enzyme has increased the total number of reactions that it is capable of catalyzing.

---

35. Which are molecules that dissociate partially or near completely into hydrogen ions with pH values lower than pure liquid water and high concentration of H^+?

A. basic

B. acidic
C. neutral
D. weak H^+ ion concentration

---

36. Which is a protein able to stretch and relax as muscles contract and relax?
    A. keratin
    B. elastin
    C. ligament
    D. collagen

---

37. Which of the following is the site a site of steroid hormone production?
    A. the pancreas
    B. the adrenal gland
    C. the thyroid
    D. the thymus

---

38. In the unbalanced oxidation-reduction reaction $CH_4 + O_2 ---> CO_2 + H_2O$, which answer choice below shows the correct, balanced half-reaction for oxygen?
    A. $O_2 ---> 2O^- + 2e^-$
    B. $2O_2 + 8e^- ---> 4O^{2-}$
    C. $4H^+ + 2O ----> 2H_2O^+$
    D. $CH_4 + O_2 ---> 1/2CO_2 + 1/2H_2O$

---

39. What type of intermolecular bond can not be broken by human digestion?
    A. electromagnetic
    B. glyosidic
    C. polar
    D. covalent

---

40. Water molecules in the liquid state will have ________ intermolecular bonding compared to the intermolecular bonding of water molecules in the solid state.
    Which of the following correctly completes the statement above?
    A. the same type of
    B. stronger
    C. a different type of
    D. no

---

41. What is the charge of an atom when the number of electrons exceeds the number of protons?
    A. neutral
    B. positive
    C. negative
    D. the charge is unknown

---

42. In a single chromosome________
    Which of the answer choices correctly completes the statement above?
    A. every DNA strand contains genes
    B. there are always two copies of every gene

C. every functional gene can be transcribed into a mRNA molecule
D. there are at least 2 alleles for every gene

---

43. Which of the sequences listed in the answer choices show the correct RNA transcript of the DNA sequence listed below?
DNA: AGC TAC CCG
RNA: ___ ___ ___
A. TCG ATG GGC
B. UCG AUG GGC
C. TCG UTG GGC
D. CTA GCA AAT

---

44. Ribosome construction occurs in which of the following locations inside of a cell?
A. rough endoplasmic reticulum
B. peroxisomes
C. lysosomes
D. nucleoli

---

45. In terms of processing of genetic information, ribosomes are to proteins as ______ is/are to DNA. Which of the following completes the analogy shown above?
A. amino acids
B. codons
C. RNA polymerase
D. DNA polymerase

---

46. In double-stranded DNA, one strand is called the "sense" strand and the other is called the "antisense" strand. Which of the following occurs during replication of double-stranded DNA?
A. The sense strand is completely replicated before replication of the antisense strand begins.
B. The antisense strand is completely replicated before replication of the sense strand begins.
C. Either the sense or the antisense is replicated before replication of the complementary strand begins.
D. Replication of both strands occurs simultaneously.

---

47. What does the hypothalamus produce that is primarily responsible for improved mood?
A. glucagon
B. dopamine
C. homeostasis
D. follicle-stimulating hormone (FSH)

---

48. Which type of immunity are lymph nodes capable of triggering?
A. innate immunity
B. adaptive immunity
C. incompatibility
D. myeloid lineage immunity

---

49. What are the two general structural categories of nitrogenous bases in nucleic acids?
A. purines and pyrimidines

B. thymine and uracil
C. nucleotides and nucleosides
D. pyrimidines and hydroxyurea

---

50. What is the R group of the amino acid, lysine?
    A. H^+
    B. -OH
    C. CH_3
    D. NH_2

ENGLISH & READING

1. Which of the following choices best completes this sentence?
   When asked if the sleeping pill had __________ him at all, the man replied that it had had no __________; nonetheless, he realized that he __________not attempt to drive his car that evening.
   A. affected; effect; ought
   B. affected; effect; aught
   C. effected; affect; ought
   D. effected; affect; aught

---

2. Which sentence makes best use of grammatical conventions for clarity and concision?
   A. Hiking along the trail, the birds chirped loudly and interrupted our attempt at a peaceful nature walk.
   B. The birds chirped loudly, attempting to hike along the nature trail we were interrupted.
   C. Hiking along the trail, we were assailed by the chirping of birds, which made our nature walk hardly the peaceful exercise we had wanted.
   D. Along the nature trail, our walk was interrupted by loudly chirping birds in our attempt at a nature trail.

---

3. Which word from the following sentence is an adjective?

A really serious modern-day challenge is finding a way to consume real food in a world of overly processed food products.
   A. really
   B. challenge
   C. consume
   D. processed

---

4. To improve sentence fluency, how could you state the information below in a single sentence? My daughter was in a dance recital. I attended it with my husband. She received an award. We were very proud.
   A. My daughter, who was in a dance recital, received an award, which made my husband and I, who were in attendance, very proud.
   B. My husband and I attended my daughter's dance recital and were very proud when she received an award.
   C. Attending our daughter's dance recital, my husband and I were very proud to see he rreceive an award.
   D. Dancing in a recital, my daughter received an award which my husband and I, who were there, very proud.

---

5. Which sentence is punctuated correctly?
   A. Since the concert ended very late I fell asleep in the backseat during the car ride home.
   B. Since the concert ended very late: I fell asleep in the backseat during the car ride home.
   C. Since the concert ended very late; I fell asleep in the backseat during the car ride home.
   D. Since the concert ended very late, I fell asleep in the backseat during the car ride home.

6. Which of the choices below best completes the following sentence? Negotiations with the enemy are never fun, but during times of war ____________ a necessary evil.
   A. its
   B. it's
   C. their
   D. they're

---

7. Which of the verbs below best completes the following sentence?
The a cappela group ___________ looking forward to performing for the entire student body at the graduation ceremony.
   A. is
   B. are
   C. was
   D. be

---

8. What kind of sentence is this? I can't believe her luck!
   A. Declarative
   B. Imperative
   C. Exclamatory
   D. Interrogative

---

9. Identify the error in this sentence:
Irregardless of the expense, it is absolutely imperative that all drivers have liability insurance to cover any personal injury that may be suffered during a motor vehicle accident.
   A. Irregardless
   B. Imperative
   C. Liability
   D. Suffered

---

10. Which of the following sentences is grammatically correct?
   A. Between you and me, I brang back less books from my dorm room than I needed to study for my exams.
   B. Between you and I, I brought back less books from my dorm room then I needed to study for my exams.
   C. Between you and me, I brought back fewer books from my dorm room than I needed to study for my exam.
   D. Between you and me, I brought back fewer books from my dorm room then I needed to study for my exams.

---

11. Choose from the answers to complete this sentence with the proper verb and antecedent agreement:
Neither of ____________ ____________ able to finish our supper.
   A. we; were
   B. we; was
   C. us; were
   D. us; was

12. Which word in the following sentence is a noun?
The library books are overdue.
   A. The
   B. library
   C. books
   D. overdue

---

13. Which of the following is a simple sentence?
   A. Mary and Samantha ran and skipped and hopped their way home from school every day.
   B. Mary liked to hop but Samantha preferred to skip.
   C. Mary loved coloring yet disliked when coloring was assigned for math homework.
   D. Samantha thought Mary was her best friend but she was mistaken.

---

14. Which of the following is NOT a simple sentence?
   A. Matthew and Thomas had been best friends since grade school.
   B. Matthew was tall and shy, and Thomas was short and talkative.
   C. Matthew liked to get Thomas to pass notes to the little red-haired girl in the back row of math class.
   D. Matthew and Thomas would tease Mary and Samantha on their way home from school every day.

---

15. Which of the following sentences is punctuated correctly?
   A. "Theres a bus coming so hurry up and cross the street!" yelled Bob to the old woman.
   B. "There's a bus coming, so hurry up and cross the street", yelled Bob, to the old woman.
   C. "Theres a bus coming, so hurry up and cross the street,"! yelled Bob to the old woman.
   D. "There's a bus coming, so hurry up and cross the street!" yelled Bob to the old woman.

---

16. Which of the following sentences is punctuated correctly?
   A. It's a long to-do list she left for us today: make beds, wash breakfast dishes, go grocery shopping, do laundry, cook dinner, and read the twins a bedtime story.
   B. Its a long to-do list she left for us today; make beds; wash breakfast dishes; go grocery shopping; do laundry; cook dinner; and read the twins a bedtime story.
   C. It's a long to-do list she left for us today: make beds; wash breakfast dishes; go grocery shopping; do laundry; cook dinner; and read the twins a bedtime story.
   D. Its a long to-do list she left for us today: make beds, wash breakfast dishes, go grocery shopping, do laundry, cook dinner, and read the twins a bedtime story.

---

17. Which of the following sentences is written in the first person?
   A. My room was a mess so my mom made me clean it before I was allowed to leave the house.
   B. Her room was a mess so she had to clean it before she left for the concert.
   C. You had better clean up your room before your mom comes home!
   D. Sandy is a slob and never cleans up her own room until her mom makes her.

18. Which sentence follows the rules for capitalization?
    A. My second grade Teacher's name was Mrs. Carmicheal.
    B. The Pope gave a very emotional address to the crowd after Easter Sunday mass.
    C. The president of France is meeting with President Obama later this week.
    D. My family spent our summer vacations at grandpa Joe's cabin in the Finger Lakes region.

19. The girl returning home after her curfew found the ___________ up the stairs to her bedroom maddening as it seemed every step she took on the old staircase yielded a loud ___________.
    Which of the following completes the sentence above?
    A. clime; creak
    B. clime; creek
    C. climb; creek
    D. climb; creak

20. By this time next summer, ____________ my college coursework. Which of the following correctly completes the sentence above?
    A. I did complete
    B. I completed
    C. I will complete
    D. I will have completed

21. Which of the following choices best completes this sentence?
    The teacher nodded her ___________ to the classroom _____________ who was teaching a portion of the daily lesson for the first time.
    A. assent; aide
    B. assent; aid
    C. ascent; aide
    D. ascent; aid

22. Which of the following sentences is grammatically correct?
    A. No one has offered to let us use there home for the office's end-of-year picnic.
    B. No one have offered to let we use their home for the office's end-of-year picnic.
    C. No one has offered to let ourselves use their home for the office's end-of-year picnic.
    D. No one has offered to let us use their home for the office's end-of-year picnic.

23. Which choice most effectively combines the information in the following sentences?
The tornado struck. It struck without warning. It caused damage. The damage was extensive.
    A. Without warning, the extensively damaging tornado struck.
    B. Having struck without warning, the damage was extensive with the tornado.
    C. The tornado struck without warning and caused extensive damage.
    D. Extensively damaging, and without warning, struck the tornado.

24. Which word in the sentence below is a verb?
Carrying heavy boxes to the attic caused her to throw out her back.

A. Carrying
B. to
C. caused
D. out

25. Which choice below most effectively combines the information in the following sentences? His lecture was boring. I thought it would never end. My eyelids were drooping. My feet were going numb.

A. His never-ending lecture made my eyelids droop, and my feet were going numb.
B. My eyelids drooping and my feet going numb, I thought his boring lecture would never end.
C. His lecture was boring and would not end; it made my eyelids droop and my feet go numb.
D. Never-ending, his boring lecture caused me to have droopy eyelids and for my feet to go numb.

26. Which choice below correctly completes this sentence?
Comets ___________ balls of dust and ice, ___________ leftover materials that ___________ planets during the formation of ___________ solar system.

A. Comets is balls of dust and ice, comprised of leftover materials that were not becoming planets during the formation of its solar system.
B. Comets are balls of dust and ice, comprising leftover materials that are not becoming planets during the formation of our solar system.
C. Comets are balls of dust and ice, comprised of leftover materials that became planets during the formation of their solar system.
D. Comets are balls of dust and ice, comprised of leftover materials that did not become planets during the formation of our solar system.

Questions 27-35 are based on the following passage about Penny Dreadfuls Victorian era Britain experienced social changes that resulted in increased literacy rates. With the rise of capitalism and industrialization, people began to spend more money on entertainment, contributing to the popularization of the novel. Improvements in printing resulted in the production of newspapers, as well as, Englands' more fully recognizing the singular concept of reading as a form of leisure; it was, of itself, a new industry. An increased capacity for travel via the invention of tracks, engines, and the coresponding railway distribution created both a market for cheap popular literature, and the ability for it to be circulated on a large scale.

The first penny serials were published in the 1830s to meet this demand. The serials were priced to be affordable to working-class readers, and were considerably cheaper than the serialized novels of authors such as Charles Dickens, which cost a shilling (twelve pennies) per part. Those who could not afford a penny a week, working class boys often formed clubs sharing the cost, passed the booklets, who were flimsy, from reader to reader. Other enterprising youngsters would collect a number of consecutive parts, then rent the volume out to friends.

The stories themselves were reprints, or sometimes rewrites, of gothic thrillers, as well as new stories about famous criminals. Other serials were thinly-disguised plagiarisms of popular contemporary literature. The penny dreadfuls were influential since they were in the words of one commentator the most alluring and low-priced form of escapist reading available to ordinary youth.

In reality, the serial novels were overdramatic and sensational, but generally harmless. If anything, the penny dreadfuls, although obviously not the most enlightening or inspiring of literary selections, resulted in increasingly literate youth in the Industrial period. The wide circulation of this sensationalist literature, however, contributed to an ever greater fear of crime in mid-Victorian Britain.

27. Which of the following is the correct punctuation for the following sentence from paragraph 1?
    A. NO CHANGE
    B. Improvements in printing resulted in the production of newspapers, as well as England's more fully recognizing the singular concept of reading as a form of leisure; it was, of itself, a new industry.
    C. Improvements in printing resulted in the production of newspapers, as well as Englands more fully recognizing the singular concept of reading as a form of leisure; it was, of itself, a new industry.
    D. Improvements in printing resulted in the production of newspapers as well as, England's more fully recognizing the singular concept of reading as a form of leisure; it was, of itself, a new industry.

---

28. In the first sentence of paragraph 1, which of the following words should be capitalized?
    A. era
    B. social
    C. literacy
    D. rates

---

29. In the last sentence of paragraph 1, which of the following words is misspelled?
    A. capacity
    B. via
    C. corresponding
    D. cheap

---

30. In the first sentence of the paragraph 2, "this demand" refers to which of the following antecedents in paragraph 1?
    A. travel
    B. leisure
    C. industry
    D. market

---

31. Which of the following sentences is the clearest way to express the ideas in the third sentence of paragraph 2?
    A. A penny a week, working class boys could not afford these books; they often formed sharing clubs that were passing the flimsy booklets around from one reader to another reader.
    B. Clubs were formed to buy the flimsy booklets by working class boys who could not afford a penny a week that would share the cost, passing from reader to reader the flimsy booklets.
    C. Working class boys who could not afford a penny a week often formed clubs that would share the cost, passing the flimsy booklets from reader to reader.
    D. Sharing the cost were working class boys who could not afford a penny a week; they often formed clubs and, reader to reader, passed the flimsy booklets around.

---

32. Which word in the first sentence of paragraph 3 should be capitalized?
    A. stories
    B. gothic
    C. thrillers
    D. criminals

33. Which of the following versions of the final sentence of paragraph 3 is correctly punctuated?
   A. The penny dreadfuls were influential since they were in the words of one commentator; the most alluring and low-priced form of escapist reading available to ordinary youth.
   B. The penny dreadfuls were influential since they were, in the words of one commentator, "the most alluring and low-priced form of escapist reading available to ordinary youth".
   C. The penny dreadfuls were influential since they were, in the words of one commentator, the most alluring and low-priced form of escapist reading available to ordinary youth.
   D. The penny dreadfuls were influential since they were in the words of one commentator "the most alluring and low-priced form of escapist reading available to ordinary youth."

34. In this first sentence of paragraph 4, which of the following words is a noun?
   A. serial
   B. novels
   C. sensational
   D. generally

35. In the last sentence of paragraph 4, which of the following words is an adjective?
   A. circulation
   B. literature
   C. however
   D. greater

36. The author wants to add a sentence to the passage that would list some of the books which were plagiarized into penny dreadfuls. Which paragraph would be the best place to add this information?
   A. Paragraph 1
   B. Paragraph 2
   C. Paragraph 3
   D. Paragraph 4

Questions 37-43 are based on the following passage about Martin Luther King Jr.

Martin Luther King Jr. was an American baptist minister and activist who was a leader in the African-American Civil Rights Movement. He is best known for his role in the advancement of civil rights using non-violent civil disobedience based on his Christian beliefs. In the United States, his racial equality efforts, and his staunchly advocating civil rights is among, undoubtedly, culturally the most important contributions made by King to last century's society.

King became a civil rights activist early in his career. In 1955, he led the Montgomery bus boycott, and in 1957 he helped found the Southern Christian Leadership Conference (SCLC), serving as its first president. With the SCLC, King led an unsuccessful 1962 struggle against segregation in Albany, Georgia, and helped organize the 1963 nonviolent protests in Birmingham, Alabama. King also helped to organize the 1963 March on Washington where he delivered his famous I Have a Dream speech. There, he established his reputation as the greatest orator in American history.

On October 14, 1964, King justly received the Nobel Piece Prize for combating racial inequality through nonviolent resistance. In 1965, he helped to organize the famous Selma to Montgomery marches, and the following year he and SCLC took the movement north to Chicago to work on eliminating the unjust and much-despised segregated housing there. In the final years of his life, King expanded his focus to include opposition towards poverty and the Vietnam War, and he gave a famous speech in 1967 entitled "Beyond Vietnam". This speech alienated many of his liberal allies in government who supported the war, but to his credit King never allowed politics to dictate the path of his noble works.

In 1968, King was planning a national occupation of Washington, D.C., to be called the Poor People's Campaign, when he was assassinated on April 4 in Memphis, Tennessee. His violent death was, not surprisingly, followed by riots in many U.S. cities.

King was posthumously awarded the Presidential Medal of Freedom and the Congressional Gold Metal. Martin Luther King, Jr. Day was established as a holiday in numerous cities and states beginning in 1971, and eventually became a U.S. federal holiday in 1986. Since his tragic death, numerous streets in the U.S. have been renamed in his honor, and a county in Washington State was also renamed for him. The Martin Luther King, Jr. Memorial on the National Mall in Washington, D.C., was dedicated in 2011.

37. In the first sentence of paragraph 1, which of the following words should be capitalized?

A. baptist
B. minister
C. activist
D. leader

---

38. Which is the best rewording for clarity and concision of this sentence from paragraph 1?

A. His efforts to achieve racial equality in the United States, and his staunch public advocacy of civil rights are undoubtedly among the most important cultural contributions made to society in the last century.
B. His efforts achieving equality in the United States, and to staunchly advocate civil rights are undoubtedly among the most important contributions culturally and societally made in the last century.
C. Racial equality and civil rights, staunchly advocated by King in the United States, are, without a doubt, last century's greatest contributions, in a cultural way, to society.
D. Last century, King made cultural contributions to racial equality and civil rights, which are undoubtedly the greatest made in the previous century.

---

39. Which of the following found in paragraph 2 should be placed inside quotation marks?

A. Montgomery bus boycott
B. Southern Christian Leadership Conference
C. March on Washington
D. I Have a Dream

---

40. In the first sentence of paragraph 3, which of the following words is misspelled?

A. received
B. Piece
C. combating
D. racial

---

41. In the first sentence of paragraph 5, which of the following words is misspelled?

A. Posthumously
B. Presidential
C. Medal
D. Metal

42. Which of the following sentences from the passage provides context clues about the author's feelings in regard to King?

A. He is best known for his role in the advancement of civil rights using non-violent civil disobedience based on his Christian beliefs. (P. 1)

B. King also helped to organize the 1963 March on Washington where he delivered his famous I Have a Dream speech. (P. 2)

C. This speech alienated many of his liberal allies in government who supported the war, but to his credit King never allowed politics to dictate the path of his noble works. (P. 3)

D. King was posthumously awarded the Presidential Medal of Freedom and the Congressional Gold Metal. (P. 5)

---

43. The author is considering adding a paragraph about King's family to the passage. Should he or she do this?

A. Yes, because it adds needed personal details to the passage.

B. Yes, because it would elaborate on information already provided in the passage.

C. No, because the passage is about King's public life and works, and information about his family would be irrelevant.

D. No, because information about his family has already been included and an additional paragraph on that topic would be redundant.

---

44. Which of the following sentences uses correct punctuation for dialogue?

A. "Hey, can you come here a second"? asked Marie.

B. She thought about his offer briefly and then responded. "I think I will have to pass".

C. "I am making pancakes for breakfast. Does anybody want some?" asked mom.

D. The conductor yelled "All aboard"! and then waited for last minute travelers to board the train.

---

45. Which of the following is a compound sentence?

A. She and I drove to the play together.

B. I woke up early that morning and began to do long-neglected household chores.

C. The long-separated cousins ran and jumped and sang and played all afternoon.

D. I trembled when I saw him: his face was white as a ghost.

---

46. Which of the following is the best order for the sentences below in forming a logical paragraph?

A. A, B, C, D, E

B. A, C, E, B, D

C. A, D, B, D, E

D. A, C, E, D, B

A. Walt Disney was a shy, self-deprecating and insecure man in private but adopted a warm and outgoing public persona.

B. His film work continues to be shown and adapted; his studio maintains high standards in its production of popular entertainment, and the Disney amusement parks have grown in size and number to attract visitors in several countries.

C. However he had high standards and high expectations of those with whom he worked.

D. He nevertheless remains an important figure in the history of animation and in the cultural history of the United States, where he is considered a national cultural icon.

E. His reputation changed in the years after his death, from a purveyor of homely patriotic values to a representative of American imperialism.

47. Which of the choices below is the meaning of the word "adopted" in the following sentence?
Walt Disney was a shy, self-deprecating and insecure man in private but adopted a warm and outgoing public persona.

A. took
B. began to use
C. began to have
D. legally cared for as one's own child

---

48. Which of the following sentences is written in the second person?

A. You had better call and RSVP to the party right away before you forget.
B. She had every intention of calling with a prompt reply to the invitation, but the week got hectic and she forgot.
C. I am utterly hopeless at remembering things, so I will set up a calendar reminder for myself to call Jan about the party.
D. "Did you forget to RSVP to the party?!" asked her exasperated roommate.

---

49. Which of the following sentences shows proper pronoun-antecedent agreement?

A. The author published several best-selling novels; some of it was made into films that were not as popular.
B. Everyone should bring their parents to the town-wide carnival.
C. Smart companies will do what it takes to hold onto its best employees.
D. Parents are reminded to pick up their children from school promptly at 2:30.

---

50. Which of the following sentences shows proper subject-verb agreement?

A. Danny is one of the only students who have lived up to his responsibilities as a newspaper staff member.
B. One of my friends are going to be on a TV series starting this fall.
C. Rice and beans, my favorite meal, reminds me of my native country Puerto Rico.
D. Most of the milk we bought for the senior citizens' luncheons have gone bad.

ANSWERS PRACTICE TEST 1

MATHEMATICS

1 C. 12%

To find the percent increase, you first need to know the amount of the increase. Enrollment went from 3,450 in 2010 to 3,864 in 2015. This is an increase of 414. Now, to find the percent of the increase, divide the amount of the increase by the original amount:

$$414 \div 3{,}450 = 0.12$$

To convert a decimal to a percent, move the decimal point two places to the right:

$$0.12 = 12\%$$

When a question asks for the percent increase or decrease, divide the amount of the increase or decrease by the original amount.

---

2 C. 78

To find the median in a series of numbers, arrange the numbers in order from smallest to largest:

69, 73, 78, 80, 100

The number in the center is the median. If there are an even number of numbers in the series, for example:

34, 46, 52, 54, 67, 81

then the median will be the average of the two numbers in the center. In this example, the median will be 53 (the average of 52 and 54). Remember: the median is not the same as the average.

---

3 D. 22

This question asks you to find the square root of 11 times 44. First, do the multiplication: 11 * 44 = 484. Now multiply each of the possible answers by itself to see which one is the square root of 484.

---

4 A. 16 gallons

Amy drives her car until the gas tank is 1/8 full. This means that it is 7/8 empty. She fills it by adding 14 gallons. In other words, 14 gallons is 7/8 of the tank's capacity. Draw a simple diagram to represent the gas tank.

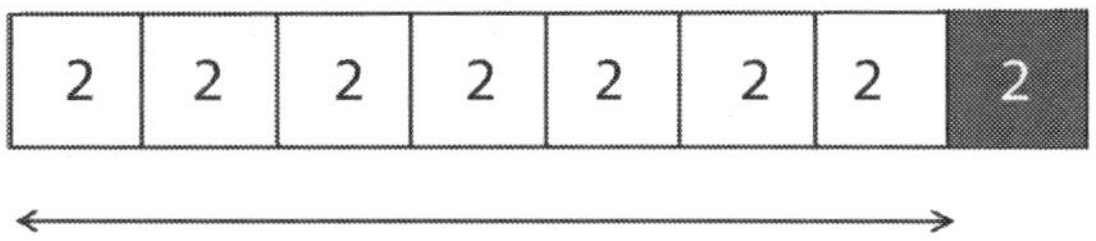

7/8 = 14

You can see that each eighth of the tank is 2 gallons. So the capacity of the tank is 2 * 8, or 16.

---

5 D. 3^4

Positive numbers are larger than negative numbers, so this limits the possible answers to 42 and 3^4. 3^4 equals 81 (3 * 3 * 3 * 3).

---

6 C. 59

A prime number is a whole number greater than 1 that can be divided evenly only by itself and 1. In this question, only 59 fits that definition. 81 is not prime because it can be divided evenly by 9; 49 is not prime because it can be divided evenly by 7; and 77 is not prime because it can be divided evenly by 7 and 11.

7 D. $\frac{(6)(9)}{2}$

The area of a triangle is one-half the product of the base and the height. Choices A and B are incorrect because they add the base and the height instead of multiplying them. Choice C is incorrect because it multiplies the product of the base and the height by 2 instead of dividing it by 2.

---

8 A. 2,595

The steps in evaluating a mathematical expression must be carried out in a certain order, which is called "the order of operations." These are the steps in order:

Parentheses: The first step is to do any operations in parentheses.

Exponents: Then do any steps that involve exponents.

Multiply and Divide: Multiply and divide from left to right.

Add and Subtract: Add and subtract from left to right.

One way to remember this order is to use this sentence:

Please **E**xcuse **M**y **D**ear **A**unt **S**ally.

To evaluate the expression in this question, follow these steps:

Multiply the numbers in Parentheses: 3 * 4 = 12

Apply the Exponent 2 to the number in parentheses: 122 = 144

Multiply: 6 * 3 * 144 = 2,592

Add: 2 + 2,592 + 1 = 2,595

---

9 B. 9

The symbol ≥ means "greater than or equal to." The only answer that is greater than or equal to 9 is 9.

---

10 C. 81

When two numbers with the same sign (both positive or both negative) are multiplied, the answer is a positive number. When two numbers with different signs (one positive and the other negative) are multiplied, the answer is negative.

---

11 B. $x = a^5$

When multiplying numbers that have the same base and different exponents, keep the base the same and add the exponents. In this case, $a^2 * a^3$ becomes $a^{(2+3)}$ or a^5.

---

12 C. $310

The costs of all these items can be expressed in terms of the cost of the ream of paper. Use x to represent the cost of a ream of paper. The flash drive costs three times as much as the ream of paper, so it costs 3x. The textbook costs three times as much as the flash drive, so it costs 9x. The printer cartridge costs twice as much as the textbook, so it costs 18x. So now we have:

$$x + 3x + 9x + 18x = 31x$$

The ream of paper costs $10, so 31x (the total cost) is $310.

13 C. 6

Solve the equation:

$$x > 3^2 - 4$$
$$x > 9 - 4$$
$$x > 5$$

We know that x is greater than 5, so the answer could be either 6 or 7. The question asks for the smallest possible value of x, so the correct answer is 6.

---

14 A. 84

First, find the number of girls in the class. Convert 52% to a decimal by moving the decimal point two places to the left:

$$52\% = .52$$

Now, multiply .52 times the number of students in the class:

$$.52 * 350 = 182$$

Of the 182 girls, 98 plan to go to college, so 84 do not plan to go to college.

$$182 - 98 = 84$$

---

15 C. $300

If the phone was on sale at 30% off, the sale price was 70% of the original price. So

$210 = 70% of x

where x is the original price of the phone. When you convert 70% to a decimal, you get:

$210 = .70 * x

To isolate x on one side of the equation, divide both sides of the equation by .70. You find that x = $300.

---

16 A. 10

Use the facts you are given to write an equation:

$$7 + 4/5n = 15$$

First, subtract 7 from both sides of the equation. You get:

$$4/5n = 8$$

Now divide both sides of the equation by 4/5. To divide by a fraction, invert the fraction (4/5 becomes 5/4) and multiply:

$$n = \frac{8}{1} * \frac{5}{4}$$
$$n = \frac{40}{4}$$
$$n = 10$$

---

17 D. 108

The ratio of the two numbers is 7:3. This means that the larger number is 7/10 of 360 and the smaller number is 3/10 of 360.

$$\frac{3}{10} * \frac{360}{1} = \frac{1080}{10} = 108$$

18 A. 20

Alicia must have a score of 75% on a test with 80 questions. To find how many questions she must answer correctly, first convert 75% to a decimal by moving the decimal point two places to the left: 75% = .75. Now multiply .75 times 80:

$$.75 * 80 = 60.$$

Alicia must answer 60 questions correctly, but the question asks how many questions can she miss. If she must answer 60 correctly, then she can miss 20.

---

19 B. 3,024 cubic inches

The formula for the volume of a rectangular solid is length * width * height. So the volume of this box is:

$$18 * 12 * 14 = 3{,}024\ cubic\ inches$$

---

20 B. Perpendicular

Lines that form a right angle are called perpendicular.

---

21 C. 15 square feet

This shape is called a parallelogram. The area of a parallelogram equals the base times the height.

---

22 D. 0.72

The simplest way to answer this question is to convert the fractions to decimals. To convert a fraction to a decimal, divide the numerator (the top number) by the denominator (the bottom number).

$$\frac{5}{8} = 0.625$$
$$\frac{3}{5} = 0.6$$
$$\frac{2}{3} = 0.67$$

The largest number is 0.72.

---

23 A. 11

If Charles wrote an average of 7 pages per day for four days, he wrote a total of 28 pages. He wrote a total of 17 pages on the first three days, so he must have written 11 pages on the fourth day.

---

24 B. 3.44 square feet

Find the area of the square by multiplying the length of a side by itself. The area of the square is 16 square feet. Now find the area of the circle by using this formula:

$$A = \pi r^2$$

The symbol p equals approximately 3.14. The letter r is the radius of the circle. In this case, r is half the width of the square (or 2), so r2 is 4. Therefore, the area of the circle is

$$A = 3.14 * 4$$
$$A = 12.56$$

To find the area of the square that is not covered by the circle, subtract 12.56 square feet from 16 square feet.

25 B. $\frac{20}{mp^2}$

To divide by a fraction, invert the second fraction and multiply.

So $\frac{20}{\text{mp}} \div \frac{\text{p}}{4}$ becomes $\frac{5}{\text{mp}} * \frac{4}{\text{p}}$

$$\frac{5}{\text{mp}} * \frac{4}{\text{p}} = \frac{20}{\text{mp}^2}$$

---

26 B. 10 miles

If you made a simple map with these three cities, it would look like this:

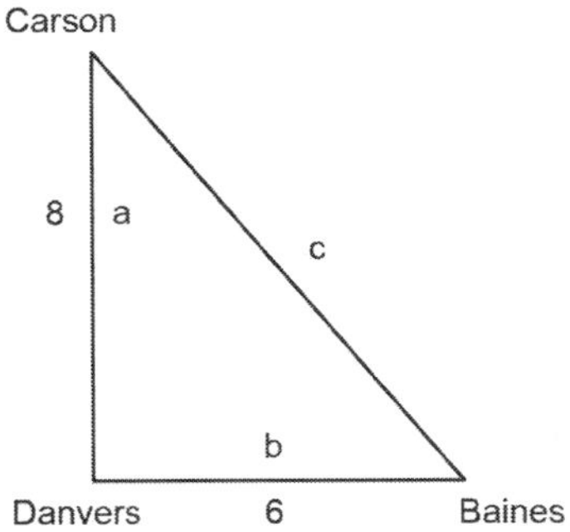

This is a right triangle. The longest side of a right triangle is called the hypotenuse. The two legs of the triangle are labeled a and b. The hypotenuse is labeled c. You can find the length of the hypotenuse (the distance between Caron and Baines) by using this equation:

$$a^2 + b^2 = c^2$$

In this case, the equation would be:

$$8^2 + 6^2 = c^2$$
$$or$$
$$64 + 36 = c^2$$
$$100 = c^2$$

To find c, ask yourself: What number times itself equals 100? The answer is 10.

---

27 C. 3/36

When you roll a pair of 6-sided dice, there are 36 possible combinations of numbers (or outcomes) that can result. There are six numbers on each of the dice, so there are 6 * 6 possible combinations. Only three of those combinations will yield a total of 10: 4+6, 5+5, and 6+4. Much of the time, probability answers will be given in the form of simplified fractions. In this case, the correct answer could also have been 1/12.

---

28 A. $144

When one person dropped out of the arrangement, the cost for the remaining three went up by $12 per person for a total of $36. This means that each person's share was originally $36. There were four people in the original arrangement, so the cost of the gift was 4 * $36, or $144.

Or alternatively:

Let 4x equal the original cost of the gift. If the number of shares decreases to 3, then the total cost is 3(x+12). Those expressions must be equal, so:

$$4x = 3(x + 12)$$
$$4x = 3x + 36$$

Subtracting 3x from both sides, we get:

$$x = 36$$

Then the original price of the gift was 4 times 36, or $144.

29 C. 120

The factorial of a number is the product of all the integers less than or equal to the number. The factorial of 5 is 5 * 4 * 3 * 2 * 1 = 120. The factorial is written this way: 5!

---

30 D. 7

In this number:
1is in the thousands place.
2is in the hundreds place.
3is in the tens place.
4is in the ones place
5is in the tenths place.
6is in the hundredths place.
7is in the thousandths place.

---

31 B. 4

The mode is the number that appears most often in a set of numbers.
Since 4 appears three times, it is the "mode."

---

32 C. 49

A perfect square is the product of an integer times itself. In this question, 49 is a perfect square because it is the product of 7 and 7.

---

33 A. (14 + 24) * 8 * 5

In the correct answer, (14 + 24) * 8 * 5, the hourly wages of Amanda and Oscar are first combined, and then this amount is multiplied by 8 hours in a day and five days in a week. One of the other choices, 14 + 24 * 8 * 5, looks similar to this, but it is incorrect because the hourly wages must be combined before they can be multiplied by 8 and 5.

---

34 D. 130,500

The population of Mariposa County in 2015 was 90% of its population in 2010. Convert 90% to a decimal by moving the decimal point two places to the left: 90% = .90. Now multiply .90 times 145,000 (the population in 2010).

$$.90 * 145{,}000 = 130{,}500$$

---

35 C. 17/24

To add 1/3 and 3/8, you must find a common denominator. The simplest way to do this is to multiply the denominators: 3 * 8 = 24. Therefore, 24 is a common denominator. (This method will not always give you the <u>lowest</u> common denominator, but it does in this case.)

Once you have found a common denominator, you need to convert both fractions in the problem to equivalent fractions that have that same denominator. To do this, multiply each fraction by an equivalent of

$$\frac{1}{3} * \frac{8}{8} = \frac{8}{24}$$
$$\frac{3}{8} * \frac{3}{3} = \frac{9}{24}$$

Now you can add 8/24 and 9/24 to solve the problem.

36 B. Serena is 7, Tom is 4

Use S to represent Serena's age. Tom is 3 years younger than Serena, so his age is S–3. In 4 years, Tom will be twice as old as Serena was 3 years ago. So you can write this equation:

$$\text{Tom} + 4 = 2(\text{Serena} - 3)$$

Now substitute S for Serena and S–3 for Tom.

$$(S - 3) + 4 = 2(S - 3)$$

Simplify the equation.

$$S + 1 = 2S - 6$$

Subtract S from both sides of the equation. You get:

$$1 = S - 6$$

Add 6 to both sides of the equation. You get:

$$7 = S, \text{ Serena's age}$$
$$4 = S - 3, \text{ Tom's age}$$

---

37 A. Length = 12, width = 4

Use w to represent the width of the rectangle. The length is three times the width, so the length is $3w$. The area of the rectangle is the length times the width, so the area is w * $3w$, or $3w^2$

$$3w^2 = 48$$

Divide both sides of the equation by 3. You get:

$$w^2 = 16$$
$$w = 4, \text{ the width of the rectangle}$$
$$3w = 12, \text{ the length of the rectangle}$$

---

38 B. 24 = 2 * 2 * 2 * 3

The prime factors of a number are the prime numbers that divide that number evenly. The prime factorization of a number is a list of the prime factors that must be multiplied to yield that number.

The simplest method of finding the prime factorization is to start with a simple multiplication fact for that number. In this case, we could have chosen:

$$24 = 6 * 4$$

The prime factorization of 24 includes the prime factorization of both 6 and 4. Since 6 = 2 * 3 and 4 = 2 * 2, the prime factorization of 24 must be:

$$24 = 2 * 2 * 2 * 3$$

---

39 A. A number greater than x

When a positive number is divided by a positive number less than 1, the quotient will always be larger than the number being divided. For example, 5 ÷ 0.5 = 10. If we solve this as a fraction, 5 ÷ (1/2) is the same as 5 * (2/1), which equals 10, since dividing by a fraction is the same as multiplying by the reciprocal.

---

40 C. x = 11

Subtracting a negative number is the same as adding a positive number. So 8 – (–3) is the same as 8 + 3, which equals 11.

41 C. The square of a number is always a positive number.

When two numbers with the same sign (positive or negative) are multiplied, the product is always positive. When a number is squared, it is multiplied by itself, so the numbers being multiplied have the same sign. Therefore, the product is always positive.

The square of a number greater than 1 is always greater than the number. But the square of a positive number less than one (for example 0.5) is always less than the original number.

---

42 B. 515

Marisol scored higher than 78% of the students who took the test. Convert 78% to a decimal by moving the decimal point two places to the left: 78% = .78. Now multiply .78 times the number of students who took the test:

.78 * 660 = 514.8 or 515 students (must be whole numbers)

---

43 D. $12

Use the information given to write an equation:

$$530 = 40d + 50$$

When you subtract 50 from both sides of the equation, you get:

$$480 = 40d$$

Divide both sides of the equation by 40.

$12 = d$, Sam's hourly wage

---

44 D. $r = \frac{p-3}{2}$

Begin by subtracting 3 from both sides of the equation. You get:

$$p - 3 = 2r$$

Now, to isolate r on one side of the equation, divide both sides of the equation by 2. You get:

$$\mathrm{r} = \frac{\mathrm{p} - 3}{2}$$

---

45 B. 40

The least common multiple is used when finding the lowest common denominator. The least common multiple is the lowest number that can be divided evenly by both of the numbers.

Here is a simple method to find the least common multiple of 8 and 10. Write 8 on the left side of your paper, then add 8 and write the result, then add another 8 to that number and write the result. Keep going until you have a list that looks something like this:

8 16 24 32 40 ...

This is a partial list of multiples of 8. (If you remember your multiplication tables, these numbers are the column or row that go with 8.)

Now do the same thing with 10.

10 20 30 40 ...

This is the partial list of multiples of 10.

Eventually, similar numbers will appear in both rows. The smallest of these numbers is the least common multiple. There will always be more multiples that are found in both rows, but the smallest number is the least common multiple.

46 D. x = 4

When you multiply or divide numbers that have the same sign (both positive or both negative), the answer will be positive. When you multiply or divide numbers that have different signs (one positive and the other negative), the answer will be negative. In this case, both numbers have the same sign. Divide as you normally would, and remember that the answer will be a positive number.

---

47 A. $2\,\frac{5}{6}$

To convert an improper fraction to a mixed number, divide the numerator by the denominator. In this case, you get 2 with a remainder of 5. 2 becomes the whole number portion of the mixed number, and 5 becomes the numerator of the fraction.

---

48 B. –10

To find the value of q, divide both sides of the equation by –13. When a positive number is divided by a negative number, the answer is negative.

---

49 A. 12

Replace the letters with the numbers they represent, then perform the necessary operations.

$$3^2 + 6(0.5)$$
$$9 + 3 = 12$$

---

50 B. 32 inches

The radius of a circle is one-half the diameter, so the diameter of this circle is 8 inches. The diameter is a line that passes through the center of a circle and joins two points on its circumference. If you study this figure, you can see that the diameter of the circle is the same as the length of each side of the square. The diameter is 8 inches, so the perimeter of the square is 32 inches (8+ 8 + 8 + 8).

SCIENCE

1 B. Cilia

Cilia that are located on the outer membrane of bronchial epithelial cells are motile hair-like extensions whose motion tends to move substances out of the airways toward the pharynx. Microvilli are found on the villi of intestinal epithelial cells. Flagella are found on sperm cells but no other cells in the human body. Dendrites are thin branching cellular extensions of neuron cell membranes.

---

2 D. bile; small intestine

Fat molecules are primarily hydrocarbon in content and are therefore not soluble in water. To absorb fats, the liver produces bile that is secreted into the duodenum. Fats are soluble in bile, so bile is able to break large fat globules into smaller droplets which can be more easily absorbed into the body. The process of fat globule dissolution is called emulsification. Amylase is a digestive enzyme that breaks down certain carbohydrates.

---

3 D. intercellular membrane binding

The role of T-helper cells in immune responses involves the binding of membrane bound molecules, usually receptors or membrane bound antigens or antibodies between the T-helper cells and other immune system cells including B-cells and antigen-presenting cells, such as macrophages. T-helper cells can produce antibodies that bind to their own membranes but do not produce antibodies that are released into the circulation (B-cells do this). T-helper cells do not directly cause lysis of other dells and do not engage in phagocytosis.

---

4 A. It passes through capillaries before returning to the internal chambers of the heart

Rationale: Blood is pumped out of the heart through either the pulmonic valve as deoxygenated blood to the pulmonary artery or secondly, through the aortic valve as oxygenated blood to the aorta. All blood, once it leaves the heart, must pass through capillaries before it returns to the internal chambers of the heart

---

5 D. continuously throughout the entire respiratory cycle

Deoxygenated blood is pumped through alveolar capillaries continuously throughout the respiratory cycle. If oxygen were not diffusing into the capillaries throughout each of the stages of the inspiratory cycle, the blood passing through the alveolar capillaries would not be oxygenated. This deoxygenated blood would return to the heart and mix with oxygenated blood, lowering the oxygen saturation level of the blood that is then pumped out of the heart through the aorta. Blood exiting the heart through the aorta is nearly 100% saturated, so there is no inspiratory phase where oxygen is not passing into the circulatory system through the alveoli into their surrounding capillaries.

---

6 A. sensory input

The integrative functions of the nervous system occur in the brain, where sensory input is utilized to create memories and to help generate thought processes. This does not require hormonal regulation. Effector cells are cells that carry out instructions from the nervous system at locations throughout the body. This is not classified as integrative neurological function. Spinal cord reflexes are, for the most part, independent of the central nervous system and are not required for integrative functions.

---

7 B. pyloric sphincter

The pyloric sphincter opens at appropriate intervals to allow stomach contents to enter the duodenum. The gastroesophageal (GE) sphincter opens only during the passage of ingested material from the esophagus into the stomach. A muscular sphincter is a generalized term for ring-like muscles that surround and contract a bodily passage or opening. The gastroduodenal sphincter is not the proper term for the pyloric sphincter.

8 C. production of antibodies

The innate immune system generates non-specific immune responses. Phagocytosis of foreign cells by macrophages, the stimulation of fever by the release of interleukins, and the release of and response to cytokines by cells involved in the innate immune responses is triggered by a wide variety of infectious agents or chemicals generated by tissue injury. The innate immune responses are then carried out through biochemical pathways and cell activities that do not require the participation of antibodies or the recognition of a specific antigens. Antibodies are produced by B-cells, which are required for activity of the humoral category of the body's adaptive immune system. B-cells do not participate in the innate immune responses.

9 A. The heart is ventral to the esophagus

The term ventral means toward the umbilical (belly button) abdominal wall versus the opposite direction, dorsal, which means, in this positional terminology, toward the spine. Proximal means toward the midline of the body, so it also can be interpreted as toward or closer to the spine, but this is contrasted with the opposite of proximal, which is described by the term distal, meaning away from the spine. Medial is used to describe relative locations toward any central axis of the body with the opposite relationship described by the term lateral, meaning to the side of that which is medial. Rostral indicates a relative position closer to the skull, with the term caudal meaning a relative position that is closer to the base of the spine.

10 A. the liver

Urea is a water-soluble, non-toxic molecule synthesized for the purpose of ridding the body of waste products generated by the catabolism of nitrogen-containing compounds such as nucleic acids and proteins. Although urea is excreted through the kidneys, it is synthesized by liver parenchymal cells.

11 D. the large intestine

All organs of the body must receive a direct arterial supply of oxygenated blood. The lungs also receive deoxygenated blood through the pulmonary artery, which is then oxygenated as it passes through alveolar capillaries. The heart receives deoxygenated blood through the superior and inferior vena cava veins, which empty into the right atrium. The liver receives deoxygenated blood through the hepatic portal vein, which carries blood that has passed through capillaries in the small intestines. The large intestine, along with most of the other organs or organ regions of the body, receives supplies of oxygenated blood only.

12 B. the diaphragm

One is not expected to know the names of all of the voluntary muscles in the body, but the major voluntary muscles, such as the biceps are expected knowledge. The masseters are the muscles that cause the lower jaw to close. This is beyond expected knowledge, but it is a higher level of anatomical knowledge that is not specifically, but as a category of superior mastery, included to distinguish the top levels of performance. At the expected knowledge level is that the diaphragm is the muscle that generates inhalation, that one can for brief periods of time voluntarily inhale or suppress inhalation, and that usually the inhalation process is involuntary, and always involuntary when one is asleep.

13 C. the small intestines

This question is often missed because most students know that the primary role of the large intestine is to absorb water. Nevertheless, 80% of water that passes through the digestive system is absorbed through the small intestine.

14 B. dendritic cells

Dendritic cells possess toll-like receptors on their cell membranes which can bind to pathogen-associated molecular patterns (PAMPs) that are present on or in a wide variety of foreign microorganisms. After recognizing and then phagocytizing a foreign immunogenic substance, dendritic cells are able to digest the substance and present the digested fragments as antigens on the outer cell membrane surface. Natural killer (NK) cells can attack virally infected and cancerous cells without interacting with other cells or other substances of the adaptive immune system. Plasma cells synthesize and secrete antibodies. The T-helper cell binds and activates the complementary T-cell to initiate the production of large amounts of antibodies

---

15 C. inadequate intake during childhood development can lead to the disease kwashiorkor

Kwashiorkor is a severe form of malnourishment that is usually fatal. It is specifically the result of inadequate protein intake that occurs in children usually after the age of 18 months. Vegetarians can obtain all required dietary protein through non-animal or animal product sources – rice and legumes are sufficient, for example. There are nine essential amino acids which must be obtained through the diet. The remaining amino acids can be synthesized by the body. The breakdown of proteins begins within the stomach.

---

16 A. Somatostatin

Somatostatin is also known as growth-hormone inhibiting hormone (GHIH). This hormone inhibits the release of growth hormone (GH) and follicle-stimulating hormone from the anterior segment of the pituitary gland.

---

17 B. 8 grams

The terms atomic and molecular weights are often used in science and equivalent to the terms atomic mass and molecular mass where the units of mass in grams is substituted for the number of AMU units. An atom with an atomic mass of 8 AMU has a corresponding atomic weight of 8 grams.

---

18 C. a phosphate group, a pentose sugar and a nitrogenous base

In both RNA and DNA molecules, the backbone of a continuous single DNA or RNA molecular chain is an alternating sequence of cyclic 5-carbon sugars (pentoses) bonded to phosphate groups (PO4). Each pentose sugar is also bonded to one of five possible nitrogenous bases. Nitrogenous bases in nucleic acids are small, cyclic nitrogen-containing molecules consisting of either one or two rings. A nucleotide is defined as a molecular subunit consisting of one of these nitrogenous bases that bonded to a nucleic acid pentose sugar and a phosphate group that is also bonded to the same pentose sugar. Any DNA or RNA segment can be built entirely from combinations of these nucleotide subunits.

---

19 D. alveoli

Alveoli are terminal sac-like, thin-walled structures of the bronchial tree. They have many capillaries within their walls. This allows for oxygen to easily diffuse from the air in the alveoli into the bloodstream. Once oxygen has arrived in the bloodstream, it then diffuses into red blood cells and binds to the molecule hemoglobin. The red blood cells carry the oxygen to all the tissues in the body via the circulatory system.

---

20 B. ribosomes

Ribosomes are protein complexes that may be free-floating within a cell's cytoplasm or, at times, attached to a cell's endoplasmic reticulum. It is simply a fact that they do not possess outer membranes, or, in fact, any membranes whatsoever. There is strong evidence that mitochondria, chloroplasts, and the nuclei of eukaryotic cells evolved from prokaryotic cells that were ingested by other prokaryotic cells but survived and evolved to their present state within the evolutionary descendants of these cells. This is a compelling explanation for why these organelles possess encapsulating membranes.

---

21 D. The mRNA segment base sequence is identical to the complementary DNA strand segment of the gene base sequence except that uracil is substituted for thymine in the mRNA base sequence

An important and common misconception regarding RNA transcriptions of a gene is that the RNA transcription is a copy of the DNA gene segment except that uracil is substituted for thymine in the RNA sequence. In fact, the RNA segment is the compliment of the gene sequence, except that in the RNA transcript, uracil is substituted for by thymine.

---

22 A. Newtons: Joule

Newtons and Joules are both measurements in the metric system.

---

23 A. valence shells

An electron shell, sometimes called a principle energy level, may be envisioned as an orbit followed by electrons around an atom's nucleus. Covalent bonds are chemical bonds that involve the sharing of electron pairs between atoms. The stable balance of attractive and repulsive forces between atoms when they share electrons is known as covalent bonding. Many molecules thus formed, through their sharing of electrons, attain the equivalent of a full outer shell, corresponding to a stable electronic configuration.

---

24 B. mRNA

Messenger RNA molecules are transcribed genetic information from DNA. After transcription, messenger RNA leaves the nucleus and travels to the ribosomes in the cell cytoplasm. Ribosomes can read the genetic code of the messenger RNA and then assemble the protein that corresponds to the genetic information contained in the messenger RNA molecule.

---

25 B. gonads

The gonads are the sexual organs of males and females of a given species that create offspring by sexual reproduction. They are the organs responsible for producing the male and female sex cells. These sex cells are called gametes. Gametes contain one chromosome of each pair of chromosomes contained in non-sex cells of the male and female of a species.

---

26 B. A single, unique three-base codon will code for only one single, unique type of amino acid

This is a question that is commonly answered incorrectly. DNA is comprised, in part, of a linear sequence of nitrogenous base subunits. These subunits can be any of four different nitrogenous bases.
These bases transmit genetic information in the form of 3-base unit sequences that are called codons. Statistically there are 64 possible 3-base sequences that can be constructed from a combination of these four different DNA bases.

---

27 B. synapse

Synapses are structures within the nervous system that permit a neuron (nerve cell) to pass an electrical or chemical signal to another neuron. The synapse is a junction between two neurons. There is a narrow space between the two neurons at the synapse, which is called the synaptic gap. One neuron releases neurotransmitters into the synaptic gap, and the neurotransmitter molecules diffuse across the gap and attach to receptor sites on the other neuron. This can cause an electrical signal in the second neuron, resulting in the transmission of neural information.

---

28 C. 5 miles

A meter is approximately 3.28 feet. An 8K race refers to a race covering a total distance of 8,000 meters. This converts to a distance in feet of 8,000 times 3.28, which is 26,240 feet. A mile is 5,280 feet. 26,240 divided by 5,280 is equal to about 4.97. Therefore, an 8K race would be 4.97 miles, or about 5 miles.

---

29 C. electric charge of zero

Electrons have an electric charge of -1, protons have an electric charge of +1, and neutrons have zero charge. Particles with opposite electric charges are attracted to one another by the electromagnetic force (particles with the same electric charge repel each other). It is the electromagnetic force that attracts electrons to an atom's positively charged nucleus. When an atom contains the same number of electrons and protons, the positive charge due to the protons in the nucleus and the negative charge of the electrons surrounding the nucleus cancel out. As a result, the atom has a net electric charge of zero.

---

30 antigen-presenting cells (APCs)

Antigen-presenting cells (APCs) are a class of immune cells that mediate the cellular immune response by processing and presenting foreign antigens that they have acquired - usually by phagocytosis or endocytosis - from the extracellular environment for recognition by certain lymphocytes such as T-cells.

---

31 B. connective tissue

An organized functional collection of a single type of cell is considered to be a tissue. Adipose cells (fat cells) are classified as a type of connective cell, and therefore adipose cell tissue is connective tissue. A syncytium is a collection of cells that have to some extent fused such that cytoplasm can circulate throughout the entire collection of cells, a gland is an organized cell structure that secretes substance through a duct.

---

32 D. increases the rate of the reaction; decreasing the activation energy

The efficiency of a reaction is the actual yield compared to the theoretical yield of products of the reaction. This is a function of the conditions under which the reaction occurs, but it is not affected by the presence of a catalyst. A catalyst increases the rate of a reaction by lowering the activation energy of the reaction. The activation energy is the difference between the energy of the reactants and the highest energy transition state between reactants and products. Lowering the energy of this transition state increases the probability that reactants will have sufficient energy to achieve the transition state so that the reaction can proceed to the final product state.

---

33 A. $1s^2\ 2s^2\ 2p^6$

The electron subshells of an atom beginning with the lowest energy subshells are the 1s, 2s, 2p, 3s, 3d and 3p subshells. The s subshells are filled when they contain 2 electrons. The p subshells are filled when they contain a total of 6 electrons. Neon, with an atomic number of 10 will in have neutral atoms with ten electrons and in the lowest energy state these will fill the lowest available energy levels. This corresponds to an electron configuration of $1s^2\ 2s^2\ 2p^6$.

---

34 C. The enzyme has increased its effect on the rate of a chemical reaction

Enzyme activity is quantified, for the biochemical reaction that the enzyme catalyzes, as the amount of product generated per unit time. In general, it indicates how fast a reaction is occurring. The major factors that affect an enzyme's ability to increase the rate of a reaction are temperature, pH at which the reaction occurs, and concentrations of the reactants and products of the reaction.

---

35 B. acidic

The pH of pure liquid water is 7. This is a neutral pH, Solutions with higher concentrations of H^+ have pH values lower than 7. These solutions are as acidic solutions.

---

36 D. collagen

Collagen is an extracellular elastic structural protein and able to stretch and relax as muscles contract and relax. Collagen in cartilage has mechanical properties intermediate between rigidity and elasticity in its role of providing a protective layer over the ends of bones at movable joints and as structural elements in the nose, ears and within the skeletal system and elsewhere throughout the body. Collagen also is a major component of ligaments and in the integumentary system where it provides the ability of skin to stretch but to resist mechanical penetration by foreign objects and to contain the internal contents of the body.

---

37 B. the adrenal gland

Steroid hormones are produced in the adrenal gland, in the gonads primarily. The pancreas produces insulin and glucagon which are peptide hormones. The thyroid hormones are also peptide hormones. The thymus is the site of T-cell maturation. It does not secrete any hormones.

---

38 B. $2O_2 + 8e^- \;--->\; 4O^{-2}$

In oxidation-reduction reactions, the reactants give product molecules that have covalent bonds, but there is a large difference in the electronegativities between the bonded atoms in the product molecules. The atoms in these molecules are not ions but they can be thought of as having strong ionic character, and that they undergo electron loss or electron acquisition as shown for the two molecules of oxygen in the answer choice B. Within a common solution environment these ions are never actually present, but if the reactants are separated into different reaction vessels and connected by an electrically conductive wire and a salt bridge, electrons will flow from the less electronegative species to the more electronegative species through the wire. This is how chemical batteries are constructed

---

39 B. glyosidic

Dietary carbohydrates are usually consumed in the form of starches contained in grains and vegetables. Starches are another polymerized form of glucose. Cellulose is a glucose polymer that has glyosidic bonds that cannot be broken by human digestion. Cellulose forms majority of non-digestible fiber in the human diet.

---

40 A. the same type of

There are no different types of intermolecular bonding that occur among water molecules in the solid phase compared to the liquid phase. The difference is that the kinetic energy of water molecules in the solid phase is insufficient to overcome the intermolecular bonds that hold the water molecules in a fixed position relative to surrounding water molecules. In the liquid phase, water molecules have sufficient kinetic energy to change position within the liquid but insufficient energy to completely break free of intermolecular bonds and thus become gas phase water molecules.

---

41 C. negative

When the number of electrons exceeds the number of protons, the ion has a net negative charge.

---

42 C. every functional gene can be transcribed into a mRNA molecule

A single chromosome can exist in two different forms. In the singular form, it contains a full set of genes; there may be more than one copy of a given gene and there may be more than one version of a given gene – which is called an allele located on the chromosome. It is not true that there are always two copies or two alleles of a gene on this version of a chromosome. In preparation for cell division, a copy of the single chromosome is made, resulting in a version of the chromosome that consists of two identical sister chromatids. In this version there are always at least two copies of every gene, but not at least two alleles for every gene. Only one strand of a double-stranded DNA molecule contains genes. The other strand contains the complementary sequence of the DNA's genes, but this strand cannot be transcribed into RNA that will code for any gene proteins. By definition, a gene is a sequence of DNA bases that can be translated into a protein, and this requires that every gene be capable of being first transcribed into a messenger RNA molecule.

---

43 B. UCG AUG GGC

In DNA, complementary base pairing occurs between adenine (A) and thymine (T) and between guanine (G) and cytosine (C). In RNA, the same complementary base relationship is true except that the complementary base of adenine is uracil (U) rather than thymine. The base sequence in choice B correctly identifies the complementary base sequence for RNA to the base sequence for DNA that is given within the question.

---

44 D. nucleoli

Nucleoli are located with the nucleus of cells. These are the organelles that are responsible for the construction of ribosomes. Peroxisomes and lysosomes are intracellular vesicles that contain specific types of substances, but they are not involved in ribosome construction. Ribosomes are attached to the endoplasmic reticular membranes in rough endoplasmic reticulum, but they are not constructed by the endoplasmic reticulum.

---

45 C. RNA polymerase

Ribosomes are the structures that physically assemble proteins by reading RNA base sequences and connecting amino acids to form a chain of amino acids, which is, by definition, a protein. RNA polymerase is the structure, in the form of an enzyme complex, that physically assembles messenger RNA molecules by reading DNA base sequences and connecting nucleotides to form a chain of nucleotides, which becomes the messenger RNA molecule.

---

46 D. Replication of both strands occurs simultaneously

The process of replication of double-stranded DNA begins with the breaking of hydrogen bonds between a small sequence of complementary base pairs at a single site on the DNA molecule This creates a gap within the DNA that allows a DNA polymerase enzyme complex to enter and to begin adding nucleotides with complementary bases to both the sense and antisense strands of the original DNA. The process differs somewhat between the two strands, but replication proceeds simultaneously on both strands.

---

47 B. dopamine

Dopamine is an organic chemical that functions as a neurotransmitter — a chemical released by nerve cells to send signals to other nerve cells. Dopamine plays a major role in "reward-motivated behavior". Most types of reward increase the level of dopamine in the brain, and a variety of addictive drugs increase dopamine neuronal activity. A variety of legal drugs work by altering the way the body makes and uses dopamine.

48 B. adaptive immunity

Lymph nodes are nodular structures that contain numerous antigen-presenting cells capable of triggering the adaptive immune system.

---

49 A. purines and pyrimidines

Purines and pyrimidines are the two structural categories of nitrogenous bases that are found in DNA and RNA. The purines are guanine and adenine; the pyrimidines are thymine, cytosine, and uracil. The major structural difference between the two is that purines have a two-ring structure and pyrimidines have a one-ring structure.

---

50 A. NH_2

NH_2 is the functional R group for the amino acid lysine.

ENGLISH & READING

1 A. affected; effect; ought

Since a verb is needed in the first blank, "affected" not "effected" (a noun) will work, but the noun "effect" is correct in the second blank. "Ought", meaning "should" correctly completes the sentence, indicating he should not drive. "Aught", meaning zero, or nothing, or none, does not make sense in this context.

---

2 C. Hiking along the trail, we were assailed by the chirping of birds, which made our nature walk hardly the peaceful exercise we had wanted.

Who was hiking along the trail? "We" were, so only option C works. The other options are dangling participles: in option b, the birds were not attempting to hike, so that doesn't make sense; in option a, again, the birds were hiking along the trail, so that makes no sense; option d is just poorly constructed and makes the meaning overall unclear.

---

3 D. processed

"Processed" modifies "food products" so that is the adjective; "really" is an adverb modifying the adjective "serious"; "challenge" is a noun, which is a person, place, or thing; "consume" is a verb, a word that shows action.

---

4 B. My husband and I attended my daughter's dance recital and were very proud when she received an award.

The most clear and concise sentence is option b; all the information is included, it is presented logically, it flows smoothly off the tongue, and it is not overly wordy.

---

5 D. Since the concert ended very late, I fell asleep in the backseat during the car ride home.

Option d is correct. "Since the concert ended very late" is a dependent clause which explains why "I fell asleep..."; since they are dependent, the only proper way to link them is with a comma.

---

6 D. they're

This question asks you to make a pronoun and antecedent agree; in this sentence, the antecedent is "negotiations"; since this is a plural noun, the pronoun must also be plural, but the blank is also missing a verb. The only option with a plural pronoun and a verb is the contraction "they're".

---

7 A. is

"Group", a singular noun, is the subject of the sentence, so a singular verb is needed. Also needed is a present tense helping verb for "looking forward". The only option that satisfies both is "is".

---

8 C. Exclamatory

An exclamatory sentence is a type of sentence that expresses strong feelings by making an exclamation. Therefore, the above sentence is an exclamatory sentence.

---

9 A. Irregardless

"Irregardless" is incorrect as it is a double-negative: the suffix "less" already indicates a lack of regard, so the addition of the negative "ir" before the correct word, regardless, is unnecessary.

10 C. Between you and me, I brought back fewer books from my dorm room than I needed to study for my exam.

"Brought" is the correct past tense form of bring; "fewer" is the correct word to describe an exact number of items, whereas "less" is used to refer to an amount of something that cannot be exactly counted, like sand or air or water; and "than" is the correct spelling of the word that shows a comparison between two things.

---

11 D. us; was

Words that follow prepositions are considered to be in the objective case; therefore "us" is the correct word here. "Neither", a single pronoun, is the subject of the sentence, so a singular verb, "was" is needed to properly complete it.

---

12 C. books

A noun is a person, place or thing. While a "library" is usually used as a noun to denote a place where people can go to borrow books, or look up information, in this sentence it is used as an adjective to modify "books", which is the only true noun in the sentence.

---

13 A. Mary and Samantha ran and skipped and hopped their way home from school every day.

A simple sentence is one that has one subject and one verb, though both the subject and verb can be compound. In this case, option a is a simple sentence, with the one subject being compound ("Mary and Samantha") and the one verb also being compound ("ran and skipped and hopped"). The other options either have more than one subject or more than one verb.

---

14 B. Matthew was tall and shy, and Thomas was short and talkative.

A simple sentence is one that has one subject and one verb, though both the subject and verb can be compound. Linked by the conjunction "and", sentence B is the only compound sentence above because it links the first sentence "Matthew was tall and shy" with the second sentence "Thomas was short and talkative".

---

15 D. "There's a bus coming, so hurry up and cross the street!" yelled Bob to the old woman.

"There's" is the subject and verb of the sentence written as a contraction so the apostrophe is needed; a comma is needed before "so" because what follows it is a dependent clause, which must be separated from the single sentence with a comma. When writing dialogue, the punctuation is included inside the quotation marks; in this case an exclamation is appropriate because Bob is warning the old woman to get out of the way of the oncoming bus; the use of the verb "yelled" is a clue that the statement by Bob is exclamatory.

---

16 C. It's a long to-do list she left for us today: make beds; wash breakfast dishes; go grocery shopping; do laundry; cook dinner; and read the twins a bedtime story.

"It's" is the subject and verb joined together in a contraction, so an apostrophe is needed. The sentence introduces a list, so it must be preceded by a colon; because the list is comprised of phrases instead of single words, a semicolon is needed to separate each item.

---

17 A. My room was a mess so my mom made me clean it before I was allowed to leave the house.

The use of the possessive pronoun "my" and the singular pronoun "I" indicates that the sentence is written from the first person perspective. "You" and "your" are second person; "her" or "him" are third person.

18 C. The president of France is meeting with President Obama later this week.
When referring to the "president of France", "president" is just a noun denoting his position, so it is not capitalized. In the case of "President Obama", "President" is the title by which he is addressed, so it is a proper noun and requires capitalization. The other options are incorrectly capitalized.

---

19 D. climb; creak
"Climb" is the proper spelling to denote ascending the stairs; "clime" refers to climate. "Creak" denotes a squeaky sound; "creek" denotes a stream or small moving waterway.

---

20 D. I will have completed
The FUTURE PERFECT TENSE indicates that an action will have been finished at some point in the future. This tense is formed with "will" plus "have" plus the past participle of the verb (which can be either regular or irregular in form). "By this time next summer" is the clue that lets you know the coursework will be done some time in the future.

---

21 A. assent; aide
The word "assent" means approval, which is what the teacher wants to do to show encouragement to novice teacher who is currently her "aide" or assistance in the classroom. "Ascent" denotes a climb; "aid" is a verb denoting the action of helping.

---

22 D. No one has offered to let us use their home for the office's end-of-year picnic.
"No one", a singular pronoun, requires a singular verb, "has". "Us" is the objective case pronoun which is needed to follow the verb "to let"; "ourselves" is the reflexive case which is not needed in this sentence; "we" is subjective. "Their" shows possession of "home"; spelled "there", this word denotes location (e.g. here or there).

---

23 C. The tornado struck without warning and caused extensive damage.
Incorporating all of the information from the four sentences logically and concisely, option C is the best choice.

---

24 C. caused
"Caused" is the verb in this sentence; "Carrying" is the subject. Though it may look like a verb, it is actually a gerund (a verb acting as a noun) which is the subject. Deleting extraneous words will help see this, so let's rewrite the sentence in its most basic form: "Carrying caused her to throw out her back." This way it is clear to see that "carrying" is the subject, and is not a verb.

---

25 B. My eyelids drooping and my feet going numb, I thought his boring lecture would never end.
This sentence most clearly concisely conveys all of the information in the four above sentences; structure is parallel and no awkward or extraneous words are included.

---

26 D. Comets are balls of dust and ice, comprised of leftover materials that did not become planets during the formation of our solar system.
"Comets" (a plural subject requiring a plural verb) "are" "comprised of" (meaning: made up of) leftover materials that "did not" (in the past) become planets during the formation of "our" solar system.

27 B. Improvements in printing resulted in the production of newspapers, as well as England's more fully recognizing the singular concept of reading as a form of leisure; it was, of itself, a new industry.

The sentence is a compound sentence (two complete subject and verb phrases), so these should be separated by a comma after newspapers. The possession of recognition of the singular concept of reading by England needs to be shown with an apostrophe plus "s": "England's".

---

28 A. era

The Victorian Era is a two-word proper noun referring to a time period in history, so "era" should be capitalized. The other words should not be capitalized.

---

29 C. coresponding

The correct spelling is corresponding.

---

30 D. market

"this demand" refers back to the "market (for cheaper literature)" in the last sentence of paragraph 2.

---

31 C. Working class boys who could not afford a penny a week often formed clubs that would share the cost, passing the flimsy booklets from reader to reader.

This sentence most clearly and concisely expresses the idea of book sharing amongst working boys who could not afford to spend a penny every week to buy the penny dreadfuls.

---

32 B. gothic

The word Gothic is a proper adjective referring to a specific genre of literature. None of the other words in this sentence should be capitalized.

---

33 B. The penny dreadfuls were influential since they were, in the words of one commentator,

"the most alluring and low-priced form of escapist reading available to ordinary youth."

The independent clause "in the words of one commentator" needs to be set off by commas on either end; and since it is a direct quote, the last part of the sentence needs to be in quotation marks. The period at the end of the sentence needs to be inside the quotation marks.

---

34 B. novels

A noun is a person, place, or thing. "Novels" is a plural noun which denotes a thing that can be read. "Serial" and "sensational" are adjectives; "generally" is an adverb.

---

35 D. greater

An adjective is a word that describes a noun. In this sentence, "greater" is an adjective describing fear. "Circulation" and "literature" are nouns; "however" is a pronoun.

---

36 C. Paragraph 3

Paragraph 3 mentions that penny dreadfuls were often plagiarized versions of other popular literature at the time, so this would be the best place to add a sentence of supporting detail about this.

---

37 A. baptist

As the word identifies King's religion, "Baptist" should be capitalized.

38 A. His efforts to achieve racial equality in the United States, and his staunch public advocacy of civil rights are undoubtedly among the most important cultural contributions made to society in the last century.

Using parallel structure and no extraneous verbiage, option A is the most clear and concise of the versions.

---

39 D. I Have a Dream

"I Have a Dream" is the title of a speech and should therefore be put inside quotation marks.

---

40 B. Piece

In this sentence, "Piece" should be spelled Peace, as in harmony or an absence of fighting.

---

41 D. Metal

In this sentence, "Metal" should be spelled "Medal", as an award or honor, not "metal" as in a naturally occurring element or raw material.

---

42 C. This speech alienated many of his liberal allies in government who supported the war, but to his credit King never allowed politics to dictate the path of his noble works. (P. 3)

The phrase "to his credit" and the description of his works as "noble" provide clues that the author has a positive perspective about Martin Luther King and the role his activism played in American history.

---

43 C. No, because the passage is about King's public life and works, and information about his family would be irrelevant.

The focus of the passage is about King's work as a minister and activist, so details about his family are unrelated to this focus and therefore should be left out.

---

44 C. "I am making pancakes for breakfast. Does anybody want some?" asked mom.

Only option C correctly includes sentence punctuation for quoted statements: punctuation for dialogue should be inside quotation marks, as is illustrated with mom asking if anyone wants pancakes; the question mark is within the quotation marks.

---

45 B. I woke up early that morning and began to do long-neglected household chores.

Option B contains two simple sentences, which when combined make a compound sentence:" I woke up early that morning" AND "I began to do long-neglected household chores."

---

46 D. A, C, E, D, B

The most logical progression of ideas is in option D. The topic of Disney's public persona is introduced, and is then contrasted with his treatment of people at work, and then the transformation of his persona from that of an American patriot to an imperialist. Finally, the paragraph is wrapped up with statements about the importance of his work and his current legacy in popular culture.

---

47 C. began to have

The sentence is discussing the contrast between Disney's private and public personas, stating that he began to have a public persona which was very different than the way he was in private.

48 A. You had better call and RSVP to the party right away before you forget.

Statements which show direct address, and use the pronoun "you" are referred to as the second person. Though the exclamation uses the pronoun you, it is a quoted statement, so it is really in the third person. Only choice A is an example of second person writing.

---

49 D. Parents are reminded to pick up their children from school promptly at 2:30.

Only D makes proper use of pronouns and their antecedents: in A, novels and it do not agree; in B, everyone is singular, so instead of their, the pronoun should be him or her; in C, companies and it do not agree.

---

50 C. Rice and beans, my favorite meal, reminds me of my native country Puerto Rico.

Choice C is the only sentence in which subject (rice and beans/meal) and verb (reminds) agree: in A, one and have lived do not agree; in B, one and are going do not agree; and in D, most (of the milk OR it) does not agree with have gone.

PRACTICE TEST 2

Round 2. You've been studying with Spire for about a month you're almost done!
Turn to the next page to begin.

MATHEMATICS

1. Change to an improper fraction: $2\ ^1/_3$
   - A. 5/3
   - B. 3/7
   - C. 7/3
   - D. 8/3

---

2. Which of the following is equivalent to 60% of 90?
   - A. 0.6 x 90
   - B. 90 ÷ 0.6
   - C. 3/5
   - D. 2/3

---

3. Convert the improper fraction 17/6 to a mixed number.
   - A. $1\ ^7/_6$
   - B. $2\ ^5/_6$
   - C. $^6/_{17}$
   - D. $2\ ^7/_6$

---

4. The decimal value of 7/11 is ________________?
   - A. 1.57
   - B. 0.70
   - C. 0.6363...
   - D. 0.77

---

5. The decimal value of 5/8 is ________________?
   - A. 0.625
   - B. 0.650
   - C. 0.635
   - D. 0.580

---

6. The fractional value of 0.5625 is ________________?
   - A. 7/15
   - B. 11/23
   - C. 5/8
   - D. 9/16

---

7. The fractional value of 0.3125 is ________________?
   - A. 5/16
   - B. 4/24
   - C. 6/19
   - D. 9/25

8. What is the value of this expression if a = 10 and b = –4:

$$\sqrt{b^2 + 2\bullet a}$$

A. 6
B. 7
C. 8
D. 9

9. What is the gr*eatest common* factor of 48 and 64?

A. 4
B. 8
C. 16
D. 32

10. Solv*e for x*: $x = {}^{3}/_{4} \bullet {}^{7}/_{8}$

A. 7/8
B. 9/8
C. 10/12
D. 21/32

11. Find the value of $a^2 + 6b$ when a = 3 and b = 0.5.

A. 12
B. 6
C. 9
D. 15

12. What is the least common multiple of 8 and 10?

A. 80
B. 40
C. 18
D. 72

13. What is the sum of 1/3 and 3/8?

A. 3/24
B. 4/11
C. 17/24
D. 15/16

14. Solve this equation: $-9 \bullet -9 =$

A. 18
B. 0
C. 81
D. –81

15. Which of the following is between 2/3 and 3/4?
   A. 3/5
   B. 4/5
   C. 7/10
   D. 5/8

16. Which digit is in the thousandths place in the number: 1,234.567
   A. 1
   B. 2
   C. 6
   D. 7

17. Which of these numbers is largest?
   A. 5/8
   B. 3/5
   C. 2/3
   D. 0.72

18. Which of these numbers is largest?
   A. −345
   B. 42
   C. −17
   D. 34

19. Find 4 numbers between 4.857 and 4.858
   A. 4.8573, 4.85735, 4.85787, 4.8598
   B. 4.857, 4.8573, 4.8578, 4.8579,
   C. 4.8571, 4.8573, 4.8578, 4.8579
   D. 4.8572, 4.8537, 4.8578, 4.8579

20. Which number is between 4 and 5?
   A. 11/3
   B. 21/4
   C. 31/6
   D. 23/5

21. Which number is not between 7 and 9?
   A. 34/5
   B. 29/4
   C. 49/6
   D. 25/3

22. If $\frac{4}{9}x - 3 = 1$, what is the value of x?

A. 9

B. 8

C. 7

D. −4½

23. What value of q is a solution to this equation: 130 = q(−13)

A. 10

B. −10

C. 1

D. 10^2

24. Solve this equation: x = −12 ÷ −3

A. x = −4

B. x = −15

C. x = 9

D. x = 4

25. Solve for r in the equation p = 2r + 3

A. r = 2p – 3

B. r = p + 6

C. r = (p - 3) / 2

D. r = p – 3/2

26. Solve this equation: x = 8 – (−3)

A. x = 5

B. x = −5

C. x = 11

D. x = −11

27. Evaluate the expression $7x^2 + 9x - 18$ for $x = 7$

A. 516

B. 424

C. 388

D. 255

28. Evaluate the expression$x^2 + 7x - 18$ for $x = 5$

A. 56

B. 42

C. 38

D. 25

29. Evaluate the expression $7x^2 + 63x$ for $x = 27$

A. 5603
B. 4278
C. 6804
D. 6525

---

30. Sam worked 40 hours at d dollars per hour and received a bonus of $50. His total earnings were $530. What was his hourly wage?

A. $18
B. $16
C. $14
D. $12

---

31. The variable X is a positive integer. Dividing X by a positive number less than 1 will yield

A. a number greater than X
B. a number less than X
C. a negative number
D. an irrational number

---

32. Amanda makes $14 an hour as a bank teller and Oscar makes $24 dollars an hour as an auto mechanic. Both work eight hours a day, five days a week. Which of these equations can be used to calculate how much they make together in a five-day week?

A. (14 + 24) • 8 • 5
B. 14 • 24 • 8 • 5
C. (14 + 24) (8 + 5)
D. 14 + 24 • 8 • 5

---

33. Seven added to four-fifths of a number equals fifteen. What is the number?

A. 10
B. 15
C. 20
D. 25

---

34. If the sum of two numbers is 360 and their ratio is 7:3, what is the smaller number?

A. 72
B. 105
C. 98
D. 108

35. Jean buys a textbook, a flash drive, a printer cartridge, and a ream of paper. The flash drive costs three times as much as the ream of paper. The textbook costs three times as much as the flash drive. The printer cartridge costs twice as much as the textbook. The ream of paper costs $10. How much does Jean spend altogether?

A. $250
B. $480
C. $310
D. $180

36. The area of a triangle equals one-half the base times the height. Which of the following is the correct way to calculate the area of a triangle that has a base of 6 and a height of 9?

A. $(6 + 9)/2$
B. $\frac{1}{2}(6 + 9)$
C. $2(6 x 9)$
D. $\frac{(6)(9)}{2}$

37. Calculate the value of this expression: $2 + 6 \bullet 3 \bullet (3 \bullet 4)^2 + 1$

A. 2,595
B. 5,185
C. 3,456
D. 6,464

38. A rectangle of length and width 3x and x has an area of 3x2. Write the area polynomial when the length is increased by 5 units and the width is decreased by 3 units. (3x+5) (x-3)

A. $3x^2 + 14x - 15$
B. $3x^2 - 4x - 15$
C. $3x^2 - 5x + 15$
D. $3x^2 + 4x - 15$

39. A triangle of base and height 4x and 7x has an area of $14x^2$, which is equal to ½ times the base times the height. Write the area polynomial when the base is increased by 2 units and the height is increased by 3 units. $\frac{1}{2}(4x + 2)(7x + 3)$

A. $14x^2 + 14x + 6$
B. $14x^2 + 14x + 3$
C. $14x^2 + 13x + 3$
D. $14x^2 + 28x + 3$

40. Momentum is defined as the product of mass times velocity. If your 1,250 kg car is travelling at 55 km/hr, what is the value of the momentum?

A. 68,750 kg m/s
B. 19,098 kg m/s
C. 9,549 kg m/s
D. 145,882 kg m/s

41. In her retirement accounts, Janet has invested $40,000 in stocks and $65,000 in bonds. If she wants to rebalance her accounts so that 70% of her investments are in stocks, how much will she have to move?

A. $33,500
B. $35,000
C. $37,500
D. $40,000

---

42. Brian pays 15% of his gross salary in taxes. If he pays $7,800 in taxes, what is his gross salary?

A. $52,000
B. $48,000
C. $49,000
D. $56,000

---

43. In a high school French class, 45% of the students are sophomores, and there are 9 sophomores in the class. How many students are there in the class?

A. 16
B. 18
C. 20
D. 22

---

44. Marisol's score on a standardized test was ranked in the 78th percentile. If 660 students took the test, approximately how many students scored lower than Marisol?

A. 582
B. 515
C. 612
D. 486

---

45. The population of Mariposa County in 2015 was 90% of its population in 2010. The population in 2010 was 145,000. What was the population in 2015?

A. 160,000
B. 142,000
C. 120,500
D. 130,500

---

46. Alicia must have a score of 75% to pass a test of 80 questions. What is the greatest number of question she can miss and still pass the test?

A. 20
B. 25
C. 60
D. 15

47. A cell phone on sale at 30% off costs $210. What was the original price of the phone?

A. $240
B. $273
C. $300
D. $320

---

48. In the graduating class at Emerson High School, 52% of the students are girls and 48% are boys. There are 350 students in the class. Among the girls, 98 plan to go to college. How many girls do not plan to go to college?

A. 84
B. 48
C. 66
D. 72

---

49. The number of students enrolled at Two Rivers Community College increased from 3,450 in 2010 to 3,864 in 2015. What was the percent increase?

A. 9%
B. 17%
C. 12%
D. 6%

---

50. Produce is usually priced to the nearest pound. A scale for weighing produce has numerical values for pounds and ounces. Which of the following weights would you expect to be priced for 15 pounds?

A. 15 pounds 14 ounces
B. 15 pounds 10 ounces
C. 14 pounds 4 ounces
D. 14 pounds 14 ounces

---

51. Which number is rounded to the nearest ten-thousandth?

A. 7,510,000
B. 7,515,000
C. 7,514,635.8239
D. 7,514,635.824

---

52. Measuring devices determine the precision of our scientific measurements. A graduated cylinder is used that has a maximum of 10 cc's but has ten increments in between each whole number of cc's. Which answer is a correct representation of a volume measurement with this cylinder?

A. 7 cc
B. 7.1 cc
C. 7.15 cc
D. 7.514 cc's

53. If a man can unload about 50 pounds in a time of 15 minutes, estimate the time and labor force to unload 2.5 tons of 50-pound blocks from a truck working 8 hours per day.

A. 1 man for 10 days
B. 2 men for 1 day
C. 4 men for 1 day
D. 5 men for 5 days

54. In rush hour, you can usually commute 18 miles to work in 45 minutes. If you believe that you can travel an average of 5 miles per hour faster in the early morning, how much time would you estimate for the early commute to work?

A. 50 minutes
B. 40 minutes
C. 30 minutes
D. 20 minutes

55. You are taking a test and you are allowed to work a class period of 45 minutes. 20 problems are multiple choice and 30 of the problems are true / false. If they have equal value, how much time would you estimate for each type of problem if you believe you are twice as fast at multiple choice problems?

A. 90 seconds per m/c; 45 seconds per t/f
B. 60 seconds per m/c; 30 seconds per t/f
C. 70 seconds per m/c; 35 seconds per t/f
D. 80 seconds per m/c; 40 seconds per t/f

56. Your interview is scheduled for 8:00 in the morning and you need to allow 20 minutes for your trip to the interview. You oversleep and leave 10 minutes late. How fast will you travel to get there on time?

A. half as fast
B. twice as fast
C. three times as fast
D. four times as fast

SCIENCE

1. Which of the following is a primary functional difference between smooth endoplasmic reticulum (SER) and rough endoplasmic reticulum (RER)?
   A. smooth endoplasmic reticulum does not participate in synthesis of products that are destined for external secretion.
   B. smooth endoplasmic reticulum does not participate in synthesis of proteins.
   C. Rough endoplasmic reticulum does not participate in synthesis of products that are destined for external secretion.
   D. rough endoplasmic reticulum does not participate in synthesis of proteins

---

2. Which of the following is a universal feature of all living cells?
   A. an external cell membrane
   B. an external cell wall
   C. a nucleus
   D. mitochondria

---

3. Which of the following terms would NOT be used to define the relative position of one body structure to another?
   A. caudal
   B. coronal
   C. ventral
   D. inferior

---

4. Which of the following identifies the type of intracellular filament that generates the whip-like motion of the flagellum of a human sperm cell?
   A. Thick filaments
   B. microfilaments
   C. microtubules
   D. intermediate filaments

---

5. What does the linear backbones of DNA consist of?
   A. alternating nitrogenous bases of thymine and uracil
   B. alternating deoxyribose sugars and phosphate groups
   C. alternating nucleotides of ribose and deoxyribose
   D. alternating nitrogenous bases and glucose groups

---

6. Which of the following could be a nitrogenous base sequence of both a single codon and a single anticodon?
   A. ACG
   B. GCT
   C. UTC
   D. AGU

7. What organelle functions with the smooth ER to process, package, and transport a variety of synthesized products throughout the cell?
   A. ribosomes
   B. the Golgi apparatus
   C. cilia
   D. mitochondria

8. Which is the major extracellular structure that provides protective and mechanical support to the outer layers of skin, hair, and nails.
   A. fibrillin
   B. collagen
   C. keratin
   D. melatonin

9. Which of the following pairs of terms correctly completes the statement below?
   In the human male reproductive system ____ cells produce ____.
   A. tunica albuginea; primary spermatids
   B. Sertoli; follicle stimulating hormone (FSH)
   C. spermatogonia; luteinizing hormone (LH)
   D. Leydig; testosterone

10. Which of the following pairs of terms correctly completes the statement below?
    In humans, the ____ joint has a greater range of motion than the ____ joint.
    A. elbow; knee
    B. sacroiliac; atlantoaxial
    C. elbow; shoulder
    D. knee; hip

11. What molecule is a component of cell membranes and a precursor molecule for the synthesis of the steroid hormones, cortisol, aldosterone, progesterone, and the sex hormones testosterone and estrogen.
    A. lipoprotein
    B. triglycerides
    C. lipid
    D. cholesterol

12. Which of the following is the primary function of pulmonary surfactant?
    A. prevention of rupture of alveoli during maximal inspiratory effort
    B. prevention of collapse of alveoli during exhalation
    C. increased solubility of oxygen in solution between alveoli and capillary endothelium
    D. decreased viscosity of bronchiolar luminal mucous secretions

13. Which cavity is enclosed by the inner walls of the thorax, abdominal wall muscles, and the inner surface bones and associated bones of the pelvis?

A. abdominal/pelvic
B. thoracic
C. ventral
D. dorsal

---

14. Which layer of the integumentary system has poor thermal conduction, thus acts as an insulator to protect against excessive heat transfer between the internal regions of the body and the external environment?

A. epidermis
B. hypodermis
C. dermis
D. stratum corneum

---

15. What is the next structure that blood will pass through after the following sequence?
right atrium → tricuspid valve → right ventricle →

A. pulmonic valve
B. pulmonary artery
C. pulmonary vein
D. right lung

---

16. Which of the following is the most likely site for the origin of a blood clot that travels to and then lodges within the right main pulmonary artery?

A. a peripheral vein located in the leg
B. the aorta
C. the left atrium
D. a main pulmonary vein

---

17. Which of the following is a lymphocyte lineage cell type?

A. eosinophils
B. plasma cells
C. monocytes
D. basophils

---

18. Dedicated or professional antigen presenting cells present antigens on their cell surfaces to T-cells in conjunction with which of the following types of cell membrane molecules?

A. Human leucocytic antigens
B. ABO glycoproteins
C. Rh-factor proteins
D. cadherin-class cell-adhesion molecules

---

19. Which is NOT a function of the sympathetic nervous system?

A. Redirection of blood flow from the intestines to the skeletal muscles
B. Suppression of peristalsis and digestion
C. Dilation of the bronchial airways
D. Reduction of the strength and contractility of the heart contraction

---

20. Which of the following is most likely to lead to a suppression of the secretion of the hormone glucagon?

A. high protein content of chyme in the stomach
B. activation of the sympathetic nervous system
C. a meal with high simple carbohydrate content
D. the release of the hormone cholecystokinin (CCK)

---

21. Which of the following is a correct cause and effect sequence of events during the digestive process?

A. CCK secretion → increased somatostatin secretion → increased pancreatic amylase secretion
B. CCK secretion → increased bile secretion → increased fat emulsification
C. secretin secretion → increased gastric mucous secretion → increased pepsin secretion
D. secretin secretion → increased gastric HCL secretion → increased pepsin activation

---

22. The male and female sex hormones are regulated by the ________ through the release of ___________, which regulates the synthesis and release of _____ and _____ by the _______ pituitary.

A. pineal; GnRh; testosterone; estrogen; anterior
B. pineal; GHIH; PRL; LH; posterior
C. hypothalamus; GHRH; testosterone; estrogen; posterior
D. hypothalamus; GnRh; LH; FSH; anterior

---

23. What type of muscle is located throughout the body particularly in the muscular layers of the respiratory airways, the walls of the digestive tract, and in the circulatory vessel wall. This muscle is not under voluntary control but regulated by the autonomic nervous system.

A. smooth
B. skeletal
C. cardiac
D. voluntary

---

24. What structures consist of the dense connective tissue?

A. collagen, keratin, and elastin
B. ligaments, tendons, cartilage, and the lower structural layers of the dermis of the skin
C. epidermal, subcutaneous, and dermal layers of the skin
D. bones, blood, plasma, and extracellular proteins

---

25. What is the electron configuration for boron (atomic number 5)?

A. $1s^2 2s^3$
B. $1s^2 2s^2 2p^1$
C. $1s^2 2s^2 3s^1$
D. $2s^2 2s^2 2p^1$

---

26. Which of the following is most likely to directly result in the accumulation of lactic acid in muscle tissue?

A. activation of the sympathetic nervous system
B. depletion of glycogen stored in the liver
C. inadequate amounts of O_2 delivered to muscle tissue
D. inadequate levels of pyruvate within muscle tissue.

---

27. Which of the following is an effect of activation of the parasympathetic nervous system?

A. increased activity of the sinoatrial node
B. decreased activity of smooth muscle contractions in the wall of the digestive tract
C. direct inhibition of deep tendon reflexes
D. contraction of smooth muscle in the walls of arterioles in voluntary muscle tissue

---

28. Which hormone has a direct effect on circulatory vessels, causing contraction of smooth muscle cells located in the walls of arteries and veins.

A. angiotensin
B. renin
C. angiotensin II
D. aldosterone

---

29. Which elemental group has the lowest electronegativity?

A. halogens
B. noble gases
C. alkali metals
D. transition metals

---

30. Which is the least abundant blood cell?

A. lymphocytes
B. erythrocytes
C. leukocytes
D. thrombocytes

---

31. Which type of chemical reaction generates a large amount of heat energy?

A. decomposition
B. dissociation
C. oxidation
D. combustion

---

32. _________ in biological processes are either fatty acids or cholesterol.

A. lipids
B. monosaccharides
C. amino acids
D. glycogen

---

33. Which of the following identifies the primary tissue type of the hypodermis and a primary function of the main cellular component of the hypodermis?

A. epithelial; mechanical barrier

B. epithelial energy storage
C. connective; mechanical barrier
D. connective; energy storage

---

34. Which of the following is NOT a hormone synthesized by the pituitary gland?
    A. prolactin
    B. melatonin
    C. oxytocin
    D. adrenocorticotropic hormones (ACTH)

---

35. Which of the following hormones has rapid effects that are similar effects associated with the activation of the sympathetic nervous system?
    A. insulin
    B. thyroid hormone (T_3 and T_4)
    C. testosterone
    D. aldosterone

---

36. Which is NOT a nonmetal element?
    A. platinum
    B. carbon
    C. nitrogen
    D. oxygen

---

37. What is the name of the process where reactants bind to the active site and site configuration changes that orients the reactants for the chemical reaction to occur?
    A. denaturation
    B. active site orientation
    C. induced fit
    D. inhibition

---

38. Among the following, which choice identifies a joint whose most general type is different from the other three?
    A. frontal-sagittal joint
    B. temporomandibular joint
    C. sternomanubrial joint
    D. sacroiliac joint

---

39. The initial filtration of blood by the kidney occurs at which of the following anatomical locations?
    A. the renal pelvis
    B. the adrenal cortex
    C. the collecting ducts
    D. the glomeruli

---

40. Which of the following is the kidney's response to exposure to antidiuretic hormone?
    A. increased secretion of urea
    B. decreased osmolality of extracellular fluid in the renal medulla

C. Increased renal tubule permeability to water
D. decreased secretion of glucose

---

41. Which of the following is the primary hormonal response of the central nervous system to an undesirably high plasma osmolarity?
   A. increased secretion of corticotropin releasing hormone
   B. decreased secretion of corticotropin releasing hormone
   C. increased secretion of antidiuretic hormone
   D. decreased secretion of antidiuretic hormone

---

42. Which of the following correctly completes the statement below?
The effect of _____ on the kidney is the release of _____by the kidney.
   A. an undesirably low plasma sodium ion concentration; renin
   B. an undesirably high plasma sodium ion concentration; renin
   C. an undesirably low plasma sodium ion concentration; aldosterone
   D. an undesirably high plasma sodium ion concentration; aldosterone

---

43. Under normal physiological circumstances, which of the following is completely reabsorbed by the kidney?
   A. glucose
   B. sodium
   C. bicarbonate ion
   D. urea

---

44. Which of the following is a physiological purpose of the sodium ion reabsorption in the kidney?
   A. sodium ion conservation
   B. potassium ion excretion
   C. concentration of urine
   D. acidification of urine

---

45. What general shape do structural proteins have?
   A. globular
   B. fibrillar
   C. elongated
   D. spherical

---

46. Which of the following is a DIRECT physiological effect of angiotensin II?
   A. increased blood pressure
   B. increased renal medullary osmolality
   C. decreased renal tubule permeability to water
   D. redistribution of gastrointestinal blood flow

---

47. What is the name for the DNA strand that is transcribed by RNA polymerase?
   A. homologous
   B. complementary
   C. sense

D. antisense

---

48. Which of the following does not participate in the immune response to viral infection?
    A. T-cells
    B. interferons
    C. chief cells
    D. plasma cells

---

49. Which of the following describes the mechanism of action of antivenom in snakebite victims?
    A. blockade of cell membrane molecular targets of snake venom toxin
    B. proteolytic destruction of the snake venom toxin molecules
    C. Non-enzymatic deamination of the snake venom toxin molecules
    D. deactivation of the snake venom toxin molecules by antigen-specific antibody binding

---

50. Which of the terms below correctly completes the following sentence?
    The influenza vaccine provides ____ immunity to the influenza virus.
    A. active innate
    B. active humoral
    C. passive cellular
    D. passive innate

---

51. Which of the pairs of terms below correctly completes the following sentence?
    Human T-cells originate from cells located in the____ and reach maturity in the_____
    A. bone marrow; cortex of the spleen
    B. bone marrow; thymus
    C. thymus; cortex of the spleen
    D. cortex of the spleen, thymus

---

52. Among the four cardinal signs of localized infection, which of the following is/are NOT the DIRECT result of increased vascular permeability?
    A. redness and swelling only
    B. redness and heat only
    C. swelling and pain only
    D. pain and heat only

---

53. Which of the following is most clearly an autoimmune disease in humans?
    A. type 1 diabetes mellitus
    B. cystic fibrosis
    C. sickle cell anemia
    D. peptic ulcer disease

---

54. Where are dietary triglycerides hydrolyzed by the enzyme lipase?
    A. endoplasmic reticulum
    B. small intestine
    C. liver
    D. stomach

55. Which of the following diagrams the chemical reaction that results in the formation of a peptide bond between two amino acids, AA_1 and AA_2?

A. $AA_1 + AA_2 \rightarrow AA_1 - AA_2 + H_2O$
B. $AA_1 + AA_2 \rightarrow AA_1 - AA_2 + CO_2 + NH_3$
C. $AA_1 + AA_2 \rightarrow AA_1 - AA_2 + 2\ glucose$
D. $AA_1 + AA_2 + NAD^+ \rightarrow AA_1 - AA_2 + CO_2 + NADH$

ENGLISH & READING

Passage 1

The United States Treasury operates a subsidiary, the Bureau of Engraving and Printing (BEP), where the nation's supply of paper money is designed and manufactured. But to call American currency "paper" money is a slight misnomer that understates its unperceived complexity and intrinsic technological sophistication. The Treasury goes to extraordinary lengths to safeguard cash from counterfeiters. One of the most fundamental ways is by printing not on paper, per se, but on a proprietary blend of linen and cotton. American money is more akin to fabric than paper, and each bill that is printed is a phenomenal work of art and masterful craftsmanship.

The most frequently counterfeited denominations are the 20-dollar bill, preferred by domestic counterfeiters, and the 100-dollar note, which is the currency of choice for foreign forgers. To make the copying of twenties more difficult, the BEP uses color-shifting ink that changes from copper to green in certain lights. Evidence of this can be seen in the numeral "20" located in the lower right corner on the front of the bills. A portrait watermark – which is a very faint, rather ethereal image of President Jackson – is also juxtaposed into the blank space to the right to his visible and prominent portrait. Additionally, there is a security ribbon, adorned with a flag and the words "USA Twenty," printed on and embedded into the bill. When exposed to ultraviolet light, the thread glows with a greenish hue. Twenties also include an almost subliminal text that reads "USA20;" this micro-printed text is well-camouflaged within the bill. With the use of a magnifying glass, it can be found in the border beneath the Treasurer's signature.

The 100-dollar bill utilizes similar security features. These include color-shifting ink, portrait watermarks, security threads and ribbons, raised printing, and micro-printing. These units of currency, dubbed "Ben Franklins" in honor of the president whose face graces it, also boast what the BEP describes as a 3-D security ribbon. The ribbon has bells and numbers printed on it. When the currency is tilted it appears that the images of bells transform into the numeral 100 and, when tilted side to side, the bells and 100s seem to move in a lateral direction.

Security threads woven into each different denomination have their own respective colors, and each one glows a different color when illuminated with ultraviolet light. Fine engraving or printing patterns appear in various locations on bills too, and many of these patterns are extremely fine. The artists who create them for engraving also incorporate non-linear designs, as the waviness can make it exponentially more difficult to successfully counterfeit the currency. The surface of American currency is also slightly raised, giving it a subtly, but distinct, tactile characteristic.

1. Which of the following conclusions may logically be drawn from the first paragraph of the passage?
    - A. Linen and cotton are more expensive printing materials than paper.
    - B. The current process of printing money is reflective of decades of modifications.
    - C. Counterfeiting of American money is an enormous problem.
    - D. The artistry inherent in the making of American money makes it attractive to collectors.

---

2. What sentence, if added to the end of the passage, would provide the best conclusion to both the paragraph and the passage?
    - A. It is clear from all these subtly nuanced features of the various bills that true artistry is at work in their making.
    - B. Yet, despite all of these technological innovations, the race to stay ahead of savvy counterfeiters and their constantly changing counterfeiting techniques is a never-ending one.
    - C. Due to the complexities involved in the printing of money, these artists are consequently well-paid for their skills.
    - D. Thus, many other countries have begun to model their money-printing methods on these effective techniques.

3. The passage is reflective of which of the following types of writing?
   A. Descriptive
   B. Narrative
   C. Expository
   D. Persuasive

---

4. This passage likely comes from which of the following documents?
   A. A pamphlet for tourists visiting the United States Treasury
   B. A feature news article commemorating the bicentennial of the Bureau of Engraving and Printing
   C. A letter from the US Treasury Secretary to the President
   D. A public service message warning citizens about the increased circulation of counterfeit currency

---

5. Which of the following is an example of a primary source document?
   A. A pamphlet for tourists visiting the United States Treasury
   B. A feature news article commemorating the bicentennial of the Bureau of Engraving and Printing
   C. A letter from the US Treasury Secretary to the President
   D. A public service message warning citizens about the increased circulation of counterfeit currency

---

6. Which of the following describes the word intrinsic as it is used in the first paragraph of the passage?
   A. Amazing
   B. Expensive
   C. Unbelievable
   D. Inherent

Passage 2

In the Middle Ages, merchants an artisans formed groups called "guilds" to protect themselves and their trades. Guilds appeared in the year 1000, and by the twelfth century, analogous trades, like wool, spice, and silk dealers had formed their own guilds. ________________________, towns like Florence, Italy, boasted as many as 50 merchants' guilds. With the advent of guilds, apprenticeship became a complex system. Apprentices were to be taught only certain things and then they were to prove they possessed certain skills, as determined by the guild. Each guild decided the length of time required for an apprentice to work for a master tradesman before being admitted to the trade.

7. The topic sentence of the above passage is
   A. In the Middle Ages, merchants an artisans formed groups called "guilds" to protect themselves and their trades.
   B. Guilds appeared in the year 1000, and by the twelfth century, analogous trades, like wool, spice, and silk dealers had formed their own guilds.
   C. With the advent of guilds, apprenticeship became a complex system.
   D. Apprentices were to be taught only certain things and then they were to prove they possessed certain skills, as determined by the guild.

8. The main idea of the passage is that
   A. wool, spice and silk dealers were all types of merchant trades during the Middle Ages.
   B. Florence, Italy was a great center of commerce during the Middle Ages.
   C. merchant guilds originated in the Middle Ages and became extremely popular, eventually leading to a sophisticated apprenticeship system.
   D. apprenticeships were highly sought after, therefore merchants had many skilled workers to choose from to assist them in their trade.

9. From the content of the passage, it reasonably be inferred that
   A. prior to the inception of guilds, merchants were susceptible to competition from lesser killed craftsmen peddling inferior products or services.
   B. most merchants were unscrupulous business who often cheated their customers.
   C. it was quite easy to become an apprentice to a highly skilled merchant.
   D. guilds fell out of practice during the Industrial Revolution due to the mechanization of labor.

10. As it is used in the second sentence, "analogous" most nearly means
   A. obsolete
   B. inferior
   C. similar
   D. less popular

11. Which of the following is the best signal word or phrase to fill in the blank above?
   A. Up until that time,
   B. Before that time,
   C. By that time,
   D. After that time,

Passage 3

Certainly we must face this fact: if the American press, as a mass medium, has formed the minds of America, the mass has also formed the medium. There is action, reaction, and interaction going on ceaselessly between the newspaper-buying public and the editors. What is wrong with the American press is what is in part wrong with American society. Is this, ___________________, to exonerate the American press for its failures to give the American people more tasteful and more illuminating reading matter? Can the American press seek to be excused from responsibility for public lack of information as TV and radio often do, on the grounds that, after all, "we have to give the people what they want or we will go out of business"? --Clare Boothe Luce

12. What is the primary purpose of this text?
   A. To reveal an innate problem in American society
   B. To criticize the American press for not taking responsibility for their actions
   C. To analyze the complex relationship that exists between the public and the media
   D. To challenge the masses to protest the lack of information disseminated by the media

13. From which of the following is the above paragraph most likely excerpted?
   A. A newspaper editorial letter
   B. A novel about yellow journalism

C. A diary entry
D. A speech given at a civil rights protest

---

14. Which of the following is an example of a primary source document?
    A. A newspaper editorial letter
    B. A novel about yellow journalism
    C. A diary entry
    D. A speech given at a civil rights protest

---

15. As it is used in sentence 4, "illuminating" most nearly means
    A. intelligent
    B. sophisticated
    C. interesting
    D. enlightening

---

16. Which of the following is the best signal word or phrase to fill in the blank?
    A. so
    B. however
    C. therefore
    D. yet

---

17. What is the author's primary attitude towards the American press?
    A. admiration
    B. perplexity
    C. disapproval
    D. ambivalence

---

18. Which of the following identifies the mode of the passage?
    A. expository
    B. persuasive/argumentative
    C. narrative
    D. descriptive

---

19. Based on the passage, which of the following can most likely be concluded?
    A. The author has a degree in journalism
    B. The author has worked in the journalism industry
    C. The author is seeking employment at a newspaper
    D. The author is filing a lawsuit against a media outlet

Passage 4

The game today known as "football" in the United States can be traced directly back to the English game of rugby, although there have been many changes to the game. Football was played informally on university fields more than a hundred years ago. In 1840, a yearly series of informal "scrimmages" started at Yale University. It took more than twenty-five years, ________________, for the game to become a part of college life. The first formal intercollegiate football game was held between Princeton and Rutgers teams on November 6, 1869 on Rutgers' home field at New Brunswick, New Jersey, and Rutgers won.

20. Which sentence, if added to the end of the paragraph, would provide the best conclusion?

A. Despite an invitation to join the Ivy League, Rutgers University declined, but later joinedthe Big Ten Conference instead.

B. Football was played for decades on school campuses nationwide before the American Professional Football Association was formed in 1920, and then renamed the National Football League (or the NFL) two years later.

C. Women were never allowed to play football, and that fact remains a controversial policyat many colleges and universities.

D. Football remains the national pastime, despite rising popularity for the game of soccer,due to increased TV coverage of World Cup matches.

---

21. Which of the following is the best signal word or phrase to fill in the blank above?

A. however

B. still

C. in addition

D. alternatively

Passage 5

Modernism is a philosophical movement that arose during the early 20th century. Among the factors that shaped modernism were the development of modern societies based on industry and the rapid growth of cities, followed later by the horror of World War I. Modernism rejected the science-based thinking of the earlier Era of Enlightenment, and many modernists also rejected religion. The poet Ezra Pound's 1934 injunction to "Make it new!" was the touchstone of the movement's approach towards what it saw as the now obsolete culture of the past. A notable characteristic of modernism is self-consciousness and irony concerning established literary and social traditions, which often led to experiments concerned with HOW things were made, not so much with the actual final product. Modernism had a profound impact on numerous aspects of life, and its values and perspectives still influence society in many positive ways today.

22. According to the passage, what is the overarching theme of the modernist movement?

A. Rejection of the past and outmoded ideas

B. Appreciation of urban settings over natural settings

C. A concentration on method over form

D. A focus on automated industry

---

23. As it is used in the passage, “touchstone” most nearly means

A. Challenge

B. Basis

C. Fashion

D. Metaphor

---

24. Which of the following statements from the passage can be described as an opinion?

A. Among the factors that shaped modernism were the development of modern societies based on industry and the rapid growth of cities, followed later by the horror of World War I.

B. The poet Ezra Pound's 1934 injunction to "Make it new!" was the touchstone of the movement's approach towards what it saw as the now obsolete culture of the past.

C. A notable characteristic of modernism is self-consciousness and irony concerning established literary and social traditions, which often led to experiments concerned with HOW things were made, not so much with the actual final product.
D. Modernism had a profound impact on numerous aspects of life, and its values and perspectives still influence society in many positive ways today.

Passage 6

The modern Olympics are the leading international sporting event featuring summer and winter sports competitions in which thousands of athletes from around the world participate in a variety of competitions. Held every two years, with the Summer and Winter Games alternating, the games are a modern way to bring nations together, ______________________ allowing for national pride, and sportsmanship on a global scale. Having withstood the test of time over many centuries, they are the best example of the physical achievements of mankind.

The creation of the modern Games was inspired by the ancient Olympic Games, which were held in Olympia, Greece, from the 8th century BC to the 4th century AD. The Ancient Games events were fewer in number and were examples of very basic traditional forms of competitive athleticism. Many running events were featured, as well as a pentathlon (consisting of a jumping event, discus and javelin throws, a foot race, and wrestling), boxing, wrestling, pankration, and equestrian events. Fast forward to the modern state of this ancient athletic competition, and we see that the Olympic Movement during the 20th and 21st centuries has resulted in several changes to the Games, including the creation of the Winter Olympic Games for ice and winter sports, which for climate reasons, would not have been possible in ancient Greece. The Olympics has also shifted away from pure amateurism to allowing participation of professional athletes, a change which was met with criticism when first introduced, as many felt it detracted from the original spirit and intention of the competition.

Today, over 13,000 athletes compete at the summer and Winter Olympic Games in 33 different sports and nearly 400 events. The first, second, and third-place finishers in each event receive Olympic medals: gold, silver, and bronze, respectively. And every country hopes to be able to go home with many of these medals, as they are truly still a point of pride for each nation to be recognized for some outstanding achievement on the world stage, however briefly.

25. Which of the following is the best signal word or phrase to fill in the blank in the first paragraph?
A. despite
B. however
C. instead of
D. as well as

---

26. Which of the following words from the last sentence of paragraph 2 has a negative connotation?
A. Shifted
B. Allowing
C. Change
D. Detracted

---

27. Which of the following statements based on the passage would be considered an opinion?
A. The ancient Olympic games were held in Olympia, Greece.
B. The Olympic games are the best example of humanity's physical prowess.
C. When the games were changed from pure amateurism to allowing professional athletes to participate, this change displeased many people.
D. Today, 33 different sports are represented at the Olympic games.

Passage 7

A day or two later, in the afternoon, I saw myself staring at my fire, at an inn which I had booked on foreseeing that I would spend some weeks in London. I had just come in, and, having decided on a spot for my luggage, sat down to consider my room. It was on the ground floor, and the fading daylight reached it in a sadly broken-down condition. It struck me that the room was stuffy and unsocial, with its moldy smell and its decoration of lithographs and waxy flowers – it seemed an impersonal black hole in the huge general blackness of the inn itself. The uproar of the neighborhood outside hummed away, and the rattle of a heartless hansom cab passed close to my ears. A sudden horror of the whole place came over me, like a tiger-pounce of homesickness which had been watching its moment. London seemed hideous, vicious, cruel and, above all, overwhelming. Soon, I would have to go out for my dinner, and it appeared to me that I would rather remain dinnerless, would rather even starve, than go forth into the hellish town where a stranger might get trampled to death, and have his carcass thrown into the Thames River.

28. Based on the passage above, the author's attitude toward his experience in London can best be described as

    A. Awe
    B. Disappointment
    C. Revulsion
    D. Ambivalence

---

29. Which type of document is this passage likely excerpted from?

    A. A travel guide
    B. A diary entry
    C. A news editorial
    D. An advertisement

---

30. Which of the following documents would likely NOT be considered a primary source document?

    A. A travel guide
    B. A diary entry
    C. A news editorial
    D. An advertisement

---

31. Based on the content of the passage, which of the following is a reasonable conclusion?

    A. The author is quite wealthy.
    B. The author has been to London before.
    C. The author is traveling to London based on the recommendation of a friend.
    D. The author will not be traveling to London again.

---

32. Which sentence below illustrates proper use of punctuation for dialogue?

    A. "I have a dream", began Martin Luther King, Jr.
    B. "Can you believe that I have been asked to audition for that part," asked Megan excitedly?
    C. "You barely know him! How can she marry him?" was the worried mother's response at her teenager's announcement of marriage.
    D. "Remain seated while the seatbelt signs are illuminated." Came the announcement over the airplane's loud speaker system.

---

33. Which of the sentences below is NOT in the second person?
   A. "I have a dream", began Martin Luther King, Jr.
   B. "Can you believe that I have been asked to audition for that part," asked Megan excitedly?
   C. "You barely know him! How can you marry him?" was the worried mother's response at her teenager's announcement of marriage.
   D. "Remain seated while the seatbelt signs are illuminated." Came the announcement over the airplane's loud speaker system.

---

34. Which of the following sentences is an example of an imperative sentence?
   A. "I have a dream", began Martin Luther King, Jr.
   B. "Can you believe that I have been asked to audition for that part," asked Megan excitedly?
   C. "You barely know him! How can she marry him?" was the worried mother's response at her teenager's announcement of marriage.
   D. "Please remain seated while the seatbelt signs are illuminated." Came the announcement over the airplane's loud speaker system.

---

35. Which of the following means "the act of cutting out"?
   A. Incision
   B. Concision
   C. Excision
   D. Decision

---

36. Which of the following refers to an inflammation?
   A. Appendectomy
   B. Colitis
   C. Angioplasty
   D. Dermatology

---

37. Which of the following refers to a cancer?
   A. Neuropathy
   B. Hysterectomy
   C. Oncology
   D. Melanoma

---

38. Which of the following conditions is associated with the nose?
   A. Hematoma
   B. Neuralgia
   C. Rhinitis
   D. Meningitis

---

39. Which of the following refers to the study of something?
   A. Gastroenterology
   B. Gastritis
   C. Psychosis
   D. Psychopath

ANSWERS PRACTICE TEST 2

MATHEMATICS

1 C. 7/3

An improper fraction is a fraction whose numerator is greater than its denominator. To change a mixed number to an improper fraction, multiply the whole number (2) times the denominator (3) and add the result to the numerator. Answer C is the correct choice.

---

2 A. 0.6 x 90

To find 60% of 90, first convert 60% to a decimal by moving the decimal point two places to the left. Then multiply this decimal, 0.6, times 90. Answer A is the correct choice.

---

3 B. $2\ {}^{5}/_{6}$

To convert an improper fraction to a mixed number, divide the numerator by the denominator. In this case, you get 2 with a remainder of 5. 2 becomes the whole number, and the remainder is the numerator. Answer B is the correct choice.

---

4 C. 0.6363...

The ratio 7/11 implies division, so the decimal value can be determined by the long division problem of 7 divided by 11. The long division results in the repeating decimal 0.6363... There may be a simpler method to find this decimal. The ratio 7/11 is the product of 7 times 1/11. The ratio 1/11 is the repeating decimal 0.0909... so multiplying that decimal by 7 is 0.6363... which provides the same answer. If it seems like the same amount of effort, remember that every fraction with 11 in the denominator can be determined in the same way. Answer C is the correct choice.

---

5 A. 0.625

The ratio implies division, so 5/8 can be determined by the long division problem of 5 divided by 8. The long division results in the decimal 0.625. There is a simpler method to find this decimal. The ratio 5/8 is the product of 5 times 1/8. The ratio 1/8 is the decimal 0.125, so multiplying that decimal by 5 is 0.625, which is the same answer. If it seems like the same amount of effort, remember that every fraction with 8 in the denominator can be determined in the same way. Answer A is the correct choice.

---

6 – D. 9/16

The numerator in the correct ratio will be equal to the given decimal times the correct denominator. It is simply a result of cross multiplying. But first, these problems can be greatly simplified if we eliminate incorrect answers.

For example, answers A and B can both be eliminated because they are both less than 0.5 or ½. If you can't see that, then multiply .5 times 15 and .5 times 23. In answer A, .5 times 15 is 7.5 so 7/15 is less than the fractional value of 0.5625. In B, .5 times 23 is 11.5 so 11/23 is less than the fractional value of 0.5625.

Now, evaluating fractional answers this way, you may look at answer C and realize that since 0.6 times 8 equals 4.8. Since 4.8 is less than the numerator and 0.6 is larger than the given decimal value, C can be eliminated. Answer D is the correct choice.

7 A. 5/16

The numerator in the correct ratio will be equal to the given decimal times the correct denominator. It is simply a result of cross multiplying. But first, the problem can be simplified if we eliminate impossible answers.

For example, answer B can be eliminated because it simplifies to 1/6 which is much less than 0.3125. If you can't see that, then divide 1 by 6 which becomes 0.167.

For answer D, the ratio 9/25 is a simplified form of 36/100 or 0.36. 0.36 is greater than 0.3125, so answer D can be eliminated.

Now, evaluating fractional answers this way, you may eliminate answer C for a very simple reason. 19 times 0.3125 will always leave a value of 5 in the ten-thousandths place because 19 times 5 equals 95. That means the product can never be the whole number 6, so answer C can be eliminated.

The correct answer is A because you have logically eliminated all the other possible choices.

---

8 A. 6

If a = 10, then 2a = 20.

Now compute the value of b^2

b^2 = (b) • (b)

b^2 = (–4) • (–4)

b^2 = 16

So now you have:

$$\sqrt{16+20} \text{ or } \sqrt{36}$$

The square root of 36 is 6. Answer A is the correct choice

---

9 C. 16

The greatest common factor of two numbers is the largest number that can be divided evenly into both numbers. The simplest way to answer this question is to start with the largest answer (32) and see if it can be divided evenly into 48 and 64. It can't. Now try the next largest answer (16), and you see that it can be divided evenly into 48 and 64. 16 is the correct answer. The other answers are also factors but the largest of them is 16. Answer C is the correct choice

---

10 D. 21/32

To multiply fractions, multiply the numerators and the denominators. In this case, multiply 3 times 7 and 4 times 8. The answer is 21/32. Answer D is the correct choice.

---

11 A. 12

Replace the letters with the numbers they represent and then perform the necessary operations.

$$3^2 + 6(0.5)$$
$$9 + 3 = 12$$

Answer A is the correct choice.

---

12 B. 40

The least common multiple is used when finding the lowest common denominator. The least common multiple is the lowest number that can be divided evenly by both of the other numbers.

Here is a simple method to find the least common multiple of 8 and 10. Write 8 on the left side of your paper. Then add 8 and write the result. Then add another 8 to that number and write the result.

Keep going until you have a list that looks something like this:

8 16 24 32 40...

This is a partial list of multiples of 8. (If you remember your multiplication tables, these numbers are the column or row that go with 8.) Now do the same thing with 10.

10 20 30 40...

This is the partial list of multiples of 10.

Eventually, the numbers will be found in both rows. That smallest common number is the least common multiple. There will always be more multiples that are common to both rows, but the smallest number is the least common multiple. Answer B is the correct choice

---

13 C. 17/24

To add 1/3 and 3/8, you must find a common denominator. The simplest way to do this is to multiply the denominators: 3 x 8 = 24. So 24 is a common denominator. (This method will not always give you the lowest common denominator, but in this case it does.)

Once you have found a common denominator, you need to convert both fractions in the problem to equivalent fractions that have that same denominator. To do this, multiply each fraction by an equivalent of 1.

1/3 • 8/8 = (8•1) / (8•3) or 8/24

3/8 • 3/3 = (3•3) / (8•3) or 9/24.

8/24 + 9/24 = 17/24

Adding 8/24 and 9/24 is the solution to the problem. Answer C is the correct choice.

---

14 C. 81

When two numbers with the same sign (both positive or both negative) are multiplied, the answer is a positive number. When two numbers with different signs (one positive and the other negative) are multiplied, the answer is negative. Answer C is the correct choice.

---

15 C. 7/10

The simplest way to solve this problem is to convert the fractions to decimals. You do this by dividing the numerators by the denominators.

2/3 = 0.67 and 3/4 = 0.75, so the correct answer is a decimal that falls between these two numbers.

3/5 = 0.6 (too small)

4/5 = 0.8 (too large)

7/10 = 0.7 (correct choice between 0.67 and 0.75

5/8 = 0.625 (too small)

Answer C is the correct choice

---

16 D. 7

In this number:

1 is in the thousands place.
2 is in the hundreds place. 3 is in the tens place. 4 is in the ones place
5 is in the tenths place.
6 is in the hundredths place.
7 is in the thousandths place.

Answer D is the correct choice.

17 D. 0.72

The simplest way to answer this question is to convert the fractions to decimals. To convert a fraction to a decimal, divide the numerator (the top number) by the denominator (the bottom number).

5/8 = 0.625

3/5 = 0.6

2/3 = 0.67

So the largest number is 0.72. Answer D is the correct choice.

---

18 D. 3^4

All positive numbers are larger than the negative numbers, so the possible answers are 42 or 3^4. 3^4 equals 81 (3 • 3 • 3 • 3). Answer D is the correct choice.

---

19 C. 4.8571, 4.8573, 4.8578, 4.8579

The numbers 4.857 and 4.858 have an unlimited set of numbers between them, and the simplest method is to start with another number after the last digit of 4.857. Therefore 4.8571 and 4.8572 are both greater than 4.857 and less than 4.858. Choices A, B, and D, include numbers that are equal to or greater than the larger of the two or less than the two numbers. Only C has all numbers between. Answer C is the correct choice

---

20 D. 23/5

The numbers 4 and 5 can be multiplied by the denominators in the answer set to see which answers are correct. Only D is correct because 20/5 and 25/5 are the numbers that are less than and greater than the answer 23/5. Answer D is the correct choice.

---

21 A. 34/5

The numbers 7 and 9 can be multiplied by the denominators in the answer set to see which answers are correct. A is correct because 34/5 is less than 35/5 and 45/5, so it can't be in between. Answer A is the correct choice.

---

22 A. 9

Begin by subtracting –3 from both sides of the equation. (This is the same as adding +3). Then:

$$\frac{4}{9}x = 4$$

Now to isolate X on one side of the equation, divide both sides by . (To divide by a fraction, invert the fraction and multiply.

9/4 * 4/9 X = 4/1*9/4

You are left with $= \frac{36}{4} = 9$. Answer A is the correct choice.

---

23 B. –10

To find the value of q, divide both sides of the equation by –13. When a positive number is divided by a negative number, the answer is negative. Answer B is the correct choice.

---

24 D. x = 4

When you multiply or divide numbers that have the same sign (both positive or both negative), the answer will be positive. When you multiply or divide numbers that have different signs (one positive and the other negative), the answer will be negative. In this case, both numbers have the same sign. Divide as you normally would and remember that the answer will be a positive number. Answer D is the correct choice.

25 C. r = (p - 3) / 2

Begin by subtracting 3 from both sides of the equation. You get:

$$p - 3 = 2r$$

Now to isolate r on one side of the equation, divide both sides of the equation by 2. You get:

$$r = (p - 3) / 2$$

Answer C is the correct choice

---

26 C. x = 11

Subtracting a negative number is the same as adding a positive number. So 8 – (–3) is the same as 8 + 3 or 11. Answer C is the correct choice.

---

27 C. 388

The value can be expanded as 7 x 49 added to 9 x 7 with 18 subtracted from the total. That becomes 343 + 63 -18 with the answer equal to 388. Answer C is the correct choice.

---

28 B. 42

The value can be expanded as 25 added to 5 x 7 with 18 subtracted from the total. That becomes 25 + 35 -18 with the answer equal to 42. There is another simple way to evaluate this expression. The expression can be rewritten as the product of two expressions (x+9)(x-2). If we substitute 5 for x then this product becomes 14 x 3 which is also 42. Answer B is the correct choice.

---

29 C. 6804

The simplest way to evaluate this expression is to rewrite it as the product of two expressions. Factoring common factors out the given expression becomes 7x(x + 9). "7x" becomes 189 and x+9 becomes 36. The product of 189 and 36 becomes 6804. In the interest of eliminating incorrect answers, the product of the values in the "ones" column is 6x9 which is 54. The correct answer must end in 4, so the correct answer must be C. Answer C is the correct choice.

---

30 D. $12

Use the information given to write an equation:

$$530 = 40d + 50$$

When you subtract 50 from both sides of the equation, you get:

$$480 = 40d$$

Divide both sides of the equation by 40.
12 = d, Sam's hourly wage
Answer D is the correct choice.

---

31 A. a number greater than X

When a positive number is divided by a positive number less than 1, the quotient will always be larger than the number being divided. For example, 5 ÷ 0.5 = 10. If we solve this as a fraction, 5÷ (1/2) is the same as 5 x (2/1) or 10 since dividing by a fraction is the same as multiplying by the reciprocal. Answer A is the correct choice.

---

32 A. (14 + 24) • 8 • 5

In the correct answer, (14 + 24) • 8 • 5, the hourly wages of Amanda and Oscar are first combined, and the total amount is multiplied by 8 hours in a day and five days in a week. One of the other choices, 14 + 24 • 8 • 5, looks similar to this, but it is incorrect because the hourly wages must be combined before they can be multiplied by 8 and 5. Answer A is the correct choice

---

33 A. 10

Use the facts you are given to write an equation:

$$7 + 4/5n = 15$$

First subtract 7 from both side of the equation. You get:

$$4/5n = 8$$

Now divide both sides of the equation by 4/5. To divide by a fraction, invert the fraction (4/5 becomes 5/4) and multiply:

$$(5/4)4/5n = 8 \bullet 5/4$$
$$n = 40/4 \text{ or } 10$$

Answer A is the correct choice

---

34 D. 108

The ratio of the two numbers is 7:3. This means that the larger number is 7/10 of 360 and the smaller number is 3/10 of 360.

The larger number is 7 • 360/10 or 7 • 36 or 252

The smaller number is 3 • 360/10 or 3 • 36 or 108

Answer D is the correct choice.

---

35 C. $310

The costs of all these items can be expressed in terms of the cost of the ream of paper. Use x to represent the cost of a ream of paper. The flash drive costs three times as much as the ream of paper, so it costs 3x. The textbook costs three times as much as the flash drive, so it costs 9x. The printer cartridge costs twice as much as the textbook, so it costs 18x. So now we have:

$$x + 3x + 9x + 18x = 31x$$

The ream of paper costs $10, so 31x, the total cost, is $310. Answer C is the correct choice

---

36 D. $\frac{(6)(9)}{2}$

The area of a triangle is one-half the product of the base and the height. Choices A and B are incorrect because they add the base and the height instead of multiplying them. Choice C is incorrect because it multiplies the product of the base and the height by 2 instead of dividing it by 2. Answer D is the correct choice.

---

37 A. 2,595

The steps in evaluating a mathematical expression must be carried out in a certain order, called the order of operations. These are the steps in order:

Parentheses: The first step is to do any operations in parentheses.

Exponents: Then do any steps that involve exponents

Multiply and **D**ivide: Multiply and divide from left to right

Add and **S**ubtract: Add and subtract from left to right

One way to remember this order is to use this sentence:

Please **E**xcuse **M**y **D**ear **A**unt **S**ally.

To evaluate the expression in this question, follow these steps:

Multiply the numbers in Parentheses: 3 • 4 = 12

Apply the Exponent 2 to the number in parentheses: 12^2 = 144

Multiply: 6 • 3 • 144 = 2,592
Add: 2 + 2,592 + 1 = 2,595
Answer A is the correct choice.

---

38 B. $3x^2 - 4x - 15$

The words in the problem tell us that the new expression for the length is 3x+5 and the new width is represented by the expression x-3. The area is represented by the product of (3x+5) (x-3). Multiplying the two binomials together with FOIL means that the first term is the product of x and 3x or 3x2. All of the multiple choices have the correct first term. However, the last term is the product of 5 and -3, or -15, which means that answer C is an incorrect answer.

Since the middle term is the difference of 5x and -9x, which is -4x, answer B is the only correct answer. If you choose to use the box method to solve these products, you will see the same results and the same factors. Answer B is the correct choice.

---

39 C. $14x^2 + 13x + 3$

The words in the problem tell us that the new expression for the base is 4x+2 and the new height is represented by the expression 7x+3. The area is represented by the product of 1/2(4x+2) (7x+3). Multiplying the two binomials together with FOIL means that the first term is the product of 4x and 7x and ½ or $14x^2$. However, the last term is the product of 2 and 3 and 1/2, or 3, which means that answer A is an incorrect answer.

The middle term is ½ the sum of 14x and 12x which is 26/2 x or 13x. Therefore answer C is the only correct answer.

---

40 B. 19,098 kg m/s

Momentum is defined as the product of mass times velocity. The conversion of 55 km/hr to meters per second means multiplying by one thousand and dividing by 3600. (seconds per hour). That value, 15.28, must be multiplied by the 1,250 kg mass. That answer is 19,098 kg m/s. Answer B is the correct choice.

---

41 A. $33,500

Janet has a total of $105,000 in her accounts. 70% of that amount, her goal for her stock investments, is $73,500. To reach that goal, she would have to move $33,500 from bonds to stocks. Answer A is the correct choice.

---

42 A. $52,000

Convert 15% to a decimal by moving the decimal point two places to the left: 15% = 0.15. Using x to represent Brian's gross salary, you can write this equation:

0.15 x = $7,800

To solve for x, divide both sides of the equation by 0.15. $7,800 divided by 0.15 is $52,000. Answer A is the correct choice.

---

43 C. 20

To solve this problem, first convert 45% to a decimal by moving the decimal point two place to the left: 45% = .45. Use x to represent the total number of students in the class. Then: .45x = 9

Solve for x by dividing both sides of the equation by .45. 9 divided by .45 is 20. Answer C is the correct choice.

44 B. 515

Marisol scored higher than 78% of the students who took the test. Convert 78% to a decimal by moving the decimal point two places to the left: 78% = .78. Now multiply .78 times the number of students who took the test:

.78 x 660 = 514.8 or 515 students (whole number answers)

Answer B is the correct choice.

---

45 D. 130,500

The population of Mariposa County in 2015 was 90% of its population in 2010. Convert 90% to a decimal by moving the decimal point two places to the left: 90% = .90. Now multiply .90 times 145,000, the population in 2010.

.90 • 145,000 = 130,500

Answer D is the correct choice.

---

46 A. 20

Alicia must have a score of 75% on a test with 80 questions. To find how many questions she must answer correctly, first convert 75% to a decimal by moving the decimal point two places the left: 75% = .75. Now multiply .75 times 80:

.75 • 80 = 60.

Alicia must answer 60 questions correctly, but the question asks how many questions can she miss. If she must answer 60 correctly, then she can miss 20. Answer A is the correct choice.

---

47 C. $300

If the phone was on sale at 30% off, the sale price was 70% of the original price. So

$210 = 70% of x

where x is the original price of the phone. When you convert 70% to a decimal, you get:

$210 = .70 • x

To isolate x on one side of the equation, divide both sides of the equation by .70. You find that x = $300.

Answer C is the correct choice

---

48 A. 84

First, find the number of girls in the class. Convert 52% to a decimal by moving the decimal point two places to the left:

52% = .52

Then multiply .52 times the number of students in the class:

.52 • 350 = 182

182 – 98 = 84

Of the 182 girls, 98 plan to go to college, so a total of 84 do not plan to go to college. Answer A is the correct choice

---

49 C. 12%

To find the percent increase, you first need to know the amount of the increase. Enrollment went from 3,450 in 2010 to 3,864 in 2015. This is an increase of 414. Now, to find the percent of the increase, divide the amount of the increase by the original amount:

414 ÷ 3,450 = 0.12

To convert a decimal to a percent, move the decimal point two places to the right:

0.12 = 12%

When a question asks for the percent increase or decrease, divide the amount of the increase or decrease by the original value. Answer C is the correct choice.

---

50 D. 14 pounds 14 ounces

When rounding measurements to the whole number value, the measurement is usually rounded up to the next larger whole number if that measurement is halfway or closer to the next higher value. In this case, since there 16 ounces in a pound, D is the correct answer.

---

51 C. 7,514,635.8239

When rounding a number to a given place value, the next lower place value is used to determine if the number is rounded up or down. The rounded value has its last significant digit in that place. Answer C has a number 9 in the ten thousandths place. Notice the difference between ten-thousands and ten-thousandths. Answer A is rounded to the ten-thousands place!

---

52 C. 7.15 cc's

When rounding a measurement, the value includes a precision of plus or minus half of the smallest increment measured. The lines on the cylinder would have the values of 7.00, 7.10, 7.20, or each tenth of a cc. The actual value of the meniscus that reads between tenths would be 7.15 cc. Answer C has a number with the correct precision.

---

53 C. 4 men for 1 day

When estimating, it is helpful to round before estimating. The summary of this problem's solution includes a rate of 200 pounds per hour (15 minute each). Two and one-half tons is 5000 pounds. 5000 pounds divided by 200 pounds per hour means 25 hours of labor is required. Answer C is the best estimate of 25 hours of labor (32). Answer A is 800 hours, B is 16 hours, and D is 200 hours.

---

54 B. 40 minutes

When estimating this answer, the basic formula of distance equal to rate multiplied by time applies. So the time required for the trip is the distance divided by the rate. 18 miles divided by ¾ (45 minutes is ¾ of an hour), is 24 miles per hour. The new rate would be 29 miles per hour (increase of 5). 18 divided by 29 is about 60% of an hour or close to 40 minutes. 30 minutes is a close answer, but that is only possible if the rate is 36 miles per hour! Estimating may require that you eliminate answers that are close to the correct answer. Answer B is the correct choice

---

55 C. 70 seconds per m/c; 35 seconds per t/f

An estimate often means that you will need to check possible answers to see if they are correct. In this example, the basic assumption is that the time for m/c problems will be twice the value for the t/f. Trying one minute for m/c and one half minute for t/f comes out to 35 minutes. So answer B is not correct. The next closest one is answer C, which comes out to 1400 seconds and 1050 seconds for a total of 2450 seconds. That is close to the allowable 2700 seconds (45 minutes). If you try answer D, the total comes out to 1600 plus 1200 or a total of 2800 seconds. That's more than the allowable total of 2700. Answer C is the correct choice.

---

56 B. twice as fast

When estimating this answer, the formula of distance equal to rate multiplied by time applies. So the speed required for the trip is the distance divided by the time. In this example 10 minutes late means half the amount of time. Dividing by one-half means that the rate must be doubled. Answer B is the correct choice.

SCIENCE

1 B. smooth endoplasmic reticulum does not participate in synthesis of proteins.

Smooth endoplasmic reticulum does not contain ribosomes. Rough endoplasmic reticulum does contain ribosomes. Ribosomes are required to synthesize proteins. Both RER and SER may be involved in the synthesis of products that are destined for transport and secretion out of the cell into the external environment.

---

2 A. an external cell membrane

An external cell membrane is a feature of all living cells. Many cells, such as plant, fungi, and bacterial cells also possess at least one outer cell wall, but human and other animal cells do not. Bacterial cells do not possess a nucleus or mitochondria.

---

3 B. coronal

Coronal refers to an axial plane of the body. The other axial planes are the sagittal and the cross-sectional planes. Caudal means nearer to the tail or the posterior part of the body. Ventral means at or nearer to the frontal surface of the body. The term inferior means near to the feet.

---

4 C. microtubules

Human sperm flagellum is constructed from and internal bundle of microtubules that interact with a microtubule organizing structure at the base of the flagellum. The individual microtubules sequentially slide back and forth within the outer envelope of the flagellum, causing a whipping motion that generates a forward motion of the sperm cells. Thick or myosin filaments are critical elements of muscle contraction, and actin microfilaments are involved in many functions that require active purposeful movement of cells and within cells, but neither are elements of the flagellum of human sperm cells. Intermediate filaments are generally structural elements of the cytoskeletal framework of a cell and do not contribute to the functioning of flagellum of human sperm cells.

---

5 B. alternating deoxyribose sugars and phosphate groups

The structure of a DNA molecule in a cell is usually the double-stranded form of DNA. This double-stranded structure is a spiraling (helical) ladder consisting of linear backbones of alternating deoxyribose sugars and phosphate groups. One deoxyribose phosphate polymer backbone forms the left side rail of the DNA ladder and another one forms the right-side rail of the DNA ladder.

---

6 A. ACG

The nitrogenous base thymine (T) occurs in DNA molecules but not in RNA molecules. The nitrogenous base uracil (U) occurs in RNA molecules but not in DNA molecules. The remaining nitrogenous bases of nucleic acids, adenine (A), cytosine (C), and guanine (G), occur in both RNA and DNA. Codons are DNA 3-base sequences and anticodons are RNA 3-base sequences. Among the choices, only choice A has a three base sequence that does not include thymine or uracil. Therefore, this is the only choice that could occur in both an RNA and a DNA sequence.

---

7 B. the Golgi apparatus

The Golgi is a highly folded series of membrane compartments that resembles a stack of pancakes. The Golgi functions with the smooth ER to process, package and transport a wide variety of products synthesized with the cell. Most often these products are packaged into secretory vesicles that are subsequently carried to the cell membrane and then secreted out of the cell into the external environment. In some types of cells, these vesicles remain inside the cell and are involved in intracellular digestion of phagocytized substances.

---

8 C. keratin

Keratin is a major extracellular structural protein in humans. It provides protective and mechanical support to the outer layers of skin and is the primary component of hair and nails in humans.

---

9 D. Leydig; testosterone

Leydig cells of the testes produce testosterone in the male reproductive system. The tunica albuginea is a fibrous outer membrane of the testis and does not directly participate in the production of any type of cells. Sertoli cells produce various substances that support the development of sperm cell precursor cells, but they do not produce FSH. Spermatogonia are cells that are progenitors of mature sperm cells. Spermatogonia do not produce LH.

---

10 A. elbow; knee

The elbow and knee joints are both synovial hinge joints that allow flexion and extension. The elbow joint is a complex hinge joint that also allows the head of the radius to pivot at the articulation of the distal end of the humerus. This allows for additional range of motion in the form of supination and pronation of the lower arm and hand. This additional range of motion is much greater than that allowed by the knee joint. The sacroiliac joint connects the sacrum (triangular bone at the bottom of the spine) with the pelvis (iliac bone that is part of the hip joint) on each side of the lower spine. It is a non-synovial ligamentous joint that has very little range of motion, less than any of the other joints listed in the choices above. The elbow and shoulder joints are both synovial ball-and-socket joints that have a much greater range of motion than hinge joints such as the knee and elbow.

---

11 D. cholesterol

Cholesterol is a four-ringed lipid-based molecule that is an important component of cell membranes and a precursor molecule for the synthesis of the steroid hormones, cortisol, aldosterone, progesterone, and the sex hormones testosterone and estrogen. It is also the precursor for the synthesis of vitamin D. Most of the cholesterol used in the body is synthesized rather that of dietary origin.

---

12 B. prevention of collapse of alveoli during exhalation

Pulmonary surfactant decreases the surface tension of the fluid layer overlying the internal surfaces of alveoli. The surface tension of fluid layers of a concave surface, such as the internal surface of a sphere, increases as the radius of sphere decreases. Without pulmonary surfactant, the surface tension of the aqueous layer within alveoli would increase as the alveoli deflate during exhalation to a point where the alveoli would completely collapse. This event would prevent reinflation of the alveoli on a subsequent inspiratory effort.

---

13 C. ventral

The ventral cavity is enclosed by the inner walls of the thorax – thoracic muscles, ribs, sternum, and thoracic vertebrae – the inner surfaces of the ventral, lateral, and dorsal abdominal wall muscles, and the inner surface bones and associated muscles of the pelvis. The ventral cavity is divided into an upper cavity – the thoracic cavity – and a lower cavity – the abdominal/pelvic cavity – by a transverse dome-shaped muscle – the diaphragm. Major contents of the thoracic cavity are the heart and lungs. Major contents of the abdominal/pelvic cavity are the intestines, associated digestive organs – liver, gallbladder and pancreas - the urinary bladder and, in females, the uterus and ovaries.

---

14 B. hypodermis

An important homeostatic function of the integument is thermoregulation, which allows the body to maintain a constant optimum internal temperature range. -The lowest layer of the integument – the hypodermis –

contains adipose tissue that has poor thermal conduction and therefore acts as an insulator to protect against excessive heat transfer between the internal regions of the body and the external environment.

---

15 A. pulmonic valve

right atrium → tricuspid valve → right ventricle → pulmonic valve

From the pulmonic valve, blood passes into the main pulmonary artery. Blood in the pulmonary artery continues to either the left or right pulmonary arteries, which then enter either the left or right lung.

---

16 A. a peripheral vein located in the leg

The pulmonary arteries are components of the right cardiovascular circulation system. Blood clots of the pulmonary arteries (thrombotic pulmonary embolisms) must originate from sites within the right heart circulation unless there is an abnormal pathway from the left to the right circulation pathways such as a direct connection between the left and right atrium. Most commonly, thrombotic pulmonary embolisms originate as blood clots in large deep veins of the lower leg. The origins listed in the other choices are all located on the left side of the heart circulation.

---

17 B. plasma cells

White blood cells or leukocytes include lymphocytes and non-lymphocytes. Lymphocytes include T-cells, B-cells and the activated form of B-cells – the plasma cells eosinophils, basophils, monocytes, and polymorphonuclear leucocytes (PMNLs) are all non-lymphocyte lineage white blood cell types.

---

18 A. Human leukocyte antigens (HLA)

The major histocompatibility complex (MHC) class I human leukocyte antigens (HLA) are generally restricted to the cell membranes of dedicated or professional antigen-presenting cells of the immune system. T-cells are activated when they bind with a class I molecule and an antigen on the surface of an antigen presenting cell. ABO and Rh factor molecules are generally restricted to red blood cell (RBC) membranes and can be a antigen that is identified as foreign by the immune system. Cadherin class cell adhesion molecules are involved primarily with structural functions related to binding with extracellular matrix molecules.

---

19 D. Reduction of the strength and contractility of the heart contraction

Sympathetic nerves release neurotransmitters to cardiac muscle and smooth muscle located in bronchial walls, intestinal tract walls, and the walls of blood vessels that generate rapid response to environmental circumstances that require aggressive and highly energetic responses (fight or flight responses.) The sympathetic effects in such circumstances include increased force of heart contractions, increased heart rate, increased blood pressure, redirection of blood flow from the intestines to the skeletal muscles, suppression of peristalsis, and dilation of the bronchial airways.

---

20 C. a meal with high simple carbohydrate content

The most common stimulus for the release of the hormone glucagon is low levels of glucose in the bloodstream. The primary effect of glucagon is on the liver, where it induces the liver to break down stored glycogen molecules into glucose molecules. The glucose molecules are secreted into the bloodstream and restore the blood glucose levels toward normal. Conversely, high blood glucose levels have the opposite effect, namely the suppression of the release of glucagon. A meal high in carbohydrates will generally result in high levels of blood glucose, because carbohydrates are composed primarily of glucose monomers. Simple carbohydrates are easily hydrolyzed by enzymes in the digestive tract to glucose molecules which in turn are rapidly absorbed into the circulation. This increases blood glucose levels and consequently tends to suppress glucagon secretion.

21 B. CCK secretion → increased bile secretion → increased fat emulsification

Cholecystokinin released from the duodenum triggers the release of bile from the gallbladder into the duodenal lumen. Bile emulsifies collections of lipids in the duodenum. Somatostatin is a hormone secreted by the duodenum and the pancreas (and anterior pituitary gland) that inhibits HCl secretion and gastrin secretion in the stomach. Secretin is a hormone released by the duodenum that inhibits HCl secretion in the stomach and stimulates the release of bicarbonate by the pancreas.

---

22 D. The male and female sex hormones are regulated by the hypothalamus through the release of gonadotropin releasing hormone (GnRh), which regulates the synthesis and release of luteinizing hormone (LH) and follicle-stimulating hormone (FSH) by the anterior pituitary.

The male sex hormone, testosterone is produced in the male gonads, the testes. Testosterone is a steroid hormone whose synthesis and secretion are regulated by the hypothalamus through the release of gonadotrophin releasing hormone (GnRh), which regulates the synthesis and release of luteinizing hormone (LH) and follicle-stimulating hormone (FSH) by the anterior pituitary. Both FSH and LH stimulate the testes to synthesize and release testosterone. Luteinizing hormone directly stimulates the production of testosterone. The female sex hormone, estrogen is produced in the female gonads, the ovaries are producing increasing amounts of estrogen. This increasing estrogen level reaches a critical level at about day 15 of the menstrual cycle. The critical estrogen level feeds back to the hypothalamus and the pituitary resulting in a rapid spike in FSH and LH levels. The LH spike stimulates ovulation.

---

23 A. smooth

Smooth muscle is the muscle type that is located throughout the body particularly in the muscular layers of the respiratory airways, the walls of the digestive tract and in the walls of circulatory vessels. Cardiac and smooth muscle are not under voluntary control but are regulated by the autonomic nervous system. Cardiac muscle is the muscle tissue that forms the heart. Skeletal or voluntary muscle consist of individual cells that have intercellular connections called gap junctions that allow the cytoplasm of cells to move freely among other cells.

---

24 B. ligaments, tendons, cartilage, and the lower structural layers of the dermis of the skin

Dense connective tissue has a high content of fibrous proteins within the connective tissue ground substance. These fibers are composed primarily of collagen and also of variable amounts of elastic fibers. Fibroblasts are distributed among the extracellular fibers. Dense connective tissue forms ligaments, tendons and cartilage and the lower structural layers of the dermis of the skin.

---

25 B. $1s^22s^22p^1$

Since at any given n electron shell level, the s orbitals are lower energy than the p orbitals, the s orbitals fill before electrons begin to occupy positions in p orbitals. For example, the electron configuration for boron (atomic number 5) is $1s^2 2s^2 2p^1$

NOT $1s^2 2s^1 2p^2$
AND NOT $1s^2 2p^3$

---

26 C. inadequate amounts of O_2 delivered to muscle tissue

Lactic acid (lactate) production in muscle tissue results from the anaerobic conversion of pyruvate (predominantly as a product of glycolysis) to lactic acid. This process generates energy but is very inefficient compared to oxidative metabolism of glucose. Inadequate oxygen supplies shift energy production to the anaerobic pathway that generates lactic acid. Additionally, oxygen is required to reduce lactate back to pyruvate. In an oxygen deficient environment, muscle tissue cannot convert lactate back to pyruvate and consequently lactate levels rise within muscle tissue.

---

27 D. contraction of smooth muscle in the walls of arterioles in voluntary muscle tissue

Parasympathetic nervous system activation produces physiological changes that are associated with resting and digestive functions. Contraction of smooth muscle in the walls of arterioles in voluntary muscle tissue redirects blood flow from voluntary muscles where it can be utilized by the digestive system. Increased sinoatrial node activity results in an increase in heart rate; decreased activity of smooth muscle contractions in the wall of the digestive tract slows peristalsis and inhibits digestive processes. Both effects are the opposite one would expect of parasympathetic effects. There are no direct autonomic effects on deep tendon reflexes. These are independent reflex arcs consisting of only a sensory receptor cell and one or two neurons in a sequence terminating on a voluntary muscle.

---

28 C. angiotension II

Angiotensin II has a direct effect on circulatory vessels, causing contraction of smooth muscle cells located in the walls of arteries and veins. This increases the force of the vessel walls on the blood within the vessels, resulting in increased blood pressure. Angiotensin II has a direct effect on the proximal tubules to increase Na^+ reabsorption. Angiotensin II is a potent vasoconstrictor and stimulates the release of aldosterone from the adrenal gland. Aldosterone causes the kidney to increase the reabsorption of sodium ion thereby helping to restore plasma ion concentrations to normal levels. Several other mechanisms can lead to the release of aldosterone.

---

29 B. noble gases

The noble gases (group VIII) have no desire for additional electrons and therefore have almost zero electronegativity.

---

30 C. leukocytes

Leukocytes (WBCs) only account for 1 percent of total blood volume.

---

31 D. combustion

All combustion reactions are self-sustaining and highly exothermic, and therefore generate a large amount of heat energy.

---

32 A. lipids

Nearly all the types of lipids in biological processes are derivatives of either fatty acids or cholesterol.

---

33 D. connective; energy storage

The hypodermis is the deepest of the three layers of the human integument. It is primarily loose connective tissue with a high content of adipocytes. One of the primary functions of the adipocytes is the storage of fat that serves as an energy reserve for the body. The adipocytes also provide some mechanical cushioning properties to the integument but they allow interstitial fluids and cells to freely pass through the hypodermis. This is the opposite of a barrier function

---

34 B. melatonin

There are no obvious methods to determine if a hormone is produced by the pituitary other than to memorize which are and which are not. Often this type of question can be answered by recognizing a hormone that is easily identified as the product of another endocrine gland. In this case, melatonin is the only significant hormone produced by the pineal gland and it is not a significant product of any other gland.

---

35 B. thyroid hormone (T_3 and T_4)

At the most general level, the activation of the sympathetic nervous system induces a high level of overall alertness and priming of the body for high energy activities. Among these effects is an elevated metabolic state. Thyroid hormones in general also induce increased metabolic activity. It is often difficult to distinguish the difference in symptoms between persons with excessive levels of thyroid hormone (hyperthyroidism) and those with extreme activation of the sympathetic nervous system, as occurs with general anxiety disorders and panic attacks.

---

36 platinum

Platinum is a transition metal. The second period group IV through VI elements - carbon, nitrogen and oxygen are all nonmetals.

---

37 C. induced fit

Enzymes are biological catalysts. They are not simple metallic surfaces but extremely complex three-dimensional protein structures. They lower activation energies of biological reactions by attracting reactants to a specific site on the enzyme known as the active site. As reactants bind to the active site, the configuration of the site changes in a manner that orients the reactants in the optimum manner for the chemical reaction to occur. This process is called the "induced fit" mechanism for enzymatic activity. The activity of an enzyme is defined as the rate at which the reaction catalyzed by the enzyme occurs. The higher the enzyme activity, the greater the rate of enzyme catalyzed reaction.

---

38 B. temporomandibular joint

Of the four choices, three are completely fused or relatively immobile non-synovial joints. The temporomandibular joint is a highly mobile synovial joint that allows for the chewing motions of the lower jaw (mandible).

---

39 D. the glomeruli

Arterial blood arrives for filtration by the kidney via the renal artery. The renal artery undergoes several branching to eventually form renal arterioles that extend throughout the renal cortex. Branches of these arterioles form tufts of capillaries that occupy an invagination of Bowman's capsule. Bowman's capsule is a balloon-like expansion of the proximal renal tubule. The combined region of capillary tufts and Bowman's capsule is called a glomerulus. There are over one million glomeruli in the renal cortex. The walls of the capillary tufts are uncharacteristically permeable to water and dissolved solutes such as electrolytes, urea, and other substances. The blood pressure inside the capillaries exceeds the pressure of the surrounding extracellular space and of the fluid within the lumen of Bowman's capsule. This pressure gradient drives water and dissolved solutes out of the capillary tufts and into the lumen of Bowman's capsule. The solution that enters the capsule lumen is referred to as a filtrate.

---

40 C. Increased renal tubule permeability to water

The effect of antidiuretic hormone on the kidney is to increase the permeability of the renal tubules and collecting ducts to water. This results in the diffusion of water out of the filtrate solution and into the renal medulla where it can be reabsorbed into the circulation by renal capillaries within the renal medulla. This concentrates urine and reduces the loss of additional water from the body that occurs through the excretory system.

---

41 C. increased secretion of antidiuretic hormone

Osmoreceptors in the hypothalamus and the pituitary gland directly detect plasma osmolality from adjacent capillaries. When plasma osmolality is undesirably high, the osmoreceptors relay this information to the pituitary. The pituitary response is to release antidiuretic hormone (ADH). As discussed in the rationale for question 40, the effect of antidiuretic hormone on the kidney is to increase the permeability of the renal tubules and collecting ducts to water. This results in the diffusion of water out of the filtrate solution and into the renal medulla where it can be reabsorbed into the circulation by renal capillaries within the renal medulla. This concentrates urine and reduces the loss of additional water from the body that occurs through the excretory system.

---

42 A. an undesirably low plasma sodium ion concentration; renin

The kidney can directly detect the sodium ion concentration of plasma within renal arterioles. A response of the kidney to an undesirably low plasma sodium ion concentration (and to low blood pressure) is the release of the hormone renin. Renin in the bloodstream leads to the production of angiotensin II. Angiotensin II is a potent vasoconstrictor and stimulates the release of aldosterone from the adrenal gland. The adrenal gland is not part of the kidney – although it does rest upon the superior pole of the kidney. Aldosterone causes the kidney to increase the reabsorption of sodium ion thereby helping to restore plasma ion concentrations to normal levels.

---

43 A. glucose

Under normal circumstances, glucose molecules that are filtered from the blood into a renal tubule are 100% reabsorbed from the filtrate. This process can be overwhelmed when blood levels of glucose are abnormally high. Glucose in the urine is an abnormal finding and often indicates the presence of type 1 or type 2 diabetes mellitus. The presence of sodium, urea, and bicarbonate ion in the urine is normal, so these are clearly not completely reabsorbed from renal tubule filtrates

---

44 C. concentration of urine

The loop of Henle is a U-shaped segment of the renal tubules. It is the mid-portion of the renal tubule – located between the proximal convoluted tubule segment and the distal convoluted tubule segment of the renal tubules. The bottom of the "U" in the loops of Henle are located in the renal medulla. The distal or ascending limb of the loop excretes sodium ion from the tubule into the adjacent interstitium of the medulla. This creates a very high osmolality of the interstitial fluids in the adrenal medulla. The renal collecting tubules pass through the renal medulla on their pathway to the sinuses of the renal pelvis. The permeability of the renal collecting tubules to water can be adjusted by various hormonal influences. The collecting tubules are impermeable to sodium and other solutes. When the tubules are maximally permeable to water, water diffuses out of the tubules into the adrenal medulla interstitium. Since this is a process of diffusion, the maximal concentration of urine or the maximum osmolality of the urine that can be produced is slightly lower than the osmolality of the interstitium of the adrenal medulla. As water diffuses out of the tubule solution, the osmolality of the solution increases. When the osmolality of the two regions are nearly equal, the driving force of the diffusion of water disappears as the concentration gradient between the two regions is eliminated.

---

45 B. fibrillar

In general, structural proteins have an overall fibrillar (fiber-like) shape - as opposed to globular proteins, which typically have enzymatic or transport functions.

---

46 A. increased blood pressure

Angiotensin II is the activated form of angiotensin hormone. Activation of angiotensin begins with the release of the hormone renin from the kidney. Angiotensin II has a direct effect on circulatory vessels causing contraction of smooth muscle cells located in the walls of arteries and veins. This increases the force of the vessel walls on the blood within the vessels resulting in increased blood pressure. Angiotensin II has a direct effect on the proximal tubules to increase Na^+ reabsorption. But this is not one of the answer choice options. Angiotensin II also stimulates the release of the hormone aldosterone which has additional effects on the kidney. These effects are indirect effects on the kidney.

---

47 D. complement proteins

The membrane attack complex is a multi-protein structure that attaches to the exterior cell membrane of disease-causing bacteria that have invaded the human body. The MAC punctures the cell membrane allowing contents of the cell to escape and external substances to enter the interior of the cell (cell lysis). This results in the death of the cell. The MAC is formed from activated protein fragments of the complement proteins (the C5b-C6-C7-C8-C9 complement proteins and protein fragments). Complement proteins circulate continuously throughout the body. Over 30 proteins and protein fragments make up the complement system When the either the innate or active immune system is activated, complement proteins may be activated in a sequential cascade, where one activated complement protein or protein fragment catalyzes the activation of the next set of complement proteins. The activation of the complement cascade also produces activated proteins and protein fragment that the phagocytosis of cells and other substances and act as cell signaling molecules that recruit immune cells to the site of an infection

---

48 C. antisense

The DNA strand that is transcribed by RNA polymerase is called the "antisense strand" The other DNA strand - the complementary strand of the sense strand - is called the sense strand. Since the base sequence of the sense strand is the complementary sequence of the antisense strand, the sense strand does not code for functional proteins and it is not read by RNA polymerase. The mRNA base sequence is identical to the sense strand DNA sequence with the exception that the nitrogenous base uracil in the mRNA base sequence replaces the nitrogenous base thymine in the sense strand of the DNA molecule.

---

49 D. deactivation of the snake venom toxin molecules by antigen-specific antibody binding

Antivenom to snake venom (and other biological venoms) is created by injecting the venom into lab animals and collecting the animal's blood serum afterwards. The injected animal will generate an active immune response to the venom that includes the production of antibodies that are targeted to antigens present on the venom molecules. In human patients, these antibodies bind to the venom molecules and in the process disrupt the venom's ability to cause injury either by altering the active sites of the venom molecule or by sequestering the venom molecules within antigen-antibody complexes which neutralize the antigen and enhance the clearance of the venom molecules from the body.

---

50 B. active humoral

The influenza virus contains viral shell proteins of the influenza virus that are recognized upon injection into the body by T-helper cells that have receptors complementary to the injected antigens. The T-cells activate B-cells with complementary antibody capability. Activation induces B-cell differentiation into plasma cells, which actively release antigen-specific antibodies into the circulation. These antibodies are short lived and will not protect against influenza infection after a few days. The exposure to the vaccine proteins antigens also results in the differentiation of some of the activated B-cells into long-lived memory cells that can generate a much stronger and more rapid antibody response to a subsequent encounter with infectious influenza viral particles. This rapid response sufficient to prevent the viral particles from infecting significant numbers of cells in the body. The antibody response is part of the active immune response (vs. the innate immune response) and is categorized as the humoral division of the active immune response (vs. the cellular cell-dependent active immune response).

---

51 B. bone marrow; thymus

All circulating red and white blood cell types of the human body originate from hematopoietic stem cells located in the bone marrow (and a few other regions in some circumstances in some individuals). Immature T-cells then migrate to the thymus early in life. These immature T-cells, as a group, have at least a few T-cells with the ability to respond to almost any possible specific molecular antigen including all the antigens that are present in the host body. In the thymus, those T-cells that can react to host antigens are detected and eliminated. Without this vital selection process, these T-cells would trigger immune system attacks against the body's own cells. This T-cell screening process continues into the early- to mid-teenage years. Afterwards the thymus progressively decreases in size and functionality.

---

52 B. redness and heat only

The four cardinal signs of localized infection are the result of the effects of various molecules that are generated by injured and infected cells and by immune cells that migrate to the site of infection. The most important of these molecules are histamines and prostaglandins. One of the effects of these molecules is to induce dilation of the local blood vessels – resulting in redness and increased heat due to increased local blood flow. Swelling is due to the accumulation of fluids and other substances that leak from the local blood vessels due to the increased permeability of the vessels induced by the infection-associated molecules. The pain associated with a localized infection is in part indirectly due to vascular permeability since increased swelling can trigger pain receptors. Pain is also a direct effect of the infection-associated molecules.

---

53 A. type 1 diabetes mellitus

Type 1 diabetes is a disease where the body produces either inadequate amounts of insulin or more commonly no insulin. In diabetes type 1, the immune system attacks the insulin-producing beta cells in the pancreas and destroys them. Cystic fibrosis and sickle cell disease are classic genetic diseases characterized by dysfunctional alleles of specific genes. Peptic ulcer disease is usually a result of chronic infection of the stomach by the bacteria H. pylori. The Nobel Prize in medicine was awarded to the physician who proved this was true.

---

54 B. small intestine

Dietary triglycerides are hydrolyzed in the small intestine by the enzyme lipase to monoglyceride molecules and fatty acid molecules. After absorption, some fatty acids are recombined with monoglycerides to reform triglycerides. Most of these triglycerides are stored in fat cells but some remain in the circulation as free triglycerides. The remainder of fatty acids are packaged along with cholesterol molecules and proteins into circulating complexes called lipoproteins.

---

55 **A.** $AA_1 + AA_2 \rightarrow AA_1 - AA_2 + H_2O$

Single chain proteins are linear amino acid polymers that are synthesized by formation of peptide bonds between individual amino acid monomers. Amino acids contain an amine group (-NH2) and a carboxylic acid group (-COOH) bonded to a central carbon atom. Peptide bonds are formed between adjacent amino acids in a polypeptide chain through a dehydration (condensation) reaction of the amine group of one amino acid and the carboxylic acid of an adjacent amino acid. Dehydration reactions produce a one or more H2O molecules as a product of each individual dehydration reaction. Amino acids can form two peptide bonds with other amino acids by forming one peptide bond through a dehydration reaction with their carboxylic acid group and the amine group of an adjacent amino acid and a second peptide bond through a dehydration reaction with their amine group and the carboxylic acid group of an adjacent amino acid.

ENGLISH & READING

1 C. Counterfeiting of American money is an enormous problem.

C is the best option as we are told that "The Treasury goes to extraordinary lengths to safeguard cash from counterfeiters."

---

2 B. Yet, despite all of these technological innovations, the race to stay ahead of savvy counterfeiters and their constantly changing counterfeiting techniques is a never-ending one.

B is the best as the main point of the passage is to emphasize the extent of counterfeiting and detail the technology used to counteract such constantly changing fraudulent activity.

---

3 C. Expository

An expository essay is one in which an idea is investigated and expounded upon, and an argument is set forth presenting evidence concerning that idea in a clear and concise manner. In this case the idea being investigated and expounded upon is anti-counterfeiting techniques.

---

4 A. A pamphlet for tourists visiting the United States Treasury

The style and specific subject matter all indicate that it is most likely from an informational pamphlet written for visitors to the Bureau of Engraving and Printing.

---

5 C. A letter from the US treasury Secretary to the President

A primary source document is one that was created and serves as a first-hand source of information or evidence about a particular time period. Only the personal letter would meet the criteria of a primary source.

---

6 D. Inherent

Technological sophistication is inherent, (or naturally found) in the making of American money, so much so that to call it "paper" does not fully reveal how complex a product it really is.

---

7 A. In the Middle Ages, merchants an artisans formed groups called "guilds" to protect themselves and their trades.

The first sentence is the topic sentence because it introduces the main idea of the paragraph.

---

8 C. merchant guilds originated in the Middle Ages and became extremely popular, eventually leading to a sophisticated apprenticeship system.

The guild system's origins and development is the main idea of the paragraph. The other options are too narrow to constitute a main idea.

---

9 A. prior to the inception of guilds, merchants were susceptible to competition from lesser skilled craftsmen peddling inferior products or services.

It can be inferred that if guilds were instituted, there must have been a need for merchants to safeguard themselves from threats to their livelihood.

---

10 C. similar

The sentence conveys to us that the spice, silk, and wool dealers were similar tradesman to that of other merchants who had set up guilds.

11 C. By that time,

The passage introduces the inception of guilds and their development over time, chronologically. From the previous sentence, it is clear that guilds grew in popularity over the centuries, until towns like Florence had 50 guilds by the twelfth century. "By that time" most clearly states this increase and development over time.

12 B. To criticize the American press for not taking responsibility for their actions

Luce is clearly criticizing the press for not taking responsibility to disseminate enlightening information to the public, and instead are blaming the public for not asking for reading matter which is "tasteful and more illuminating".

13 A. A newspaper editorial letter

Given the paragraph's opinionated style and serious, critical tone, it most likely excerpted from a longer letter printed in the op/ed section of a newspaper.

14 C. A diary entry

The diary entry (which would likely provide firsthand thoughts, feelings and opinions about current life or world events as witnessed by the author) would qualify as a primary source document of evidence or information of a particular time period.

15 D. enlightening

Illuminating reading matter is that which would be enlightening and provide necessary information to the public.

16 C. therefore

Luce is using a cause and effect argument here, but she is questioning the excuse of the press to not do their job as a result of certain demands of the public, which would "therefore exonerate the American press for its failures to give the American people more tasteful and more illuminating reading matter".

17 C. disapproval

Luce clearly disapproves of the press and their practice of serving up a lack of news to the public, "on the grounds that, after all, "[they] have to give the people what they want or [they] will go out of business".

18 B. persuasive/argumentative

Luce utilizes several modes of writing here, but overall, she is critical of the American press, and is arguing that they are at fault for not giving the American public useful information or "illuminating reading matter".

19 B. The author has worked in the journalism industry

The author clearly has an understanding of the business of the media, as well as its public responsibility to inform citizens, so it can be concluded that she likely has worked in the journalism industry. None of the other statements can reasonably be concluded based on the content of the passage.

20 B. Football was played for decades on school campuses nationwide before the American Professional Football Association was formed in 1920, and then renamed the National Football League (or the NFL) two years later.

This statement adds additional information to the paragraph about the progression of the game of football in the US and therefore, appropriately concludes the paragraph. The other statements discuss topics not directly related to football, or add additional information that is slightly off topic.

21 A. however

The sentence is explaining that, despite the appearance of football as a sport on some college campuses, and annual scrimmages occurring at Yale, 25 years passed before it became a regular activity in college life. "However" shows this contrast best.

22 A. Rejection of the past and outmoded ideas

From the paragraph it is clear that modernism is mainly concerned with rejecting the ideas of the past – like the science of the enlightenment, and old ideas about religion – and instead focusing on creating what was "new".

23 B. Basis

Pound's suggestion to "Make it new" was the basis, or touchstone of the Modernist movement's outlook and approach to interpreting the world and society.

24 D. Modernism had a profound impact on numerous aspects of life, and its values and perspectives still influence society in many positive ways today.

The author's description of Modernism's influence as being "positive" is clearly an opinion about the nature of the influence. The other statements are factually based, providing general information about the Modernist movement.

25 D. as well as

This sentence discusses all of the positive benefits that result from the continuation of the Olympic games in the present day, so "as well as" is the correct signal phrase to convey this idea, in a list form.

26 D. Detracted

The idea that allowing professional athletes to participate in the games would cause people to believe it "detracted" from the intentions of the original, is a negative notion, as it suggests that this would take away from the games, instead of adding something positive.

27 B. The Olympic games are the best example of humanity's physical prowess.

This statement is the opinion of the author, as there is no indication that this idea has been tested or proven in any way, but is simply what the author believes or feels.

28 C. Revulsion

The author uses words like "moldy smell" and "black hole" to describe his rented room in the inn, and "heartless" and "hideous" to describe the environment of London, adding that he "would rather even starve" than go out to find himself a meal in the "hellish town where a stranger might get trampled to death". These are very strong negative sentiments that clearly indicate his revulsion to the city.

29 B. A diary entry

The personal and frank tone that the author uses to describe his hotel room and his private fears about going out into the city of London for dinner suggest that this would have been written in a journal or diary.

30 D. An advertisement

A primary source document is one that was created from first-hand experience under a period of study of a particular event, moment in time, situation etc. A travel guide, diary entry and news editorial could all potentially be primary sources which chronicle one of the aforementioned. The only one that would likely NOT qualify as a primary source is the advertisement, as usually advertisements are meant to persuade one to engage in an experience, purchase a product or the like, and are often not completely based in personal experience and may not even be factual.

---

31 D. The author will not be traveling to London again.

It is clear that the author is unhappy with his lodging and finds London a generally disagreeable place, so it is likely that he would not travel to London again. The other statements are not reasonable conclusions that can be made from the content of the passage.

---

32 C. "You barely know him! How can she marry him?" was the worried mother's response at her teenager's announcement of marriage.

Sentence punctuation always is inside quotation marks; therefore, option C is punctuated correctly for dialogue.

---

33 A. "I have a dream", began Martin Luther King, Jr.

Second person uses the pronoun "you" or features direct address. Though punctuated incorrectly, it is clear that only the first sentence is not written in the second person; the use of "I" illustrates first person.

---

34 D. "Please remain seated while the seatbelt signs are illuminated." Came the announcement over the airplane's loud speaker system.

An imperative statement is one that gives a command. Though punctuated incorrectly, it is clear that option D is imperative: the announcement is commanding the passengers to remain seated.

---

35 C. Excision

The prefix "ex" means out, so that is our clue here. "Excision" refers to a surgical procedure done to cut out something unwanted or unnecessary.

---

36 B. Colitis

The suffix "itis" is one that refers to inflammation, so "colitis" is an inflammation of the colon.

---

37 D. Melanoma

The suffix "oma" refers to a tumor or cancer, so "melanoma" refers to a cancer of the skin (coming from melanin, that which gives our skin its color). "Oncology" is the study of cancer, but it does not refer to cancer itself.

---

38 C. Rhinitis

The root "rhino" refers to the nose or nasal area, so "rhinitis" is an inflammation of the nasal passages.

---

39 A. Gastroenterology

The suffix "logy" refers to the study of some discipline or area; therefore, gastroenterology is the study or examination of the gastrointestinal area of the body.

FINAL THOUGHTS

Congratulations!

If you're reading this, that means you have successfully completed your first experience with the Spire Study System, a fresh new approach to studying. You've proven that you're one of the free thinkers of the world, willing to try new things and challenge the conventional wisdom.

We sincerely hope you enjoyed the Spire Study System for the NLN-PAX (...well, as much as anyone can enjoy studying – you know what we mean).

If we succeeded and you're impressed with the Spire Study System, or if you have suggestions about how we can improve, we'd love to hear from you! Our inbox is always open: contact@spirestudysystem.com. Better yet, tell your friends about us. And be sure to look for our upcoming books. We can't wait to bring the Spire Study System to more students!

Best Wishes,

Your study partners at Spire

Made in the USA
Coppell, TX
01 September 2020

36171610R00149